THE MILITARY AND THE PRESS

Medill School of Journalism
VISIONS *of the* AMERICAN PRESS

GENERAL EDITOR
David Abrahamson

Other titles in this series

HERBERT J. GANS
Deciding What's News: A Study of CBS Evening News,
NBC Nightly News, Newsweek, *and* Time

MAURINE H. BEASLEY
First Ladies and the Press: The Unfinished Partnership of the Media Age

PATRICIA BRADLEY
Women and the Press: The Struggle for Equality

DAVID A. COPELAND
The Idea of a Free Press: The Enlightenment and Its Unruly Legacy

THE MILITARY AND THE PRESS

AN UNEASY TRUCE

Michael S. Sweeney

Foreword by Roy Gutman

MEDILL SCHOOL OF JOURNALISM

Northwestern University Press
Evanston, Illinois

Northwestern University Press
www.nupress.northwestern.edu

Printed in the United States of America

10   9   8   7   6   5   4   3   2   1

ISBN 0-8101-2299-5

Library of Congress Cataloging-in-Publication Data

Sweeney, Michael S.
  The military and the press : an uneasy truce / Michael S. Sweeney ;
foreword by Roy Gutman.
     p. cm. — (Visions of the American press)
   Includes bibliographical references and index.
   ISBN 0-8101-2299-5 (pbk. : alk. paper)
  1. War correspondents—United States. 2. War—Press coverage—
United States. 3. Censorship—United States.
I. Title. II. Series.
 PN4784.W37S94 2006
 070.4'3330973--dc22

                                             2006002781

  ∞ The paper used in this publication meets the minimum
requirements of the American National Standard for Information
Sciences—Permanence of Paper for Printed Library Materials,
ANSI Z39.48-1992.

*To Patrick S. Washburn, Joseph Bernt,
and Katherine Bradshaw, my mentors and friends.*

CONTENTS

FOREWORD

Roy Gutman

War reporting, as Michael Sweeney so ably demonstrates in this impressive consideration of the genre, may be the ultimate journalistic challenge. War, after all, is the most complex of all human activities as well as the most destructive. It provides many of the milestones of history and is the stuff of the daily news. For reporters, it is the most daunting of assignments, whose intricacy, deception, secrecy, and immensity exceed that of any other story. Since the end of the Cold War, it has become clear that reporters will have to improve their war coverage if their aim is to continue producing relevant journalism.

In the unknown world we are moving into, reporters need to wear multiple thinking caps: to think like military personnel and understand how they operate, to have a good grasp of how military power is implemented for the country's national interests or its foreign policy goals, and then to step back and ask whether those interests and goals as defined are genuine and important and worth the resources, manpower, and sacrifices they will require.

It isn't enough to travel with the troops and report their day-to-day battles, though that is an indispensable element of any journalism of war coverage. Nor is it enough to report what the commanders are saying or, if one wins their confidence, to measure their actions against the intelligence they are working from and the resources at their disposal. The U.S. military is more than a tool in the hands of policy makers, for it plays a role in the policy game to the extent that policy makers allow it. Sound military advice, such as whether to strike a foe preemptively, to avoid a conflict, or to fight through a proxy, can save the country an enormous setback. Unsound advice or silence in the face of a weak plan allows the nation to proceed straight down a path of disaster.

Since the end of the Cold War, the American military establishment has been adapting slowly at best to the new world order, and this sluggishness is hindering the United States in playing its role efficiently as the uncontested power of its day. By no means is it certain that an enlightened debate on the use of military power in this era will facilitate a more rapid adaptation, but critical reporting on the use of power and on the crises that may generate a need to use it will surely improve the climate for serious decision-making.

Under the leadership of then-chairman of the Joint Chiefs of Staff, Colin Powell, the U.S. military was on the wrong side in the Balkan wars of the early 1990s. For decades American forces were preparing to fight a conventional war in Germany's Fulda Gap, but in the early post–Cold War era they resented being asked to stage a messy intervention to save innocent civilians in the rugged terrain of the Balkans. Although members of the Joint Chiefs proposed sending U.S. troops to distribute food in Somalia in late 1992, they balked at the assignment to halt the "ethnic cleansing" in Bosnia. The word was out: "We do deserts, not mountains." The top leadership had bought into the fallacy that Serb forces had tied down Germany's Wehrmacht during World War II, seemingly unaware that it was a communist maverick at the head of a guerrilla force of disparate ethnic groups who took on the Third Reich. They also had forgotten how the nerve endings that tied the nations of Central Europe to one another made it possible for an assassination in Sarajevo to escalate into World War I. They thought genocide could go unnoticed. Some senior military figures even tried to redefine the facts to suit their preference for not getting involved. The errors were driven not by willful ignorance but by old-school ties. The U.S. military had forged good liaisons with a Yugoslav force and did not recognize how it had changed beyond recognition, from being a defender of an independent communist state to being an ultranationalist aggressor that used its power to foster Europe's worst war crimes since World War II.

In the second half of the 1990s, the U.S. military showed almost no interest in Afghanistan under the Taliban and the bitter civil war between the Islamist regime and veteran guerrilla fighter Ahmed Shah Massoud. Military scholars largely failed to monitor or learn from the Afghan civil war; they were unaware of the role the war played in Osama bin Laden's training process and the role bin Laden's forces played in the war. Military planners resisted preparing for an intervention until after the September 11, 2001, attacks in the United States, and then it took them two months to develop a plan. Once again, the top command focused on maintaining the best possible liaison ties, this time with the Pakistan military. But Pakistan's military had lost its way and was backing a dangerous Islamist regime that offered bin Laden not only sanctuary but also freedom to target U.S. civilians. Further, the military establishment failed to recognize that maintaining bases in Saudi Arabia long after the first Gulf War played directly into the hands of bin Laden, who could recruit and train thousands of his countrymen to die fighting the United States on the grounds that U.S. forces were occupying the land of the "Two Holy Places."

Officials in parts of the U.S. government recognized as early as 1998 that bin Laden had effectively hijacked the Taliban regime and was operating a state-within-a-state. But top military officials said they were unaware of this development. An elected president, Bill Clinton, was responsible for allowing bin Laden to retain his sanctuary in Afghanistan and for putting the onus for intelligence gathering on the Central Intelligence Agency and the Federal Bureau of Investigation, but Clinton made his judgment based on military advisers' counsel that the military had no role to play. It was completely upside-down advice. The FBI could never take the lead role in countering al-Qaeda. As an FBI agent told the joint congressional inquiry in December 2002, it was "like telling the FBI after Pearl Harbor, 'go to Tokyo and arrest the Emperor.'" A military solution was necessary, the agent said, because "[t] he Southern District . . . [the pertinent New York FBI office] doesn't have any cruise missiles." The news media did no better than the U.S. government in Afghanistan and in many ways missed the story of the prelude to September 11.

A decade later in Iraq, where the U.S. military brilliantly refought the first Gulf War, this time marching all the way to Baghdad but against a greatly weakened foe, military leaders failed to anticipate the possibility of an "asymmetrical" response by irregular forces or to plan for the peace. A generation after Vietnam and having said the United States would never fight another guerrilla-style war, military leaders found themselves up against exactly that. They viewed peace-keeping and peace building as noncombat activities that someone else would perform. In fact, as the Iraq invasion was getting under way, the Army was in the process of dismantling its Peacekeeping Institute at the Army War College in Carlisle Barracks, Pennsylvania, whose job it was to plan for stability after the combat was over. The U.S. military handily triumphed in the combat phase but lost the peace in the first three years after the intervention, not so much in the number of U.S. troops killed as in the failure to ensure a stable, secure environment that would prevent a relapse into violence.

Iraq was par for the course. According to one study, of eighteen regime changes brought about by U.S. military intervention in the twentieth century, only five produced stable democracies: Italy, Japan, West Germany, Grenada, and Panama (reported in the January 15, 2003, *Christian Science Monitor* under the caption "The 'Morning After' Regime Change"). The reason, says Ray Salvatore Jennings, is that the U.S. military and political establishments are "congenitally unable to stay the course in such matters."

So what is the job of reporters in this new era? They should be smart and sufficiently educated in military affairs so as to have a framework to understand what they are seeing and hearing. They should know the difference between strategy, operations, and tactics. They should be able to report the big picture and the scene on the ground that illustrates it. They have to think beyond the moment.

Reporters also need to have the self-confidence to ignore the judgment of the government and the military establishment and operate as the distant early-warning system of trouble ahead. If the U.S. government turns a blind eye to events that are highly newsworthy—be it the genocide in Rwanda (Africa) in 1994, the overrunning of Srebrenica (Bosnia) in 1995, or Massoud's loss of his main base at Taloqan (Afghanistan) in 2000—or defines a U.S.-manufactured event as important, such as the toppling of the Saddam Hussein statue after the fall of Baghdad, it is the media's task to analyze skeptically the official perspective, collect the pertinent facts, and let the American public decide for itself.

On the whole, militaries feel very ill at ease when the media are present. Embedding reporters in the tactical units during the invasion of Iraq was a major exception to this rule and a positive development all around; but the result was reportage, not journalism, for there was no way to investigate and tell the complete story. The major stories of the Iraq invasion were those that the media missed: the absence of weapons of mass destruction despite purported intelligence information that they existed; the failure of the civilian and military leadership to plan for irregular warfare and for stabilizing the peace: and the existence of abuses at Abu Ghraib and other detention centers.

In covering war, whether the United States is involved or the conflict is between other parties, reporters should apply the same principle as is used in covering politics: If the door is closed, if officials don't want us there, if they say something is unimportant but refuse to say what it is—that is where I want to be. At the same time, war reporters must be aware that especially in the age of coordinated "spin," they can rarely get a full story on the day it occurs or even a few days later. Instead, they must return to the scene again and again until sufficient facts are available to give a well-rounded account. One reporter won a Pulitzer Prize after the 1990–1991 Gulf War by touring U.S. military bases in Germany and asking soldiers who won medals to describe the basis of their commendation. He learned from this that the war had lasted longer than officially announced, and he uncovered major operations that no one had previously disclosed.

To cover war nowadays, a reporter should have a grasp of Carl von Clausewitz's writings (especially *On Strategy*), of guerrilla warfare, of the laws of armed conflict and how they work, and of the foreign policy aim that should underlie every use of force. Most important is to be able to step back and examine what is going on with detachment and to remain self-critical until one figures out what is really happening. It will, of course, require tremendous effort, and clearly this is one of the central lessons to be drawn from Mike Sweeney's thoughtful history of war correspondents. But nothing short of such an effort will generate real journalism.

PREFACE

It was Riley Mack Tidwell's moment in the nation's spotlight, and he could not speak. The six-foot-five-inch former trucker from Texas, still trim at seventy-one, had put on his gray suit, cowboy boots, and cream-colored cowboy hat for the biggest fling ever in Dana, Indiana, the boyhood home of Ernie Pyle.

Pyle—a farm boy who hated farm work—had left his rural home as soon as he could for a job that would let him see the world. He studied journalism at Indiana University, toured Japan with the school's baseball team, just missed the chance to serve in World War I, and turned his attention in the 1920s to the work that best suited him: newspapering. He became the rarest of wartime journalists, receiving five thousand fan letters a year as he reported from North Africa, Italy, France, and the Pacific, before dying during one of World War II's final battles. On April 18, 1995, exactly fifty years after a Japanese machine gunner put a bullet through Pyle's brain, Dana and the Ernie Pyle State Historic Site gathered his legion of friends and admirers to dedicate a museum to his memory.

Tidwell—who played a central, albeit anonymous, role in Pyle's most famous column—was there. So was I. I first read Pyle's World War II columns when I took a basic newswriting class at the University of Nebraska in 1978, and I learned more in another class taught in part by Peter Maslowski, an excellent war historian and author. Pyle's words from the front lines in Italy and France still packed an emotional punch many years after they had been written. They made me proud to be a journalist. They made me want to know more about Pyle, about journalism, and about the role of the press in wartime. Perhaps reading the work of Ernie Pyle was the first step toward the genesis of this book.

It would take sixteen years for the seeds of inquiry to be planted—and for me to ask questions, as curious journalists are supposed to do, about Pyle. I had left a job as an editor at the *Fort Worth* (Texas) *Star-Telegram* to pursue a doctoral degree in journalism at Ohio University. "PhD" was the stamp I needed on the academic passport that would allow me to teach journalism at the university level. My wife and I had taken a giant leap of faith in order for me to go back to school. We quit our jobs in Texas and moved halfway across the country.

In my second year in Athens, Ohio, while taking and teaching classes during the day and studying at night in a stiflingly hot cinderblock apartment, I enrolled in an oral history class taught through the School of Telecommunications. Oral history seemed intuitively like what I had been doing for years at newspapers in Texas and Missouri: conducting detailed interviews on tape, transcribing them, and constructing stories—or, to use a stuffier academic phrase, "narratives"—to share with audiences. The main difference seemed to be that journalists wrote on daily deadlines about recent events, whereas historians took a much broader period as their canvas and worried mainly about the publish-or-perish deadlines of promotion and tenure.

Dr. David Mould's oral history class required that students produce a lengthy term paper on an original subject, using primary sources including formal interviews. I chose to try to flesh out Pyle's story of Henry T. Waskow, a Texas army captain who died in Italy in December 1943. Pyle's column about the "beloved captain," quietly honored in death by his men, had gripped American readers as few war stories ever had. Pyle described how an unnamed soldier—Tidwell, as it turned out—had retrieved Waskow's body from the heights of Mount Sammucro and brought it down atop a mule. Tidwell's devotion to his captain came through in Pyle's description of his quietly holding Waskow's dead hand and fixing the torn cloth around his fatal wounds.

Over the 1994–1995 Christmas break, my wife, son, and I drove to visit my parents in Kansas City. We made a side trip down Interstate 35 to North Texas, where we still had friends. In Belton, Killeen, and other towns between Waco and Austin, I found and interviewed a handful of Waskow's friends and family members, including his younger sister, Mary Lee, who brought a packet of news clippings and photographs to the Bell County Courthouse to share with me. Several weeks later, the research resulted in a long and much-footnoted term paper as well an A from Dr. Mould.

I sent a copy of the paper to the Ernie Pyle State Historic Site for its files. Quite unexpectedly, in return I received an invitation to attend the ceremony observing the fiftieth anniversary of his death. I leaped at the chance. I took a couple of days off from classes and drove across the tabletop plains of Indiana to join thousands of Pyle's fans for a celebration of his life. While working on the term paper under Ohio's quarter system, which gave me ten weeks to complete the project, I only had the chance to interview Tidwell by phone. The conversation was interrupted by his raspy cough. I ignored it at the time, but it turned out to be significant.

For many attendees at the ceremony, their trip to Dana truly would be a matter of last respects. Survivors of carnage at Anzio, Normandy, Okinawa, and hundreds of other places less familiar had seen their ranks reduced by disease, old age, lingering wounds, and other afflictions visited with equanimity upon the heroic and the ordinary. For Tidwell, the final adversary was cancer. Two weeks after vowing to drive eight hundred miles to western Indiana from his home in Gallatin, Texas, for the celebration of Pyle's life, he got the news from his doctor. It was bad: Cancer had invaded his esophagus and liver. "Y'all fix me up," Tidwell demanded, as he had an appointment and he had to keep it. Later, he would recall, "Whatever I could say or do to help Ernie, I wanted to do it." The best the doctor could do was insert a tube into Tidwell's stomach and prepare him for the worst. Six months, the doctor told him. But it was enough.

At lunch on the big day, Tidwell's right hand rearranged the chicken and noodles on his plate while his left arm, encased in a brace, rested on the edge of the VIP table. Tidwell, by virtue of his presence in Pyle's most famous column, belonged in Dana with the hundreds of others whose lives had intersected with America's favorite wartime journalist. They included journalist Andy Rooney, actor William Windom, and Shirley Hufstedler, a neighbor who had helped Pyle build a fence around his New Mexico home and grew up to become the federal government's first secretary of education. In addition, as many as fifteen thousand admirers packed the town of six hundred to honor the journalist who, more than any other, constructed the popular image of the American infantryman as an ordinary and unsung hero.

A powerful wind began to stir the dust and spread the ripe smell of rain on the horizon. Dark clouds rumbled overhead as Tidwell and the other VIPs finished lunch and made their way down Indiana Highway 71, Dana's main street, to the State Historic Site. Gusts threatened to topple a tent erected on the museum's immaculate lawn, once even lifting a support pole off the ground, but a hundred determined dignitaries ignored the weather and filed into their seats. Many more, some in wheelchairs or on crutches, waited outside the tent and stole glances at the skies. The Indiana Army National Guard Thirty-eighth Infantry Division Band played the national anthem, snapping the veterans to attention. Afterward, one white-haired septuagenarian, seated in a motorized wheelchair at the edge of the tent, said, "He honored us, and I'm here to honor him."

Perhaps the most anticipated moment came right before Tidwell's turn to speak. Windom, who had created a one-man theatrical show about Pyle, stood to deliver some of the best quotations from Pyle's newspaper columns. He read from the story about Captain Waskow. Then he introduced Riley Tidwell to the crowd. This big, rawboned Texan was the man, Windom said, who fetched Waskow's body down the mountainside above San Pietro, Italy, in 1943, at a cost of his left arm and hand being peppered with German shrapnel. He was the one who straightened Waskow's collar as the body lay near a low stone wall. He was the one who pulled

Waskow's jacket over the gaping torso wound and then covered the body. Tidwell approached the microphone, his face flushed, his lower lip trembling.

"I came here . . . to talk of Ernie Pyle," Tidwell began. "But . . . I can't." His voice breaking, he tried again, barely above a whisper.

"What can I say . . . except God bless you all for being here." Raising his right hand to screen his face from the crowd, he sat down, pulled out a handkerchief, and dabbed at his eyes.

The crowd rose as one, hands pounding in applause. Tidwell had said nothing, and yet, everything. The sentiment was right. God bless you all: Those who fought the good fight. Those who knew and loved the man who best chronicled it. Those who, like Tidwell, knew they might not see another reunion. Those who, like all veterans of America's wars, were marching, marching, over the final hill. Tidwell died not long after the celebration of Ernie Pyle. I was glad to have met him.

An interviewer is never sure when approaching war veterans whether they are willing to share memories from darker days. Almost without exception, those whom I approached for an interview about Pyle were gracious and accommodating. I wondered, what was it about Pyle's style of wartime journalism that appealed to civilians, government officials, troops, and other journalists? What might journalists today learn from Pyle? What would Pyle say if he witnessed the press coverage of America's most recent wars?

Only a tiny fraction of this book is about Pyle. And Pyle probably wouldn't approve of what I have written. He avoided the spotlight, and he didn't like to write about the big picture. He preferred to focus his attention on chronicling the small, everyday details of war. This book, however, takes a much broader view of war than the one Pyle embraced. It examines the context in which wartime journalism is created, distributed, and understood. After my trek down a long and wandering academic road, my curiosity about Pyle has led me to examine how the press and military interact during wartime; how censorship, publicity, and propaganda shape the news; and what constitutes good and bad combat journalism.

In writing this book, I wanted to set forth what has been wrong, and what has been right, about American wartime journalism. It is my hope that the narratives of history in this book will inform the future of press-military relations. In this way, the legacy of Pyle and the rest of America's combat journalists may expand our collective wisdom, and, I hope, Americans may have a fuller and more accurate picture of war.

MICHAEL S. SWEENEY

ONE

ON THE SHOULDERS OF GIANTS: WAR CORRESPONDENTS BEFORE WORLD WAR I

"After reading this over I ought perhaps to say that the position of the real correspondents is absolutely the very best. . . . Generals fight to have us on their staffs and all that sort of thing, so I really cannot complain, except about the fact that our real news is crowded out by the faker in the rear."
  —Richard Harding Davis at Rough Riders headquarters, Cuba, to his brother Charles, June 29, 1898

For the best American war correspondents—and Richard Harding Davis was among the best—the twilight of the nineteenth century seemed to promise a golden dawn for the twentieth. The rebellion in Cuba and the brief Spanish-American War that followed had been good for most journalists. The American army fighting in 1898 accredited up to seven civilian journalists per publication. As many as five hundred reporters and photographers covered the war. They observed, wrote about, and photographed much of the offensive, including actual combat.

"I expect to make myself rich on this campaign," Davis wrote his family before going to Cuba to cover the invasion. He was right. *The Times* of London paid him the princely sum of $400 a week, plus expenses, while he also earned ten cents per word from *Scribner's* magazine for everything he could send the editors.

In securing his own fame and fortune, Davis also popularized the Rough Riders and their flamboyant leader, Colonel Theodore Roosevelt. Davis's nationalistic and heroic narratives helped construct the colonel's identity as the perfect man for the age: active, athletic, and decisive. "Roosevelt, mounted high on horseback, and charging the rifle-pits at a gallop and quite alone, made you feel that you would like to cheer," Davis wrote of Roosevelt's charge during a battle near San Juan Hill.

The close relationship that blossomed between Davis and the Rough Riders helped create the mythology surrounding Roosevelt. Whether it was proper for a journalist to get so close to the soldiers he covered was not a question given serious attention in the American press.

Davis enjoyed the freedom to wander and to report. William Shafter, commanding general of the army in Cuba, allowed correspondents into the thick of fighting and considered press access crucial to maintaining public support for the war. "I recognize that, with a people like ours, it may be better to risk the injury their news even under censorship may do than cause the dissatisfaction their exclusion would give rise to at home," Shafter wrote in a popular American magazine six months after war's end.

Not that censorship posed much of a problem for enterprising journalists. Although the navy cut the telegraph cable linking Key West and Havana, and censors controlled crucial telegraph offices in New York, Washington, D.C., and Florida, correspondents could ship handwritten reports in private dispatch boats to the mainland or an island such as Jamaica or could submit short cables to military scrutiny. Given the one-sided nature of the battles, the censors usually had little to delete. Most reporters supported the war outright and silenced themselves out of a sense of patriotism, or they avoided sensitive topics they knew would fall under the censor's blue pencil.

GENESIS OF THE PRESS POOL

Within six years, however, press-military relations changed dramatically and permanently. Davis, writer Jack London, and other American correspondents who traveled to Korea to cover the Russo-Japanese War in 1904 expected conditions for reporters to be much the same as they had been in Cuba. London looked forward to imitating his hero, Stephen Crane, who had reported for the *New York World* during the Spanish-American War. London said he wanted to be "right in the thick of it," living dangerously and filing thrilling stories to press baron William Randolph Hearst's newspaper syndicate in America. Instead, the Japanese subjected correspondents to the most severe censorship the world had seen to that point.

Journalists were not permitted within four miles of combat. They were not allowed to wander without a military escort, print anything that might disturb morale, file any information to the telegraph without getting a censor's stamp of approval, or attempt to circumvent the censorship system by leaking news through unofficial channels. Unfortunately, the official channel wasn't much of a pipeline. A Japanese army spokesman gave out news once a day to one representative of the press, who was expected to share with his colleagues. This restrictive system, the origin of the modern press pool, eliminated competition among reporters and ensured that everyone who read the news got the same sanitized version. "This was like standing outside the inclosure and having a man on the fence tell you who has the ball on whose fifteen-yard line," wrote one American correspondent.

Reporters criticized Japan's press control for creating boring news—or no news at all. But what the correspondents condemned, the Japanese military celebrated. By eliminating any potentially negative news, the Japanese army increased morale on the home front and built confidence among foreign investors. The plan worked so well that it created a new paradigm for press-military relations: Just as news could be a weapon of war, so too could orchestrated silence and carefully controlled propaganda.

The new tactics of wartime press control spelled doom for the freewheeling Davis and his peers. Between 1898 and 1904, Davis had witnessed the role of war correspondent change from independent yet supportive observer to what he called "a prisoner and suspected spy." Japan had buried the war reporter, he said, and he predicted future armies would copy its methods of controlling and exploiting the press for propaganda value. Thus, at the dawn of the twentieth century, the parameters of the press-military-government relationship had been set. It could be free and open, as in Cuba, or closed and controlled, as in Korea.

Or anything in between.

ROLE OF THE WARTIME PRESS

In the same way government and military strategists constantly replay the last war to find better ways to conduct the next, likewise journalists and their military overseers scour the record as they try to build upon the lessons of the past. From the Mexican–American War of 1846–1848, the first hostilities covered by full-time professional journalists, to the most recent international conflicts, the news media and military have pursued their own agendas, each hoping to gain from the other.

For the journalist, war sells the news. But news gathered from battlefields and wartime governments also has the higher goal of fulfilling the press's modern role as the Fourth Estate. News provides American citizens with information to help them make informed decisions about their leaders. For the soldier, however, news is primarily a tool or a weapon. Information shared through the mass media can bolster military and civilian morale, raise enlistments, boost the armed forces' budget, undermine the enemy's confidence, and hasten the end of conflict. Or it can compromise battlefield security, wreck the civilian base of support, and topple the government leadership directing the war effort. From the military point of view, a reckless press can turn victory into defeat.

For officials in government, who decide when and where to go to war, news provides information that ideally contributes to intelligent military decisions. However, as the first rule of having power is to stay in power, politically elected and appointed leaders also seek to shape information in the press to serve their own interests. During most of the twentieth and early twenty-first centuries, the press and military observed an uneasy truce. Journalists and soldiers generally cooperated during wartime, although conflicting interests kept their relationship in flux. When their aims brought them into conflict, the press lost most of the battles. After all, journalists carry notebooks while soldiers carry guns.

In World War II, the press, military, and government acted in relative harmony despite the functioning of the largest federal bureaucracies of censorship and propaganda in American history. The reasons behind the general success of their relationship thus merit two chapters in this book, compared with one for most other wars. In the conflicts since World War II, tensions have become more apparent. Methods of press control have grown to include the reinstatement of press pools and new restrictions on access to combat, governments producing their own publicity to avoid traditional news editing, and self-censorship for overtly patriotic and economic reasons.

During Operation Iraqi Freedom in 2003, however, the pendulum swung toward a more open and trusting relationship—at least on the battlefield. Journalists who had been denied access to the front lines in previous wars found themselves in the thick of fighting. They enjoyed as close a view of combat as anything Richard Harding Davis experienced in Cuba. Still, some observers feared the press and the military had grown too close, objecting that their embrace would impart the same kind of patriotic, positive spin that shaped dispatches from the Spanish-American War. And critics of the administration in Washington worried about whether the press that traditionally had acted as a check on government had grown too timid or too ossified to challenge the rationale for going to war in the first place.

As a new century unfolds, America has come full circle. From censorship to access to the danger of losing its independent voice, the press is grappling with issues that surfaced more than a hundred years ago. The critical issue for the press in the decades ahead will be whether it can fulfill its traditional role as the public's neutral and skeptical observer or will acquiesce to growing pressure to conform to government and military agendas. For the military, the issue remains whether it can trust the American news media to disseminate accurate, important, and timely information without compromising security. If they do not reach some permanent understanding, America's news media and armed forces may find themselves at a tipping point in their relationship.

In this book I examine the evolution of American press-military relations and the uses of news in wartime. As I recount our history and look toward our future, I focus on the following questions: How have the news media portrayed America's armed conflicts, and how have these portrayals affected the conduct of war? How has news coverage of war interacted with public opinion? How have the three central actors—government, military, and press—shaped their relationship? Finally, what *should* the American press do in modern warfare, and what might the future hold?

THE COLONIAL-REVOLUTIONARY
PERIOD

The American press and military have grown up together. Like siblings, they have experienced both harmony and discord. If the past is prologue, the future will have more conflict and coercion than calm.

The first American newspaper, *Publick Occurrences Both Forreign and Domestick,* set the tone in 1690 by carrying war news in its first and only edition. Publisher Benjamin Harris wrote about the abduction of two children by Indians, rumors about the king of France sleeping with his son's wife, and a militia's expedition against the French and Indians in Canada. The Massachusetts governor and members of the colony's ruling council shuttered Harris's paper. Some feared the loose cannon of an unfettered press. Others objected to his paper's violent and salacious content. Still others saw unacceptable political intrigue in the possible alliance of Harris and the fiery cleric Cotton Mather.

The American press did not experience explicit military censorship until 1725, during one of the periodic Indian wars. A Massachusetts Order-In-Council issued on May 13 of that year declared, "The printers of the newspapers of Boston be ordered upon their peril not to insert in their prints anything of the public affairs of this province relative to the war without the order of the government."

Censorship has continued, in some form, in every war the United States has fought. Those who argue that a free press strengthens the nation by exposing its mistakes to public scrutiny have opposed wartime censorship, with varying success. During the Revolutionary War, anti-British papers took an active role in supporting combat. They relayed crucial information of battles to an eager public, stirred up political passions, and helped unite the thirteen colonies into one nation. One of the signers of the Declaration of Independence, Francis Hopkinson, considered a supportive press crucial to military victory because "by influencing the minds of the multitude, [it] can perhaps do more towards gaining a point than the best rifle gun or sharpest bayonet."

Colonial printers had no reporters. They gathered news through letters, official proclamations, and clippings from other papers—including those published in enemy-held territory. They occasionally printed news of troop movements, which raised security concerns for America's leaders, but such news apparently did little to affect the course of the war. More influential were the publications that sought to boost colonial morale or sow doubts among the British and their loyalist supporters. Printers such as Isaiah Thomas, publisher of the *Massachusetts Spy* and a member of the Sons of Liberty (a secret network that had fought the odious Stamp Act), aimed to raise public confidence in the Revolution through spirited and opinionated accounts of battle.

"On the nineteenth day of April, one thousand, seven hundred and seventy-five, a day to be remembered by all Americans of the present generation, and which ought and doubtless will be handed down to ages yet unborn . . . the troops of Britain, unprovoked, shed the blood of sundry of the loyal American subjects of the British King in the field of Lexington," Thomas wrote.

The breakdown in British authority freed most colonial papers from the restrictions of licensing by the crown. Patriotic newspapers joyfully publicized their support for independence without immediate fear of retaliation. Thomas

Paine's "Crisis" essays, urging Americans to stand fast during their initial setbacks to the British army, first trumpeted their opening line, "These are times that try men's souls," in the pages of Pennsylvania newspapers. Among the loyalists, printer James Rivington accused the American rebels of having lost their sense of direction and predicted their defeat by the better-equipped and better-financed British. Rivington scoffed at reports of the key British defeat at Saratoga in 1777. The rebels had made up the story, he said, "with a view to inlist men." Rivington could spread his loyalist views because he published in New York, which was safely in British hands for most of the conflict. Two years earlier, however, the Sons of Liberty had exercised an effective form of censorship by destroying his press to silence him.

Other printers faced reprisals if their opinions offended whichever army occupied their town. John Mein, who published the *Boston Chronicle,* tried to be nonpartisan as relations with the British became difficult. However, neutrality and objectivity—qualities that mark most modern, professional journalism—did not exist in colonial newspapers. Given the push and pull of public debate, particularly in Boston, those qualities probably were next to impossible to achieve. Mein's paper grew openly pro-British as he publicly opposed Sam Adams's Sons of Liberty. A mob attacked his paper and he fled to England.

The press, exulting in its freedom to criticize the British government, helped win America's freedom. It is no surprise, then, that the leaders of the new country recognized the power of the press in shaping public debate. The constitution of nearly every new state forbade limits on press freedom. As delegates debated the creation of a federal Constitution in

1787, however, its backers initially disdained an explicit guarantee of press freedom. Alexander Hamilton, drumming up support for the Constitution in a letter to the people of New York, argued that constitutional guarantees of press freedom were essentially meaningless. "What is the liberty of the press? Who can give it any definition which would not leave the utmost latitude for evasion?" he wrote in Federalist No. 84. "I hold it to be impracticable; and from this I infer, that its security . . . must altogether depend on public opinion, and on the general spirit of the people and of the government." Despite such arguments, Anti-Federalists insisted on insertion of a Bill of Rights, including a press guarantee, into the Constitution as the price of their support.

The Constitution and Bill of Rights provide no explicit guidance on press–military relations. At first glance, the first of the ten amendments that made up the Bill of Rights, ratified in 1791, seems clear in its intent: "Congress shall make no law . . . abridging the freedom of speech, or of the press."

Many have argued that "no law" meant exactly that. In practice, the meaning of the amendment as written by James Madison has been subject to debate. One recent study found no consensus in what the signers of the Declaration of Independence, Articles of Confederation, and the Constitution thought about the meaning of press freedom. "Few of us, I believe, have distinct ideas of its nature and content," Benjamin Franklin declared in summing up the debate in 1789.

Interpretations of the First Amendment, and how it might affect press–military relations, vary. Some endorse the ideas of jurist Sir William Blackstone. In his *Commentaries on the Laws of England* (1765–1769), Blackstone defined press freedom as forbidding "prior restraint," which referred to governmental prohibition of publication. He said the press instead could be held accountable by subjecting it to post-publication prosecution for sedition and libel. Under this view of the First Amendment, if a newspaper had a story of some value to the enemy—such as the time and place of a future military assault—no censor could march into the newsroom and break the printing plates. However, the newspaper could face postpublication penalties, including charges of treason. The framers of the Constitution defined that term as waging war against the United States or providing aid and comfort to its enemies.

Another view held that the amendment expanded press freedom further than Blackstone envisioned, although not to the point of being absolute. Supreme Court Justice Oliver Wendell Holmes Jr. said in 1919 that speech and publications were protected unless they constituted "a clear and present danger" to society. Publications could express antiwar sentiments, but if these interfered with the country's ability to conduct war, the publishers could be subject to prosecution.

A final view is the most extreme: The press cannot be restricted by the government in any way. Press-military historian Jeffery A. Smith has argued that the historical record of the debates over ratification, as well as the wording of the Constitution itself, favors such an interpretation. Wartime officials might be justified in refusing to reveal some sensitive information, but a separate, independent press must be absolutely free of the government's prior restraints or subsequent penalties. "Both the government's ability to maintain any secrecy and the freedom of journalists to go about their work naturally involved some risks, but the [Constitution's] concept of the 'consent of the governed' required that the people be informed and that the government be accountable," Smith wrote.

Perhaps the toughest test of the First Amendment occurred within a few years of its ratification. President John Adams's Federalist Party, worried over domestic political threats as well as foreign intrigue during America's undeclared 1797–1798 conflict with France, won passage of the Alien and Sedition Acts. These consisted of four separate laws. The first three dealt with immigration, but the last outlawed criticism of the American government. It banned "false, scandalous and malicious writing" against the government, Congress, and the president. Offenders faced up to two years in prison and fines of up to $2,000. The Federalists ignored the First Amendment in favor of political expediency: The law shut down proper debate during a time of national crisis by prosecuting dissidents for seditious libel.

The Alien and Sedition Acts established truth as a defense, but the truth of Anti-Federalist claims proved impossible to demonstrate to the satisfaction of Federalist judges. Prosecutors indicted fourteen people before the law expired in 1801, the year Thomas Jefferson succeeded Adams as president and issued pardons. Victims of prosecution included Franklin's grandson, Benjamin Franklin Bache, who published a well-documented story about a bribe taken in the secretary of state's office, and the unfortunate Luther Baldwin of New Jersey, who publicly wished that the wadding of a cannon fired during an act of celebration "were lodged in the president's posterior."

Newspapers in the late eighteenth and early nineteenth

centuries contained little that modern readers would recognize as news, as publishers filled their pages mostly with political opinions and a litany of commerce. They appealed to the mercantile classes with a mix of advertisements, shipping reports, and business news. Newspapers sought profit by selling relatively expensive copies, at several cents each, to a small but wealthy clientele. Subscription income supplemented political patronage and accounted for about one-third of the cost of publishing. Advertising helped, but rates were too low to break even.

The press enjoyed a powerful voice under such a system, but its power was integrated with class and politics. Beginning in the 1830s, however, a new economic formula expanded readership while simultaneously making the press more independent. The new press had greater freedom of political expression, but had to be more sensitive to broad public opinion in order to remain profitable. This was a simple matter of audience demographics. If a paper could make money by taking partisan payments and selling a small number of expensive copies to rich readers, it also could make money—perhaps a lot more—by cutting its ties to party politics and selling a large number of cheap copies to a politically and socially diverse audience. Of course, this change in newspaper economics required advances in technology and literacy, as well as free thinkers who could exploit them.

TECHNOLOGICAL ADVANCEMENTS

The technological changes alone were stunning. Since the introduction of Johannes Gutenberg's movable type in the mid-fifteenth century, printers created pages one at a time by inserting paper into a modified wine press and squeezing it against a bed of inked, raised letters. In the hands of a master, such presses could produce about 125 papers in an hour. Newspaper circulation could not grow beyond that rate of production; even if more readers wanted to buy the paper, printers could not create enough copies to satisfy demand.

The application of steam power to Gutenberg's invention changed that. By 1840, the *New York Sun* was printing 4,000 pages an hour on a steam-driven press. Engravers also carved drawings on blocks of wood, which were integrated into publications and created the first illustrated newspapers. Frank Leslie, who once worked for celebrated showman P. T. Barnum, capitalized on the appeal of cheap reproductions and created *Frank Leslie's Illustrated Newspaper,* which enjoyed an astonishing circulation of 100,000 copies per week by 1860. Technology also improved the gathering and distributing of news as railroads began stitching the continent together, starting in 1828, and the telegraph began transmitting information at the speed of light in 1844. A leading publisher of the age described the technological revolution as "the annihilation of time and space," while predicting it would cause "a greater change in some of the social institutions than anyone now imagines."

The number of American papers quadrupled between 1825 and the start of the Civil War, when 2,500 titles were published in the United States. Meanwhile, literacy rates reached well above 80 percent for white men and women by midcentury.

Beginning in 1833, publishers began pricing newspapers at a penny to take advantage of the broadest possible readership. Publisher Benjamin Day of the *New York Sun* fed his readers a diet of human interest and crime stories. Two years later, publisher James Gordon Bennett of the rival *New York Herald* went beyond Day's formula to institute professional news-gathering routines. Bennett covered the courts, the docks, the stock exchange, city hall, and nearly anywhere else he thought he could find a story to sell. Bennett bragged his paper would be "the organ of no faction or coterie" and prided himself on industry, brevity, and readability.

Advertisers as well as immigrants and the working class embraced the concept. A press unaligned with a particular political party could appeal to a vast spectrum of readership. Its freedom from party politics gave it the latitude to criticize or applaud government actions, including military interventions, as Bennett saw fit. The model he helped create has existed to the present day.

Bennett employed full-time foreign correspondents. American newspapers had carried foreign news before the 1830s, but they had to clip it from other papers or wait for fresh intelligence to arrive aboard incoming ships. Bennett hired correspondents in London, Paris, Rome, and other European cities, as well as writers in Mexico, Canada, and the Republic of Texas.

Within a few years, telegraph lines sped the collection and distribution of news across great distances. By the late 1840s, however, with telegraph wires stretching only as far west as Petersburg, Virginia, Bennett and other Eastern publishers had to rely on steamships, railroads, and private pony-express systems to publicize the reports from the Mexican–American War.

THE FIRST EMBEDDED REPORTERS

The Mexican-American War was the first war covered by professional war correspondents. More than a dozen witnessed and wrote about the campaigns of Zachary Taylor in northern Mexico and Winfield Scott's march from Vera Cruz to Mexico City in the south. Correspondents created their own courier service to hasten dispatches to the Mexican coast, where they were picked up by steamships bound for New Orleans. The system of spreading war news to waiting readers proved so effective that President James K. Polk learned of the American landing at Vera Cruz not through official channels but via a message cabled to him by the *Baltimore Sun*. News of the first major engagement, at Monterrey, reached New Orleans newspapers in eight days, well ahead of government couriers.

Troops and officers welcomed nearly all correspondents among their ranks, and the American public eagerly read published accounts of far-off battle. Penny papers in New Orleans sent three celebrated reporters: George Wilkins Kendall, James L. Freaner, and Christopher M. Haile. To say that these and other journalists enjoyed freedom on the battlefield would be an understatement. They wandered almost without restriction and did not have to submit their dispatches to military censors. They did not practice detachment.

Kendall, who filed more than 200 war dispatches, charged into battles with American soldiers and once captured an enemy flag. He gathered news while occasionally serving as aide-de-camp, military courier, and judge over soldiers accused of civil crimes. General William J. Worth cited

Kendall for gallantry during the fighting at Molino del Rey. Freaner killed a Mexican officer and took his horse, earning the reporter a new nickname: "Mustang." The battlefield even had room for a celebrated female correspondent, Jane McManus Storms, who wrote for the *New York Sun* under the byline Cora Montgomery. She felt sufficiently free to criticize the shortcomings of the army in print.

Likewise, Kendall openly questioned the actions of American military commanders during the assault on Mexico City, arguing in the New Orleans *Picayune* that they caused too many casualties. American officers "contend that no result has been gained commensurate with the immense loss we have sustained in battle," he wrote. He documented the army's inadequate supplies and assailed what he saw as too much leniency in the terms of surrender at Monterrey.

Papers published within the war zone controlled by the army felt the lash of postpublication censorship. At least five American and five Mexican papers were suppressed for criticizing the conduct of the war. Polk's official newspaper, the *Union,* labeled war-zone complaints as "treason." Polk was happy to allow martial law to silence civilian opposition even though the legal authority to do so on foreign territory had not been clearly established.

THE CIVIL WAR

Thirteen years after the end of the Mexican-American War, the Civil War opened with war correspondents routinely at the scene of battle. The growth of telegraph communications, extending over nearly 50,000 miles of lines in the eastern United States, simplified and accelerated correspondents' ability to report the news. Telegraph wires made war reporting more extensive, more immediate, and more of a potential threat to commanders in the field. It came as no surprise that military censorship expanded during the Civil War.

In the South, the Confederate Congress forbade publicizing troop and ship movements in 1862, and censorship grew stricter as the war progressed. Nevertheless, Southern reporters could criticize the conduct of the war as long as they avoided questioning Southern independence or the institution of slavery. Peter W. Alexander, one of the better Southern correspondents, condemned drunkenness in the Confederate Army and applauded the uprooting of incompetence. He also assailed the invasion of Maryland, which culminated at the Battle of Antietam, as a mistake. Most Confederate papers needed no lecturing to maintain their support for the war. Editors censored their pages to build morale and avoided using words such as "retreat" to describe their soldiers' falling back from Union offensives.

Southern censorship at least had consistency. Union censorship was often haphazard as well as heavy-handed. The Union government had suggested a voluntary form of self-censorship early in the war, but this strategy lacked clear guidelines and quickly failed. The government then turned to a rigid system imposed upon journalists after they had written or published their stories.

President Abraham Lincoln did not worry about the First Amendment; he and his cabinet ignored it or rationalized its subjugation to concerns about public safety. The House of Representatives investigated the rationale for telegraphic censorship in late 1861 and in particular asked whether such censorship "has not been used to restrain wholesome political criticism." During debate, Congress authorized Lincoln to take control of the telegraph to maintain public safety. He did so in February 1862 and turned over day-to-day control of the wires to his secretary of war. Further restrictions followed, including the suspension of habeas corpus, but the Supreme Court let Lincoln run the war without interference.

Union correspondents faced strict censorship of any information transmitted over telegraph lines, and stories deemed inappropriate could be delayed or killed. Army meddling mangled the news of the first Battle of Bull Run in 1861. Early reports characterized the fighting as a Union victory and passed quickly over the telegraph lines. When the battle turned into a rout by the Confederates, General Scott halted transmissions. As a result, the next day's papers announced a Northern victory when the opposite was true. Simon Cameron, Lincoln's first secretary of war, reacted to the defeat at Bull Run by issuing a proclamation to subject correspondents to military discipline. The order, approved by Lincoln, cited the fifty-seventh article of war as approved in 1806, which essentially put reckless or disloyal civilian journalists on the same legal footing as spies. It provided for punishments up to the death penalty if correspondents provided intelligence to the enemy. In the end, no journalists had to pay that penalty during the war. Yet the fact that news leaked across the lines was inescapable. Confederate General Robert E. Lee said he regularly scanned Union papers for news he could use to his advantage.

Friction began building newspapers' distrust of military authority even before the notorious Edwin Stanton replaced

Cameron as war secretary. Stanton ran censorship as his own fiefdom. He jailed reporters, lowered Union casualty figures in wired dispatches, and canceled reporters' passes to restrict their movements. One recent study of Stanton's heavy-handed control of the telegraph office even argued, compellingly, that his shaping of the nation's news through press releases contributed significantly to the modern form of newswriting in which the lead paragraph gives a who-what-when-where-why summary of events.

Generals in the field were often hostile to reporters. Henry W. Halleck expelled reporters from his camp, and William Tecumseh Sherman, labeling free speech and free press "relics of history," ordered the press not to print anything that excited hatred or undermined the government's authority. "They come into camp, poke about among the lazy shirks and pick up their camp rumors and publish them as facts, and the avidity with which these rumors are swallowed by the public makes even some of our officers bow to them," Sherman said. "I will not. They are a pest and shall not approach me and I will treat them as spies, which in truth they are." The Union government shut down newspapers that printed information it deemed offensive. The *New York Journal of Commerce* and the *New York World* were shuttered for two days after publishing a forged letter in which President Lincoln purported to call for a draft of 400,000 more men.

A few Union war journalists had first-class talent. *New York Tribune* reporter George Smalley's account of the Battle of Antietam, *New York Times* reporter Sam Wilkeson's emotional recounting of his finding his own son among the dead at Gettysburg, and *Tribune* reporter Henry Wing's scoops about the Battle of the Wilderness and the surrender at Appomattox rank among the best news stories of the war. With nearly 500 journalists in the field for the North alone, some of the reporting had to be good. But as Civil War journalism historian J. Cutler Andrews noted in his survey of Union army correspondence, "Sensationalism and exaggeration, outright lies, puffery, slander, faked eye-witness accounts, and conjectures built on pure imagination cheapened much that passed in the North for news."

While many abuses undoubtedly occurred, the *New York Times* argued that an even greater sin would have been to prohibit coverage of the war. Despite its faults, the press acted as a check upon military excess, it said: "More harm would be done to the Union by the expulsion of correspondents than those correspondents now do by occasional exposures of military blunders, imbecilities, peccadilloes, corruption, drunkenness, and knavery, or by their occasional failure to puff every functionary as much as he thinks he deserves."

Drawings or engravings that suggested or explicitly provided a moral message often accompanied news accounts of battle. Photographs ostensibly could not distort reality and therefore made excellent fodder for propaganda. In truth, Civil War photographers manipulated and sometimes faked compositions for greater impact.

Photographic processes had improved from the single-print daguerreotypes taken during the Mexican-American War, which could not be reproduced. By the Civil War, improvements allowed multiple paper prints from plate-glass negatives. A ready market arose for mass production of photos in stereoscopic prints and small cards that could be collected in albums. Reproductions in newspapers and magazines still required an intermediary step between the print and the plate—an artist had to transfer a photographic image to an engraving to prepare it for the press. Many publications therefore skipped photography and sent sketch artists into the field. *Frank Leslie's Illustrated Newspaper* published about 3,000 Civil War sketches. The halftone process, which converted photographs directly into images ready for printing, did not become widely available until 1900.

Actual photographs of the war, while not appearing in newspapers and magazines, still caused a sensation. Combat proved too fast and furious to be captured by the cumbersome cameras; instead, photographers required live subjects to freeze in place for several seconds. The dead needed no instruction to lie motionless and consequently dominated many postbattle scenes. For the first time, Americans far from battle could witness the carnage of war. "Mr. Brady has done something to bring home to us the terrible reality and earnestness of war. If he has not brought bodies and laid them in our door-yards and along streets, he has done something very like it," the *New York Times* wrote of the Antietam photographs displayed in Mathew Brady's Broadway studio in 1862. "At the door of his gallery hangs a little placard, 'The Dead of Antietam.' Crowds of people are constantly going up the stairs; follow them, and you find them bending over photographic views of that fearful battle-field, taken immediately after the action. . . . Here lie men who have not hesitated to seal and stamp their convictions with their blood—men who have flung themselves into the great gulf of the unknown to teach the world that there are truths dearer than life."

The public found the photographs, taken by Alexander Gardner and James F. Gibson for Brady's studio, both fascinating and repulsive. Gardner produced a book of war photos in 1866 in which he pasted actual prints onto the pages. Although he said he wanted the book to "speak for itself," his captions nevertheless extolled Union virtues and portrayed Confederates as wicked traitors who paid for their perfidy with their lives. Gardner also repositioned Confederate corpses around the Gettysburg battlefield to make his photographs more dramatic and potentially profitable.

The Civil War helped solidify the new economics of the press as independent and business-oriented. "Only the press could provide information about the course of the war, policy, and potential outcomes of the conflict—and hence, some sense of whether the nation might endure," said journalism historian Hazel Dicken-Garcia. "It was indispensable in providing information needed by a whole nation." By war's end, the United States had become addicted to the news, and the news industry had cemented its status as a business.

The benefits of such a paradigm are clear: The press can make a lot of money, and be independent of government pressure, if it attracts enough readers and advertisers. On the other hand, if the press puts its business interests ahead of the public that it serves, it compromises its independence and may ultimately fall out of favor. "Herein lies a danger," a critical Ohio newspaper publisher wrote about the news business in 1893. "It will be a sorry day for journalism if our leading papers pass out of the control of trained, professional newspaper men, and their policy be dictated and guided by men who look upon the business of journalism as the pork packer does upon his. . . . Is it not already foreshadowed—a press pandering to the low and vicious, to the love of scandal for the sake of larger money returns?"

The business model of the press rejected the overt censorship of the colonial era, when licensers allowed publication only by authority. It substituted a range of subtler restrictions. In order to sell, news had to be interesting. The news media had to make a profit, resulting in a tendency to avoid stories that would offend readers and advertisers. In addition, competition among the nation's many papers put a premium on being first with the news. During the Civil War, American newspapers competed to be the first with big news from the battleground and score a circulation coup; however, the rush contributed to many inaccurate reports of battle. Finally, the news media during wartime looked to skirt any overt confrontation with government and military officials that might cut their representatives off from gathering the most sensational, regular news imaginable: war. These influences usually are taken for granted. They become most apparent only when violated. Wartime reporting that validates some portion of the enemy's point of view or challenges the underlying assumptions of America's war rationale breaks these unwritten rules and invites retaliation.

SPANISH-AMERICAN WAR

By the time of the Spanish-American War, when the top magazines and New York papers enjoyed circulations of more than a million, self-censorship and competition for the most sensational, profitable news had become an established part of war journalism. Faking the news became a common way to attract readers. Before America entered the war against Spain, one of Hearst's reporters, Frederick W. Lawrence, invented news about a nonexistent army of 25,000 Cuban insurgents and some "Amazon" warriors. In Lawrence's imaginative stories, the rebel army marched on two cities and burned both in a single night. Sharp-eyed readers of Hearst's *New York Journal* might have questioned Lawrence's reporting if they had consulted an atlas: The cities lie more than three hundred miles apart.

Wartime newsreels also were faked. Cameras were bulky, lenses were short, and film speeds were slow, all of which made the creation of actual combat footage extremely difficult. Some newsreel photographers captured real-life scenes in Cuba, but others resorted to fabrications.

The Edison Company faked short films of a Rough Riders skirmish and the infantry at El Caney. The competing Vitagraph Company shot actual footage of the assault on San Juan and Kettle hills but found it less than satisfying. Vitagraph camera operators J. Stuart Blackton and Albert E. Smith decided to spice up their newsreel coverage of the war by re-creating the Battle of Santiago Bay, in which the American navy destroyed the Spanish fleet. The hoaxers made cardboard cutouts of the ships and nailed them to blocks of wood. They set the little boats in a container of water on top of a table and simulated shellfire and explosions by touching off tiny pinches of gunfire. To reproduce the smoke of battle, an off-camera friend puffed mightily on a cigar. Producing the entire film cost Vitagraph only $1.98; it played to packed houses in New York.

Photographers in Cuba published no photographs of identifiable American corpses during the war. One, J. C.

Hemment of Hearst's *New York Journal,* watched the body of an American officer being removed from the forward torpedo room of the wreck of the USS *Maine* but "had not the heart to photograph it." Burr William McIntosh, photographing the war for *Leslie's Weekly,* went ashore during the invasion of Cuba and saw much of the same action as Richard Harding Davis. While at an American supply base, he learned that Hamilton Fish, blue-blooded son of the former secretary of state, had been killed at Las Guasimas. Arriving on the scene, he found Fish's blanket-covered body next to another victim of the battle. McIntosh decided not to uncover the body before photographing it. "My first impulse was to steal a picture of the face while no one was looking; but I didn't, and I am glad of it," McIntosh wrote. Like the rest of the photographers, he viewed the dead as heroes.

McIntosh considered it unethical to picture the dead in ways that detracted from their noble sacrifice. He underscored his respect for Fish by photographing a group of men sitting nearby—including Davis and Roosevelt—talking and laughing. "The photographs were taken with a heart filled with resentment," McIntosh continued. "It was all 'war,' and time has shown me that one should be able to drink to 'the next one who dies,' but I felt a resentment toward certain of those men, who were joking with that boy's body lying within a few feet of them."

Davis also censored himself. In a letter to his brother, he laid out the problems of the army in Cuba: lack of proper uniforms and shoes, lack of training with firearms, and unsanitary conditions. "I could go on for pages, but it has to be written later; now they would only think it was an attack on the army," Davis said. He kept such news out of print "because, if I started to tell the truth at all, it would do no good, and it would open up a hell of an outcry from all the families of the boys who have volunteered."

The Spanish-American War was short, one-sided, and well-supported on the home front. Reporters who touted it as "The People's War and the Soldier's Campaign" did not need prompting to adopt jingoistic attitudes. Nearly all who covered the war endorsed America's aims, celebrated its soldiers, and presented a romantically distorted view of conflict. They did this mostly through selective observation and self-censorship, independent of overt control.

RICHARD HARDING DAVIS, STAR CORRESPONDENT

None approached war more romantically than Richard Harding Davis. The most famous reporter in an age described by Irvin S. Cobb as "the time of the Great Reporter," Davis embodied the clean-cut, patriotic, masculine ideal characterized by the drawings of Charles Dana Gibson. He came from a literary family. His mother, Rebecca Harding Davis, was a celebrated writer. When her son Richard was born in 1864, followed by two siblings in the next eight years, she poured herself into raising creative, moral children. She doted on her eldest son, turning him into a mama's boy. Richard, however, struggled in grade school and at Lehigh and Johns Hopkins universities. He rarely applied himself to the subjects being taught. Instead, he began dressing and acting the part of a rich dandy and expressing himself in print. He wrote for college publications and eventually secured jobs at newspapers in Philadelphia. There he interviewed Walt Whitman and covered the Johnstown flood of 1889. Moving to New York, he got a job at Charles A. Dana's *Evening Sun* and began writing fiction on the side.

Davis rose to become one of New York's most famous writers, specializing in accounts of show business and the slums. The publication of his short stories and novels, including the best-selling adventure tale *Soldiers of Fortune,* secured his fame as well as enough income to keep him in tailored suits and expensive dinners from Delmonico's. Despite his success, he longed to write about war. He accepted an offer from Hearst and traveled to Cuba in January 1897 to investigate the islanders' revolt against Spain. During his travels, where he was welcomed by the Spanish authorities, he witnessed a firing squad execute a young insurgent in Santa Clara province. The resulting news story, "The Death of Rodriguez," demonstrated his skill as an observer of detail as well as his penchant for romanticizing conflict. The farm boy met his fate with heroic nonchalance and a cigarette dangling from his lips. Davis's story ended with the boy's bullet-riddled body in the grass next to the cigarette that "still burned, a tiny ring of living fire, at the place where the figure had first stood." The boy seemed to sleep in the wet grass, with "the blood from his breast sinking into the soil he had tried to free." Thus was born the Hollywood cliché of the last cigarette for the condemned man.

Later that year, Davis briefly covered the short Greco-Turkish War. The state of press-military relations may have reached an all-time high during that conflict—at least according to reporters on the scene. Davis marched with troops and picnicked with the generals. During one encounter, a Greek commander "seriously apologized for not bombarding while I was there," Davis wrote, "and I said not to mention it."

America sided with the Cuban revolt and went to war against Spain after the mysterious destruction of the *Maine* in Havana harbor in 1898. Returning to Cuba to write for *The Times* of London, *New York Herald,* and *Scribner's,* Davis reveled in the press's freedom of movement and freedom of action near the front lines. American journalists ran guns, acted as spies, and scouted the enemy.

Even William Randolph Hearst, the millionaire publisher, joined the action. He jotted down the story of an assault from a wounded eyewitness as Mauser bullets from Spanish troops pinged around them and then jovially observed that it had been "a splendid fight." He also sailed on his own yacht to inspect the burned hulks of Spanish warships in Santiago harbor and ransack them for souvenirs. "Can't you mind your own business?" an officer demanded of Hearst and his assistants after they boarded their yacht. "Not very well, sir, and be good newspapermen," Hearst replied.

For his part, Davis directed the Rough Riders' return fire against Spanish snipers at Las Guasimas and shot twenty rounds from a carbine at a Spanish shack. "I thought as an American I ought to help," he told his brother. In Puerto Rico as the war wound to a close, Davis entered the town of Coamo ahead of occupying troops and accepted its surrender with comic-opera gravity. No wonder he declared his support for this "merry war."

A competitor, Poultney Bigelow of the *New York Herald,* ranked as one of the first to question the war's conduct when he exposed logistical problems in the embarkation city of Tampa, Florida. "Nobody dares complain for fear of appearing unpatriotic," he wrote. "Still it will do no harm to hear a little of the truth." His reports resulted in loss of his army credentials.

Davis criticized Bigelow's stories as "untrue" and "unAmerican," but he knew better. After apparently wrestling with his conscience, Davis wrote his own exposé of mismanagement as the army prepared to attack Santiago. In a report dispatched to the *Herald,* Davis described the campaign in Cuba as "prepared in ignorance and conducted in a series of blunders. . . . This is written with the sole purpose that the entire press of the country will force instant action at Washington to relieve the strained situation." The *Herald* labeled Davis's report too inflammatory and withheld it from publication for several days. By the time it appeared in print, the Spanish fleet had been destroyed and the troops in Cuba were on the verge of surrender. It was only after the war, when American citizens learned of the army's blunders as well as woefully inadequate health care—deaths from disease outnumbered combat fatalities fourteen to one—that public opinion swung against the army's leaders.

ON THE EVE OF TOTAL WAR

Despite their different tactics, the American military in Cuba and the Japanese military in Korea had the same goals in their press relations. Both sought to use journalists to boost public confidence among citizens and soldiers. The United States expected a short and successful war against Spain and had public opinion on its side. A free press, catering to the tastes of an enthusiastic American public, could be expected to report swift and heroic victories and downplay the war's logistical and tactical mistakes.

The American military accepted the potential risks of open news coverage in 1898 in return for its benefits. Generally upbeat news contributed to greater support. Like feedback in an amplifier, boosting a signal and then using the output to push the signal even higher, good press and good feelings increased together.

Of course, the process could work both ways. When a nation's citizens disapprove of a particular war, the news media enjoy greater freedom to criticize without suffering economic, governmental, or military pressure. Negative publicity feeds the growth of negative public opinion, and vice versa.

That is what the Japanese army feared in 1904. Fighting a European power for the first time, it was unsure of its chances of victory on the field. To lessen or erase the impact of bad news from the front, the Japanese government and army instituted rigid censorship before the fighting started. National harmony remained high. The system succeeded even though Japan's relatively easy victory over Russia, which shocked Europe and America, suggested the censorship plan wasn't crucial. The rest of the world noted not only Japan's rise to military power but also its innovative incorporation of the news media into an overall wartime strategy. Thus in 1904, the free and open youth of combat journalism came to an end, replaced by the hard realities of the twentieth century.

As wars that ensued grew to encompass millions of soldiers and national economies retooled to support long-term

combat, press controls also grew more extensive and sophisticated. Some were overt, some subtle. Some were imposed
from without, some emerged from within. Regardless, the
institutions of publicity, propaganda, and censorship remade
the political map of the world as wartime governments
became more adept at shaping information for public
consumption.

Early in the twentieth century, all of the modern elements
of press-military-government relations were in play. The
American government had precedents for military control of
civilian correspondents and their papers; military censorship
of news from war zones had become the norm; and most
journalists had adopted a rationale for self-censorship that
extended beyond strict concerns over operational security.
The next step, the creation of systematic propaganda,
awaited the outbreak of such total war that governments insisted on enlisting journalists as full-fledged participants.
Within a decade of the Russo-Japanese War, such a war
came. With it came huge armies, big government, and a
massive effort to control the press.

TWO

WORDS AS WEAPONS: WORLD WAR I PROPAGANDA AND CENSORSHIP

"If people really knew, the war would be stopped tomorrow. But of course they don't know and can't know. The correspondents don't write and the censorship would not pass the truth."
— David Lloyd George, British prime minister, privately to C. P. Scott, editor of the *Manchester Guardian,* December 28, 1917

World War I drove a wedge of doubt and suspicion between wartime journalists and their sources. The American press lost a measure of independence in support of fighting total war. Afterward, in balancing the ledger of gains and losses, journalists questioned their sacrifice.

"Total war" meant exactly what the phrase suggested: the harnessing of every resource to achieve victory. Conscription put millions in uniform. Factories retooled from civilian to military production. And a new combat zone, the home front, emerged. To win the fight at home, governments mobilized public opinion through widespread, systematic control of information. Too much was at stake, they reasoned, to allow the press any significant degree of freedom. But it would be an exaggeration to say Uncle Sam drafted American journalism into service. The press enlisted to fight World War I. With few exceptions, newspapers and magazines agreed not only to abide by broad censorship guidelines but also to spread government-approved messages. It was "the first press agents' war," according to the *New York Times*—the first time nations conducted mass media campaigns aimed at whipping their citizens into a frenzy as well as gaining favorable wartime press coverage in foreign countries.

The government-inspired hysteria extolled all things American and demonized all things German, portraying the kaiser's soldiers as wild beasts, Huns, gorillas, rapists, sadists, and menaces to Christian civilization. Only after the war did Americans learn how much the Allied governments had selectively informed them.

PROPAGANDA: COMMISSION AND OMISSION

A combination of military censorship at the front and "voluntary" censorship at home kept the news in line. Those who tested America's tolerance for free expression found themselves arrested and charged with crimes under sweeping federal laws. Hundreds went to prison. Postal inspectors barred newspapers and magazines from the mail if they challenged government propaganda. Vigilante mobs pressured naysayers to fall in line or face violence. Together, government agencies and their public supporters violated a laundry list of constitutional rights. "Efforts to curtail civil liberty in the United States came from so many different directions, the citizen failed to realize how close he came to losing civil liberty entirely," said World War I censorship historian James R. Mock.

The assault on independent thought began with Britain's first offensive act of the war. It shaped how America received and interpreted news of the war in Europe. On the evening of August 4, 1914, while Britain still was officially at peace, its 213-foot cable-laying ship *Telconia* slipped out of port and headed for continental Europe. Germany already was fighting Russia and France, and its invasion of neutral Belgium during the march toward Paris had prompted Britain to issue a last-minute war ultimatum. As Britain's midnight deadline passed for a German withdrawal, the *Telconia* churned toward the port of Emden in accord with war plans that had been drawn up two years earlier. On August 5, the ship hauled up from the ocean floor five cables connecting German telegraph offices with France, Spain, the Canary Islands, and the Americas. The crew cut four, leaving only the cable to Brazil because it was partly owned by Americans. A year later, the British cut that one, too. Thus, during the crucial opening weeks of war, when Americans were forming opinions, Britain improved its communication security and enjoyed a monopoly on direct telegraphic traffic to the United States. German attempts to influence the New World had to rely on the slower or less dependable mail ships and radio transmissions.

"It all turns on which side gets the news in first; for the first impression sticks," lamented the German ambassador to the United States. While that was true, he neglected to point out the chief drawback of German propaganda: No matter how much Germans complained of British spin, they could not ignore that their soldiers had taken the offensive and their armies had overrun neutral Belgium.

Domination of the channels of communication between Europe and America gave Britain a continuing advantage as it targeted American opinion. Still, the work was difficult at first. In the war's early months, most Americans endorsed President Woodrow Wilson's declaration of neutrality in word and deed. A *Literary Digest* poll in November 1914 found 105 newspaper editors to favor Britain and its allies; 20 to favor Germany and its allies; and a majority of 242 who proclaimed strict neutrality. Faced with entrenched attitudes, the British Foreign Office established a secret War Propaganda Bureau at Wellington House, a former insurance office. The bureau, headed by Charles Masterman, quietly sought to influence neutral nations to hate the Central powers and support the Allies.

The branch dedicated to American opinion, headed by Sir Gilbert Parker, papered the United States with pamphlets, cartoons, books, printed speeches, and slanted news stories. Parker concentrated on sympathetic Americans in positions of power and prestige. His office compiled lists of names of influential figures in schools, government offices, industry, and the news media. At its peak, the American contacts numbered 260,000. In addition to mailing letters to prominent Americans, the propaganda bureau placed its materials in libraries, YMCAs, and universities. Weekly reports, circulated in-house and titled *The American Press Résumé,* tracked successful efforts to place British propaganda in U.S. papers and magazines. "The pro-Ally *Philadelphia Public*

Ledger writes an editorial upon the pamphlet 'Treasury Romances' prepared by Wellington House," a typical *Résumé* report told Parker's agency.

Britain and France severely limited journalists' access to the western front in 1914 and 1915, preventing independent coverage of the war that might undermine propaganda. Field Marshal Lord Herbert Kitchener, who hated journalists, ordered them arrested and expelled if they should be found wandering British lines in 1914. In their place, he dispatched a British officer, Colonel Earnest Swinton, to send the press a series of official reports from the front. Swinton called himself "Eye-witness." Sarcastic editors sniffed at his columns' patriotic pabulum and dubbed them "Eye-Wash."

After initially following a similar policy forbidding journalists from the front, France found a craftier solution to the problem of press control. The Bureau de la Presse announced that reporters would be allowed to tour the French sector under restrictions similar to those adopted by the Japanese in 1904: strict censorship, military escorts, and press conferences with a designated spokesman. Once the reporter had the approved facts in hand, he would be allowed to write a story—but only in French. To guarantee fluency in the language, reporters took a grammar test. The exam proved so difficult that no American applicant could pass it.

The fierce restrictions on journalists didn't crack until former President Theodore Roosevelt complained to Sir Edward Grey, the British foreign secretary, in January 1915. "The only real war news written by Americans who are known to and trusted by the American public comes from the German side; as a result of this, the sympathizers with the cause of the Allies can hear nothing whatsoever about the trials and achievements of the British and French armies," Roosevelt wrote.

A few weeks later, the British Expeditionary Force agreed to accredit five British newspaper reporters and take them on a carefully guided tour. Incredibly, only one American journalist received accreditation—*one* reporter to cover the entire war, for *all* American readers. That reporter, Frederick Palmer, filed a censored pool report for the Associated Press, United Press, and International News Service.

In such a nearly airless atmosphere, rumors expanded into atrocity stories. Such stories were not unique to World War I; they formed an integral part of the religious propaganda of the Crusades as well as many subsequent conflicts. However, total war created a greater need to persuade ordinary citizens to fight. Whereas professional armies fought at the pleasure of governments, the task of indoctrinating young conscripts to kill required a massive moral adjustment. World War I propaganda relied heavily on the creation and exploitation of ethnic hatred; stories of atrocity provided a ready tool.

Such stories centered on three main topics: massacres, such as the Turkish genocide in Armenia; mutilations, including the supposed amputation of children's hands, bayoneting of Belgian babies, and crucifixion of a Canadian soldier; and the mistreatment of war prisoners and civilians, including rape and torture. Some were true, some false, and some open to interpretation. After the Germans executed English nurse Edith Cavell on charges of helping French and British soldiers escape from Belgium, she posthumously enlisted in the British atrocity propaganda campaign. The press called her sentence "judicial murder," even though she freely admitted her actions. Likewise, the press framed the German torpedoing of the passenger liner *Lusitania* in March 1915 as an atrocity, even though Germany had warned neutral nations that its submarines might attack any ships traveling in the war zone near Britain.

On occasion, propagandists created atrocity stories of pure fiction and circulated them throughout the world. The British allegation in April 1917 that the German army rendered soldiers' corpses into soap remains the most infamous example. The chief of British Army Intelligence, Brigadier General J. V. Charters, deliberately switched the captions of two captured photographs to promote the lie. One picture showed dead horses being sent to a soap factory; the other showed dead Germans en route to burial. Charters sent the newly captioned photo of "German cadavers on way to the soap factory" to Shanghai, certain it would assault the Chinese reverence for the dead. From there, the story spread throughout the world. *The Times* of London seemed to find independent corroboration in a German dispatch, which it reprinted, that referred to the German army's *Kadaververwertungsanstalt*. The paper translated that mouthful as a "Corpse Exploitation Establishment" that converted cadavers into war matériel. Germany protested that "kadavers" would hardly refer to human bodies, but to no avail. In the passion of war, the story of German disregard for the dead fit Britain's needs too well to go gently into that good night. Not until several years later did Charters admit his hand in the fabrication.

Atrocity stories spread not only because they resonated with readers saturated in propaganda but also because censorship severely limited journalists' investigations. Only once in the early months of the war did an independent voice cast doubt on an atrocity allegation. As the German army marched through Belgium, hard-to-confirm reports of mass torture and mutilation reached the Allies. The accounts seemed plausible, given Germany's undeniable torching of the ancient Belgian university town of Louvain, where scores of civilians died.

Five American newspaper correspondents, including the nationally respected Irvin S. Cobb of the *Saturday Evening Post,* managed to witness the initial German offensive in Belgium and get their accounts to American readers. They confirmed that civilians had been shot but said the Germans acted in retaliation for sniper attacks. "After spending two weeks with and accompanying the troops upward of 100 miles, we are unable to report a single instance unprovoked," the correspondents said. "Everywhere we have seen Germans paying for purchases and respecting property rights, as well as according civilians every consideration." Cobb insisted he was no apologist. As a neutral observer, he felt it his duty to report the facts. In a book rushed into print in 1915, Cobb reiterated he found nothing to confirm the stories of depravity. "As for Uhlans [Prussian light cavalry] spearing babies on their lances, and officers sabering their own men, and soldiers murdering and mutilating and torturing at will—I saw nothing," Cobb said. "I knew of these tales only from having read them in the dispatches . . . cabled to American papers [through British censorship]."

Americans debated whether the correspondents had been duped by their German escorts. That argument received a boost in May 1915 when Wellington House published "Report of the Committee on Alleged German Atrocities" under the chairmanship of a respected British historian, Viscount James Bryce. Bryce loaned his prestige to a report that, in retrospect, rests on an extremely shaky foundation. The report's evidence lay in 1,200 statements, many from Belgians who had fled their country for Britain. None of the statements was taken under oath. Many, if not most, were recorded by British agents who did not speak Flemish, the language of many refugees. None of the Belgians was named. Anonymity shielded them and their families from reprisals, but it also conveniently protected them from taking responsibility for their words.

Nevertheless, American newspapers treated the so-called Bryce report as gospel. The *New York Times* proclaimed in a front-page headline, "German Atrocities Are Proved, Finds Bryce Committee." In summarizing the 30,000-word report, the *Times* accused Germany of "deliberate and systematically organized massacres of the civil population." An editorial assured readers that Bryce and his colleagues, as "men of high character and standing," deserved complete trust. Bryce's report said the original depositions would be preserved for later validation, but exhaustive searches after the war failed to find them. They had conveniently disappeared after serious scholars attempted to confirm the atrocity allegations.

AMERICAN CENSORSHIP EFFORTS

America entered the war in April 1917 after Germany's resumption of unrestricted submarine warfare and the public revelation of its pursuit of an alliance with Mexico. Censorship of the American news media began almost immediately.

At home, the federal government quickly created a federal office that supervised a system of self-censorship, augmented by subtle and not-so-subtle threats. Abroad, American military censorship began with the arrival of the first Yankees in France that summer. Both forms of press control guaranteed a narrow view of combat conditions for American readers.

The American War Department had started planning for censorship shortly after the beginning of the war in Europe in 1914. Researchers investigated press restrictions in other countries and made recommendations to the chief of staff. Their report, published in 1916 as "The Proper Relationship Between the Army and the Press in War," characterized the armed forces' needs as "paramount" when compared with those of the press and public and warned of the potential for critical news accounts to damage military efficiency.

The mass media's power to gather information and disseminate it quickly frightened military planners enough for them to demand total control over war news. The War Department named a young major, Douglas MacArthur, as military censor. Ironically, the man who would earn fame as a general in the Pacific during World War II as a result of favorable press coverage had few kind words for journalists in 1916. He said reporters' accounts of battles, including names of particular units in the lines, "furnish information to the enemy that will enable him to detect the strength and location and intended movements of our own troops." Unshackled press criticism of military leaders would undercut discipline, MacArthur added. He proposed strict military control of the press in combat zones and hoped that domestic newspapers would make compromises with the War Department in America's best interests.

Arthur Bullard, a young foreign correspondent for *Harper's Weekly, Outlook,* and *Century* magazines, read MacArthur's report and dispatched a different plan for America's wartime press to Colonel Edward M. House, Wilson's closest adviser. Bullard, who would go on to serve as a liaison to Russia during the war, argued that responsible press criticism would help, not hurt, morale. Overzealous military censorship, he said, would produce "systematic falsification of Public Opinion" as well as protect incompetents in authority. Truth, however painful, would support the government because democracy required "trust [in] the people to sort the true from the false."

The actual system of publicity, propaganda, and censorship that emerged on the home front beginning in April 1917 lay somewhere between MacArthur's and Bullard's proposals. The federal government recognized the press's key role in total war. However, rather than control it with an iron fist, the president and Congress attempted to influence it with a combination of carrot and stick. A new federal office, the Committee on Public Information (CPI), provided the carrot: a steady supply of war news, ready for publication, in the form of 6,000 government press releases, coupled with a domestic censorship system that avoided outright prior restraint. The stick consisted of a series of federal laws, beginning in 1917, that punished journalists and other civilians who refused to play by the government's rules.

Wilson created the CPI by executive order on April 14, 1917. He placed the secretaries of war, navy, and state on its board and named George Creel, an enthusiastic Wilson supporter and Colorado journalist, as its chairman. Josephus Daniels, an erstwhile newspaper publisher who had become navy secretary in 1913, said Wilson foresaw two purposes for Creel's committee: to mobilize the mind of America and to fight for the "verdict of mankind." Both required maximum publicity, he said, as Wilson believed that to *form* public opinion, he first had to *inform* it. Creel echoed that sentiment, portraying the creation of public support as the result of expression, not suppression.

In practice, however, Creel encouraged the silencing of those who questioned their government. A typical CPI pamphlet, "The German Whisper," told Americans to give the Justice Department the names of anyone spreading antiwar statements. One of the first major CPI campaigns targeted expansion of the armed forces and replacement of neutrality with prowar hysteria. Wilson had campaigned in 1916 on a platform of having kept America out of the war. Pacifism gripped much of the country even after Congress declared war, with only 73,000 Americans enlisting in the ensuing six weeks. The government turned to conscription and a propaganda campaign to increase civilian support for the war. "There was no part of the great war machinery that we did not touch, no medium of appeal that we did not employ," Creel said in a postwar report to the president. "The printed word, the spoken word, the motion picture, the poster, the signboard—all these were used in our campaign."

It was true: Virtually every piece of war information that reached a typical American family carried the endorsement of the U.S. government. Creel's agency distributed 75 million copies of prowar pamphlets; coordinated and released war news from the army and navy; organized a bureau of 75,000 speakers to give four-minute prowar talks around the country; mobilized artists, advertisers, photographers, and motion picture producers; and performed myriad other tasks targeting specific groups at home and abroad. The committee also issued the federal government's first daily newspaper, the *Official Bulletin,* at Wilson's specific request. It reached a peak circulation of 115,000. Newspapers received it for free and dissected it for stories.

The CPI's Division of News made itself indispensable to the press. It released lists of casualties and interviews with high-ranking government and military officials. It institutionalized the distribution of government press releases, resulting in an average of six pounds of official circulars arriving in California newsrooms every day. It also operated a clearinghouse for press questions about the war.

Creel touted his office's ability to produce unbiased, factual news and noted that critics questioned the accuracy of only four of the CPI's press statements. Although technically true, that claim ignores the skewing of information in other materials. Pamphlets and other CPI releases took information out of context, highlighted militaristic German statements while ignoring others, and presented some information as fact when it was open to doubt. The committee released a regular column for publication headlined "The Daily German Lie," along with a pamphlet titled "The Kaiserite in America," both of which treated wild rumors (e.g., Wilson's secretary had been shot for treason) as part of a systematic, domestic German propaganda campaign. "You have met him, Mr. Citizen," the "Kaiserite" pamphlet warned Americans. "Or you have met a man who has just met him—and who still carries about in his conversation the peculiar accent of German propaganda. The agents of the Imperial German Government are busily spreading throughout the country all sorts of poisonous lies and disquieting rumors and insidious criticisms of the Government and its war-work. . . . Watch for the stories . . . and nail them at sight. In that way, you will be doing as good work for your government as the inventor of the lie is trying to do for his Imperial master in Potsdam."

More egregiously, Creel's official listing of all CPI pamphlets failed to mention the most notorious, "The German-Bolshevik Conspiracy," which purported to prove German supervision of Russia's 1917 Bolshevik Revolution. American and British experts already had declared the pamphlet's sources to be forgeries, but Wilson and Creel decided to publish it nevertheless. When the *New York Evening Post* publicly discredited the pamphlet, Creel sent a letter to the editor accusing the paper of "having given aid and comfort to the enemy," the constitutional definition of treason. Later examinations established beyond doubt that the *Post* was right.

The CPI also urged American newspapers to avoid publishing stories that might undermine the Bryce report. "The Daily German Lie" column linked support for the report's authenticity to a War Department request for a ban on publishing atrocity rumors. "That he [Germany] has been guilty of atrocities has been clearly proven," the "German Lie" said of America's adversary. "The request is designed to prevent vitiation of the unimpeachable case which has been established against him by the British Bryce report and the findings of other official agencies which have investigated instances of his cruelty. Publication of charges of atrocities that are not susceptible of proof would enable him to make a propaganda attack upon the proven cases." By helping stifle criticism of the "unimpeachable" Bryce report, the CPI contributed to its acceptance and the disillusionment that later greeted its dismissal as false propaganda.

THE PRESS AND SELF-CENSORSHIP

Coupled with his office's outpouring of publicity, Creel aimed to control the press through a system of self-censorship that avoided a First Amendment showdown. In May 1917, the CPI issued a censorship card—edited by Wilson himself—to American newspapers and magazines. It summarized the government's requests for self-restraint on publishing stories that had not gone through official censorship channels. The card placed news in three categories: dangerous material that should not be published, such as news of current military operations "except that officially given out"; questionable news accounts, such as rumors and stories focused on the technology of warfare, which journalists were asked to clear with the CPI before publication; and material that had no bearing on the war and therefore could be published as the editor saw fit.

Creel hoped that the press could be coaxed into self-censorship through appeals to common sense and patriotism. "It was not servants we wanted, but associates," Creel wrote in his war memoir. "Better far to have the desired compulsions proceed from within than to apply them from without." While self-censorship proved effective—the small number of violations never was linked to any casualties—the press grumbled at Creel's imperious manner. Creel antagonized journalists with his thin skin, his arrogance, and his refusal to compromise. "Voluntary" censorship took on the coloring of government coercion.

"I ask . . . for an instant reply to your attitude," he wrote to the publisher of *The Story of the Great War,* a set of books he considered disloyal. "Above all, I wish to know the name of the man responsible for the preparation of the material that is so peculiarly German in its very essence. . . . I must insist that changes be made." Creel also roared at press baron William Randolph Hearst over a story about the defense of troop transports. He demanded that Hearst name his sources and proclaimed publication of the story illegal. Creel's bark had a bite. He sat on federal boards that could deny exportation of published materials, including films, or cut off newsprint to recalcitrant editors.

If Americans ignored Creel's threats, they could be prosecuted under three federal laws passed during the war to control speech and press. The first, the Espionage Act of 1917, provided sentences of up to twenty years in prison and fines as high as $10,000 for statements that disrupted the work of the army or navy or were otherwise deemed disloyal. Publications that contained such expression could be withheld from the mail and lose their second-class mail permits, which usually were essential to profits. U.S. Navy Secretary Daniels called the law the "Big Stick behind voluntary censorship."

America's postmaster general, Albert Burleson, enthusiastically invoked the law about seventy-five times by mid-1918. In particular, he targeted socialist newspapers. Many lost their licenses; others he coerced into self-censorship with threats. Among the victims was the National Civil Liberties Bureau, which was denied use of the mail. A postal inspector rejected the bureau's "Freedom of Speech and the Press" pamphlet as an inappropriate wartime publication.

The Supreme Court upheld the Espionage Act in a 1919 decision, *Schenck v. United States,* in which it famously proclaimed that the First Amendment did not protect a man from falsely shouting "fire" in a crowded theater. Justice Oliver Wendell Holmes Jr. ruled that freedom of expression cannot be absolute in wartime. Instead, words must be weighed to decide if they "are of such a nature as to create a clear and present danger that they will bring about the substantive evils that Congress has a right to prevent." Curiously, *Schenck* focused on the distribution of a leaflet that urged peaceful opposition to the draft, not the "substantive" panic envisioned by the theater analogy. The decision nevertheless created a major limitation on First Amendment freedom that stands to this day.

The scope of the Espionage Act broadened in 1918 with a second law, known as the Sedition Act. It punished expressions of contempt for the president, the government, the Constitution, and a host of other supposedly disloyal opinions, including those uttered casually or impulsively instead of deliberately. The Justice Department prosecuted 2,168 people under the two laws and convicted 1,053, including twenty-four who received twenty-year prison terms. The most famous victim was Socialist party leader Eugene V. Debs, who ran for president in 1920 from his cell. The Sedition Act expired the following year.

The third punitive federal law, the Trading with the Enemy Act of 1917, allowed the president to censor mail entering and leaving the United States and required foreign-language papers to file English translations of war-related articles before mailing. That requirement placed a heavy burden on the budgets and deadlines of small, foreign-language papers. One journalist who refused to follow the law, the publisher of the German-language *Herold* of Wisconsin, died in prison. His crime was failure to translate an editorial that criticized the army's smallpox vaccination program.

The postmaster general won the Supreme Court's endorsement of his power to revoke second-class permits in a case filed by the Socialist *Milwaukee Leader,* which had criticized the president and government. Justice John H. Clarke's opinion said, "The Constitution was adopted to preserve our Government, not to serve as a protecting screen for those who while claiming its privileges seek to destroy it."

AMERICAN CENSORSHIP AT THE FRONT

Across the ocean, the army imposed a system of combat-zone censorship that proved ruthlessly effective. Accreditation required reporters to swear they would "convey the truth to the people of the United States" while avoiding topics that might provide valuable information to the enemy. They had to post a bond, subject to forfeit for any violation of accreditation rules, including censorship, and deposit $1,000 with the adjutant general in Washington to offset expenses in the field. They received passes and identification cards, just as did military officers, but reporters enjoyed the freedom to move without military escorts. Correspondents wore Sam Browne belts, green arm bands adorned with the letter C, and uniforms without the insignia of rank, to show their subservience to army control yet indicate they were not to take or give salutes.

Correspondents were allowed to carry small cameras. However, field censorship virtually killed objective photojournalism. Trench warfare produced particularly vivid images, but the American government deemed them too gruesome to share with the public. Concentrated shellfire, barbed wire, poison gas, machine gun bullets, and the mud and filth contrasted with the romantic view of war left over from the end of the nineteenth century. Jimmy Hare, a veteran combat photographer, observed that the British War Office was especially fearful of the effect of war pictures. As he observed in 1915, "to so much as make a snapshot without official permission in writing means arrest."

Not much changed after American troops appeared in France in 1917. Authorized photography remained the responsibility of the Army Signal Corps and, to a lesser extent, the other service branches. General John Pershing, commander of the American Expeditionary Force, loosened the rules in December 1917 only after learning the army could not control French official photographs that circulated overseas or clandestine picture-taking. Pershing decided to allow civilian photographers to undergo the same accreditation process as reporters.

Photographic censorship first fell to the Paris office of the CPI. In May 1918 photographic censorship shifted to an army office, the newly formed photographic subdivision of military intelligence. It took charge of creating official army photographs as well as censoring civilian photojournalism. Army officials held up any photograph that indicated a specific location, military unit (including any unit insignia), or details about weaponry. Photographs deemed likely to hurt morale or "cause unnecessary and unwarranted anxiety to the families of men at the front," including images of war's horrors, were suppressed. Also censored were photographs of black and white soldiers relaxing together, which censors feared would anger Southerners.

Civilian combat photographers quickly learned what would pass muster and began censoring themselves, either by avoiding forbidden subjects or withholding offensive negatives until after the war. As a result, bland and happy images circulated in America. Only a few pictures of wounded Americans—already receiving aid for their injuries—received the censor's approval. Not one photograph of a dead American soldier's body appeared in print while the war was being fought.

FREDERICK PALMER, JOURNALIST AND CENSOR

In choosing the military censor to oversee American print reporters in Europe, Pershing made a shrewd choice: Frederick Palmer, who had been the lone American correspondent accredited to the British front in early 1915. On April 4, 1917, the day Congress declared war, Colonel House recommended Palmer for the job in a private note to President Wilson. House reasoned that Palmer already knew the conditions at the front, had great experience as a war correspondent, and had no affiliation with any particular American paper or magazine. Pershing shared House's assessment that Palmer's background made him the perfect candidate for the job. Pershing offered the position to Palmer after appealing to his sense of duty. In taking the commission in late June, Palmer traded an offer of $40,000 from the *New York Herald* for a major's salary of $2,400 per year.

Palmer knew, only too well, that static war produced few

headlines. "Unless some new way of killing developed, even the English public did not care to read about its own army," Palmer wrote. He knew many aspects of warfare were routinely kept from print even though their existence was common knowledge to both armies. And he knew firsthand that censorship had increased with every war since the mid-1890s.

"More and more, perhaps, they [correspondents] were being used as the personal perquisite of generals and statesmen in war time to screen their errors and promote their individual ambitions," he wrote. "Where the mirror which he held up formerly reflected photographic actualities, it now reflected a drawing out of focus to inflame the war spirit." Palmer penned those comments after the war. When he accepted Pershing's offer, he still clung to his idealism. This war would end all wars, he thought, and he relished the opportunity to play a small role in it. What he did not realize was the extent to which military censorship would cause him to distort the news.

Palmer's background was the opposite of Richard Harding Davis's life of privilege. Palmer was born in 1873 in the Pennsylvania oil country and grew up on a tenant farm in upstate New York. He took up journalism to help pay the family's bills. When the *New York Press* asked him to be a full-time European correspondent, Palmer said he "found nothing personally distasteful in the suggestion." Thus began a career in which he covered nearly every major war from the Greco-Turkish conflict of 1897 to the Pacific campaign against Japan at the end of World War II. Despite his life of globe-trotting, he insisted that the last time he felt truly free to cover the sweep of war was during the final battle of his first conflict, when he was twenty-four years old.

Palmer missed the Spanish-American War while covering the Yukon gold rush. However, he arrived in the Philippines in time to observe the native insurrection against the American occupation, which started shortly after the Spanish defeat. The Filipinos had rallied against Spain in expectation of independence; instead, they chafed at living under an American army of occupation. Palmer observed Filipino guerrillas revolutionizing strategy and tactics.

"You can't wrestle when you can't lay hands on the other fellow," an American soldier told him. Likewise, when Palmer asked an American general whether a particular victory would "break the backbone" of the insurrection, the general replied, "I am not yet convinced that this rebellion is a vertebrate organism." Hundreds of thousands of Philippine islanders died, many of them victims of American brutality, as the army crushed the rebellion through mass killings and burnings. The American governor-general, Elwell S. Otis, controlled the press accounts of the slaughter with full approval of President William McKinley. Otis told his chief censor to "let nothing go that can hurt the Administration" and shaped the news to keep the American public in the dark about the true state of affairs.

Palmer covered the Boxer Rebellion in China, the Russo-Japanese War, and a brief 1912 war in the Balkans. As World War I censor, he initially believed the press and military could work together. He saw his own position as a bridge between the two and pressed for greater access for reporters. He applauded when nineteen American correspondents quickly received accreditation to cover the American Expeditionary Force. "Following the same ratio to the number of troops, the British Army would have had three thousand correspondents," he said.

PRESS-MILITARY FRICTION

As the American presence swelled in 1918, Pershing permitted the press corps to grow as well. Up to twenty-five reporters fell under the direct supervision of the army's press division. In addition, one accredited correspondent won approval to go with each division, allowing hometown papers to cover hometown heroes. "Visiting" correspondents were housed in Paris and given tours of the front. Although the total numbers are imprecise, World War I journalism historian Emmet Crozier listed more than thirty journalists accredited to the army and dozens more who visited the front.

Four reporters had their credentials suspended for violating accreditation agreements. The American Expeditionary Force (AEF) dismissed Wythe Williams of the *New York Times* for filing a story to *Collier's Weekly* magazine without clearing it through censorship. Williams protested that he was free to do so, as the article did not mention the AEF. However, the army said it embarrassed France by blaming a military defeat on French politicians. It made no difference that the source of the story was Georges Clemenceau, the French prime minister. Also dismissed was Reginald Wright Kauffman of the *Philadelphia North American,* who chafed under regulations. He smuggled uncensored criticism of conditions at the front to his paper by sending his letters to the home of another opinionated war observer, Teddy Roosevelt—reasoning the censors would not open mail addressed to a former president. A third reporter, Westbrook Pegler of United Press, was removed at Pershing's request for his aggressive attempts to inform Americans about a severe shortage of supplies. Pegler described how lack of proper clothing and warm housing contributed to the American death toll in the winter of 1917–1918 and also how censorship kept the home front from learning about avoidable military errors. Heywood Broun also lost his credentials after documenting the lack of preparedness in the lines. He waited until he returned to the United States, thus avoiding the censor's stranglehold on the telegraph, to write his exposé. "Supply Blunders Hamper First U.S. Units in France," blared the headline on Broun's *New York World* article.

The army insisted on censoring news that might injure morale as well as alert the enemy to advantages in combat. Reporters were forbidden to write that grateful French civilians gave wine to American soldiers because of fears it might offend the temperance movement. News of the transfer of the first American units to the front lines in January 1918 was kept out of American papers for seventeen days, long after the British, French, and Germans knew. Censors gave no reason for the delay, but correspondents speculated that the government wanted to downplay any news that made it clear that American troops had been in France for six months without seeing any action.

Palmer played a key role in at least two controversial censorship decisions. In the first, he prevented correspondents from giving a full picture of Americans capturing their first prisoner. A nineteen-year-old German mail carrier had wandered into the wrong lines in the dark and surprised two

Americans. They shot him, and one stabbed him with his bayonet after he fell. Palmer allowed the story of the capture to go out on the wires but deleted reference to the fatal stab wounds. In the second, he refused to allow correspondents to write about a common but unpleasant fact of trench warfare: soldiers slit enemy throats at night. Palmer silenced news of German "mutilations," reasoning that if America were really making an idealistic war to end war, "the inculcation of hate to fester in the minds of future generations was a poor way of attaining our object." In the end, Palmer despised his role as apologist. In the final volume of his war memoirs, published in 1921, he wrote that in the censor's office, "one must suffer agony as he strangled the truth and squirm with nausea as he allowed propaganda to pass." Above all, he said, the grand illusions of war could not be challenged.

Perhaps Palmer's distaste for the job affected his relations with accredited journalists. By early 1918, reporters complained of Palmer's being aloof, stuffy, and hidebound. Meanwhile, army officers questioned his efforts to liberalize censorship. Caught in the middle, Palmer stepped down in late winter 1918. His last official act as censor, before joining Pershing's general staff, was to carry orders from the War Department to Pershing authorizing a relaxation of censorship rules, partly in response to domestic complaints. Military censors exercised a lighter touch for the duration of the war and allowed more war news to be sent home faster.

Still, censorship colored the news from Europe, even after the end of hostilities. On Armistice Day, four American reporters went off on their own to inspect conditions in Germany, only to eventually run afoul of postcombat censorship. They reasoned that the end of the war meant they no longer had to answer to military discipline. Surveying the devastation of no-man's-land and determined to avoid future carnage, they vowed to tell the truth at any price. "If the angel of the Lord had appeared before us on the battlefield and said to each one, 'Would you give your life to prevent another such war?' all four of us would gladly have gone out and died," wrote one of the four, George Seldes of the Marshall Syndicate. The others were Lincoln Eyre of the *New York World,* Cal Lyon of the Newspaper Enterprise Association, and Hal Corey of the Associated Newspapers syndicate. In addition, Frederick A. Smith of the *Chicago Tribune* joined the "runaway" correspondents for a time.

The reporters took two Cadillacs and crossed into Germany in late November. They were greeted by a Workers and Soldiers Council, which had assumed local control in a mutiny. Council members ordered Field Marshal Paul von Hindenburg to submit to an interview with the correspondents. Gruffly and impatiently—he complained of suffering a headache, not to mention having lost a world war—Hindenburg answered the American reporters' questions.

When Seldes asked about what broke the long stalemate on the western front, he received an unequivocal answer: "The American infantry in the Argonne won the war. I say this as a soldier, and soldiers will understand me best. . . . The day came when the American command sent new divisions into the battle and when I had not even one broken division to plug up the gaps. There was nothing left to do but ask for terms."

American military censors refused to pass the story when the correspondents returned to the army. They faced a court-martial until Eyre produced a letter from Colonel House that endorsed their independent review of conditions in Germany. Nevertheless, Hindenburg's frank admission of the Germans' military defeat remained censored until the end of December 1918. By the time of its release, many other reporters had entered Germany and filed their own reports. The runaways' account received scant attention. Seldes, who lived to be 104, wrote in his 1987 memoir that if Pershing's censors had passed the Hindenburg confession in November 1918, it probably would have made headlines throughout the world. It would have given the lie to Corporal Adolf Hitler's claim that the German army did not lose the war but rather had suffered a stab in the back by civilian groups.

It is, of course, impossible to sweep clean the board of history, set up the pieces, and play the game again. Still, it is intriguing to imagine how the world might have been different if the correspondents' accounts of the Hindenburg interview had been freed for immediate publication. With the main plank removed from the platform on which he rose to power, would Hitler have become chancellor of Germany in 1933—or been in a position to launch the globe into World War II?

THREE

A FREE AND PATRIOTIC PRESS: JOURNALISTS AND THE HOME FRONT IN WORLD WAR II

"The principal battle ground of this war is not the South Pacific. It is not the Middle East. It is not England or Norway, or the Russian steppes. It is American opinion."
—Archibald MacLeish, March 19, 1942

World War I censor George Creel had some advice for his successor: Don't muzzle the press. "Secrecy is essential in connection with many activities of the war machine, although the need is often exaggerated beyond the bounds of common sense," he wrote in a popular magazine in 1941, "but censorship of the press in *any* form is not the answer, never was the answer, and never will be the answer. . . . Just as it failed in the first World War, so it will fail again."

He was wrong. Voluntary censorship of the news media in World War II exceeded all expectations. The American Civil Liberties Union declared in 1945 that censorship during the war "raised almost no issues in the United States." Furthermore, the head of the Knight newspaper chain called the office in charge of domestic censorship of the news "the best-run bureau in Washington."

Censorship succeeded despite an initial lack of direction from the president. Franklin D. Roosevelt preferred to split authority among competing government agencies while distancing himself from internal debates. One of his administrative assistants, James Rowe, said Roosevelt "liked conflict, and he was a believer in resolving problems through conflict." Although this created confusion among subordinates, it allowed Roosevelt to hear different views, float potential solutions in the press, and ultimately decide his course of action.

"I am a juggler," Roosevelt said. "I never let my right hand know what my left hand does." As war broke out in Europe after Germany's invasion of Poland on September 1, 1939, Roosevelt took little significant action on wartime press policy. He navigated between a widespread sense that America should stay out of foreign wars and his own belief in the need to help Britain fight German aggression.

Having seen the excesses of the Creel committee during World War I, when Roosevelt served as assistant secretary of the navy, the president was loath to reestablish a wartime agency that concentrated powers over information, propaganda, and censorship. Americans had grown more sophisticated, and more skeptical, between the wars. Exposés of Britain's Wellington House campaign had appeared during the 1930s. Widespread claims that British propaganda had lured the United States into the previous war, along with historians' attacks on the Bryce report, fed American fears of a repeat performance. At the same time, the expansion of consumer culture and its accompanying advertising boom in the 1920s had raised awareness of how the mass media influenced attitudes toward everything from toothpaste to political candidates to foreign affairs.

The public also had been educated in the techniques of political propaganda through publicity and discussion groups run by the Institute for Propaganda Analysis, a citizens organization created in 1937 by Columbia University professor and World War I reporter Clyde R. Miller. The institute highlighted how easily a propagandist could sway opinion by playing on emotions instead of reason. As war broke out in Europe, the institute was teaching Americans how to recognize such government propaganda techniques as the selective use of facts to slant the news, euphemisms to disguise unpleasant truths, and epithets to demonize one's enemies through name-calling and the use of symbols linked to cultural values.

CENSORSHIP BY FORCE AND SUGGESTION

Roosevelt decided to split the war-information system into three pieces: a voluntary domestic news censorship program, run by civilians; a mandatory censorship operation for news originating in the combat zones, overseen by the armed forces; and a global propaganda and publicity campaign aimed primarily at wartime morale. The resulting bureaucracy created a measure of confusion about which government office had final jurisdiction over particular issues. Censors and propagandists clashed over what information to release, and civilian and military censors occasionally disagreed over whether a story or photograph compromised

American security. The trade-off, however, was that blurred lines of authority among agencies left none with absolute power. The arrangement allowed the president the latitude to shape war news as he saw fit.

Roosevelt was both an elitist and a commoner. He had been born into a wealthy family and educated at prep school and Harvard University, yet he projected a populist image. He felt comfortable with power but avoided abusing it so much that he might tarnish his democratic image. As a "juggler," Roosevelt liked having things both ways—despite his professed support for the rule of law, he believed the Constitution had to bend in times of stress. His wartime attorney general, Francis Biddle, recalled, "If anything, he thought that rights should yield to the necessities of war. Rights came after the victory, not before."

Publicly, Roosevelt praised the importance of a free press, as in a radio address to the *New York Herald Tribune* forum in October 1940: "The constant free flow of communication among us—enabling the free interchange of ideas—forms the very bloodstream of our nation. It keeps the mind and the body of our democracy eternally vital, eternally young." Yet, Roosevelt prickled at press criticism and disliked the publishers who opposed his New Deal programs. The president tolerated internal criticism as the nation grappled with the Depression, but he sought unity when discussion turned to international crises. He endorsed strong management of the news during wartime, including widespread censorship.

Even before America entered the war, it experienced war-related censorship. The War Department began limiting access to reporters in mid-1940 by requiring its press office to approve interviews with top officers. When questioned about the policy, presidential press secretary Stephen Early explained that if the White House didn't want a particular story published, the press should honor that request. Behind the restriction stood a 1938 law and 1940 executive action allowing the president to decide which information about the armed forces he could keep secret in the name of national security.

As the country's first line of defense, the navy experienced one of the war era's first clashes over freedom of information. Navy Secretary Frank Knox issued 5,000 copies of a memo on the last day of 1940 asking the mass media not to publicize the movements of ships and planes, the development of secret weapons, and other sensitive topics. The American Newspaper Publishers Association endorsed the plea, as did the American Society of Newspaper Editors. The difficulties in the plan became obvious that spring. Knox followed up his initial request to ask the media to avoid stories about British ships in American ports, as Britain's defense had become tied to America's interests under the Lend-Lease Act. In April 1941, the battle-damaged HMS *Malaya* docked in New York Harbor. Anyone in southern Manhattan, including German officials working in their Battery Park consulate, could see the ship. Two newspapers, the *Herald Tribune* and the *Daily News,* defied Knox and published the story on the assumption that the public already had access to the information.

That spring the Joint Army–Navy Public Relations Committee tried to write prewar censorship into law. It sent Roosevelt a "Basic Plan for Public Relations Administration" that would have provided for complete federal censorship of all forms of mass media, including radio and Hollywood movies. The president killed it and chastised the board for its naïveté in thinking that its proposal could gain congressional or public approval.

The Japanese surprise attack on the installations at Pearl Harbor on December 7, 1941, prompted a swift reassessment of the country's need for a war-information program. The army and navy imposed martial law in Hawaii; censored radio, telephone, and cable communications between the mainland and the islands; and suppressed details about the devastation.

Roosevelt asked Federal Bureau of Investigation Director J. Edgar Hoover to coordinate censorship immediately after the attack. Hoover directed a national syndicate to withdraw a newspaper column detailing the losses at Pearl Harbor by investigative reporters Drew Pearson and Robert S. Allen before it could be printed. The column revealed more about the damage than military and government officials had released to the public. Hoover also threatened Pearson with jail. "I told Edgar he was nuts, that there was no law by which he could put me in jail," Pearson wrote in his diary. "He admitted all this, said that Steve Early . . . had called him up and asked him to throw the fear of God into me."

The Pearson-Hoover exchange highlighted the government's difficulty in censoring the news media during World War II. Roosevelt and his cabinet shied from overtly challenging the press's First Amendment immunity from government-imposed prior restraint. Nevertheless, Roosevelt sought ways to halt journalists whom he considered reckless, subversive, or seditious. Unlike during World War I, no journalist went to prison in World War II for violating the Espionage Act. Instead, Roosevelt used a combination of administrative controls and intimidation to shape domestic news as he saw fit. The government's strongest actions came early in 1942, when the outcome of the war remained in doubt. In April 1942, the government's administrators of censorship, publicity, and postal communication met to discuss Roosevelt's desire to restrain "isolationists" in the mass media. Chief on the list was the anti-British, anti-Jewish, anti-Roosevelt magazine *Social Justice,* run by Catholic priest Charles Coughlin. The federal group agreed to take as much action against publications as possible without compromising due process. First, federal censors monitored questionable publications for content that might reveal secrets to the enemy. Next, the postmaster general decided whether to bar publications from the mail under the Trading with the Enemy Act. As a final step, the group consulted government information experts about the possible propaganda value of punishing the publications, although Biddle alone decided whether to pursue charges under the Espionage Act.

The system proved restrained yet effective. *Social Justice* had its mail permit suspended that month, and the magazine ceased publication for good after Biddle arranged for a Catholic friend to contact Coughlin's bishop in Detroit and put forward the case for suppression. The bishop, apparently upset by the attention Coughlin's magazine and equally inflammatory radio program had called to the church, ordered the priest to give up his mass media voice or his priesthood. Coughlin chose the former.

Social Justice was one of more than 17,000 publications examined by postal authorities between December 7, 1941, and June 30, 1945. For each one, officials prepared a legal opinion about its possible violation of federal law. However, counting *Social Justice,* only six publications had their second-class mail permits revoked during the war. Two of the six had their permits restored in 1944. The six publications targeted over the forty-four months of American combat compared with roughly 100 publications subjected to post office suppression during the nineteen months America fought in World War I.

Significantly, Biddle did not prosecute a single African-American newspaper despite a widespread campaign in the black press that embarrassed the government by publicizing blacks' second-class citizenship. The *Pittsburgh Courier,* an influential black paper, began the "Double V" campaign in February 1942, calling for victory against America's enemies abroad and at home. The latter included those who would fight for freedom from fascist tyranny but deny human rights to dark-skinned Americans. Although the army withheld some black publications from its bases, and it was "a rare day" in 1942 when the FBI didn't try to intimidate a black editor, the government never revoked a black paper's second-class permit or initiated prosecution. No doubt the Negro Newspaper Publishers Association's decision to pledge loyalty to Roosevelt in 1942 helped the black press maintain good relations with the White House.

Throughout the war, the nation's news media policed themselves. A new federal office, created nine days after the attack on Pearl Harbor, supervised the wartime censorship. Roosevelt chose not to follow his usual method of cobbling together older agencies or adding a new function to an existing program. Instead he fashioned the civilian Office of Censorship out of whole cloth. It supervised two kinds of censorship: absolute, mandatory control of information originating in war zones or crossing the nation's borders; and voluntary self-censorship of the nation's domestic mass media. The former included censoring mail, telephone, and cable communications, as well as assisting the armed forces, where needed, in controlling combat journalists and photographers.

The Office of Censorship mainly left combat-zone censorship to authorities in the armed forces, assuming that on-the-scene officers would know best what information compromised operational security. However, civilian censors acted as advocates for disgruntled journalists and pushed for the release of more information when journalists complained of excessive military censorship. In 1943 the Office of Censorship chastised "volunteer firemen" in civilian agencies who tried to censor information of no value to the enemy, and it scolded the press for agreeing to submit to excessive requests.

Roosevelt began shaping the definition of appropriate censorship topics in announcing the creation of the Office of Censorship. He said that although Americans abhorred censorship, the government found it necessary "that prohibitions against the domestic publication of some types of information, contained in long-existing statutes, be rigidly enforced. . . . [T]he government has called upon a patriotic press and radio to abstain voluntarily from the dissemination of detailed information of certain kinds, such as reports of the movements of vessels and troops. The response has indicated a universal desire to cooperate."

Those words had been written for the president by Byron Price, whom Roosevelt named censorship director. Price had to run domestic censorship without the aid of prepublication or prebroadcast legal restraints. Given the highly competitive nature of the news business, as well as the fierce independence of journalists, the job must have seemed as difficult as Creel had suggested. Nevertheless, domestic self-censorship proved extremely effective. For the duration of the war, only one journalist deliberately violated one of Price's requests for censorship—the manager of radio station KFUN in Las Vegas, New Mexico, who briefly refused to provide translations of his Spanish-language programs. Hundreds of censorship violations did occur in newspapers, magazines, and radio broadcasts, but they resulted from journalists not receiving or understanding the Office of Censorship's requests. No combat losses were ever traced to any of the violations.

Many of the censorship violations came to the attention of the Office of Censorship when a newspaper or radio station questioned information in a competing publication or broadcast. Out of patriotism and a competitive demand for equal treatment by the censors, the press kept itself in check. A wartime public opinion poll revealed that seven in ten Americans agreed with the amount of news censorship. One in ten thought it too strict and two in ten not strict enough.

Price had the option of recommending Espionage Act prosecutions to the Justice Department to enforce censorship, but he avoided overtly punitive controls. Biddle pursued only one Espionage Act case against a journalist in World War II (detailed in Chapter 4), which focused on press-military relations in the combat zone. Price also examined the possibility of imposing prior restraint. A Supreme Court ruling in 1931 suggested that some news stories could be so sensitive the government might prevent their publication rather than limit itself to postpublication penalties. The ruling in *Near v. Minnesota* said the print media enjoyed freedom from the threat of prepublication censorship except for a short list of topics, such as advance news of troop ship sailings. In addition to avoiding a debate on the constitutional issues involved in pursuing that option, Price refused to create the bureaucracy necessary to screen all war-related stories before publication or broadcast. Instead, Price and Roosevelt decided to inform journalists about the need for censorship and then trust them to do the right thing.

BYRON PRICE, CENSOR AND PRESS ADVOCATE

Price's background and personality made him an excellent choice to lead a domestic campaign to embrace self-censorship. He had a small-town-boy's trust in democracy, two years of service as an infantryman in World War I, and a professional understanding of the news media. Price had been a reporter, political columnist, and executive news editor of the Associated Press (AP). He knew hundreds of journalists from coast to coast. He also viewed censorship with suspicion and, when administered unwisely, with contempt. Finally, he refused to allow his administration to be compromised by other agencies. "There is no such thing as joint responsibility," the tart-tongued Price had told War Secretary Henry Stimson in 1941. Curiously, given Roosevelt's management style, Price enjoyed nearly complete freedom to run censorship as he saw fit. He was limited only by the fact that his office, having been created by Roosevelt, could not veto the president's occasional censorship rulings.

Price championed a free press and referred to the AP as his "religion." He loved reading, writing, and editing the news. Born in Topeka, Indiana, in 1891, he played as a child at creating a newspaper about his family. He wrote for his high school and college papers as well as *Crawfordsville Journal* in Indiana, where he attended Wabash College. After graduation, he worked for United Press and the AP, its larger rival, before joining the American Expeditionary Force in World War I. He helped break the news of Woodrow Wilson's incapacitating illness during a cross-country train trip in 1919 and then turned to political coverage. As the author of "Politics at Random," a column containing his observations, he met many of America's top politicians, including Roosevelt before he became president. This background instilled in Price an appreciation of the First Amendment antithetical to the censor's supposed dour desire for control. He "always considered a censor an official to be regarded with a fishy eye," a 1942 profile said.

He enjoyed nothing more than poker and plain food. He famously portrayed a diapered baby in the capital's annual Gridiron Show and happily reminisced about chasing chickens on his parents' farm for the *Washington Post*. The paper's accompanying photograph portrayed Price preparing to eat a fried chicken leg. By contrast, Price's hobbies suggested an intellectual depth. He was an excellent bridge player and raised irises. He read Walt Whitman and Mark Twain voraciously and collected first editions of his favorite books.

Price drew up the blueprint of domestic self-censorship during his first four weeks on the job. He set up a Press Division and a Broadcasting Division and staffed both with veteran journalists. They gathered suggestions from government and military officials about the types of news that might compromise the war effort if published or broadcast. The lists of sensitive topics included troop movements and locations; ship movements and locations; plane disposition, movement, and strength; details about fortifications; and sensitive war production information, such as news about raw materials or factories that could help saboteurs. Also on the list were weather stories that would give an advantage to enemy ships and planes in combat; photographs and maps of secret military areas; and a "general," catch-all category that included advance news of the president's movements, details of casualty lists, and the location of national treasures. On January 15, 1942, the Office of Censorship published these lists as the *Code of Wartime Practices for the American Press* and the *Code of Wartime Practices for American Broadcasters.* They were mailed to thousands of reporters and editors coast to coast.

The codebooks received four updates and reprintings during the war as well as dozens of supplements as issues arose. One ad hoc memo in 1943 urged total censorship of news about atomic energy; censors carefully crafted the statement to prevent publicity about the Manhattan Project without calling attention to the possibility of building an atomic bomb.

News of atomic research occasionally surfaced in the nation's press and radio, but such leaks proved inconsequential. The bomb's successful production remained a widely kept secret despite investigative reporter Pearson having uncovered the story as early as 1943, and *New York Times* science reporter William L. Laurence being drafted by General Leslie Groves to be the official chronicler of the bomb's

development. Laurence joined the Manhattan Project and
kept its secrets through the final week of the war. He also
helped the army lie about its test explosion at Alamogordo,
New Mexico, on July 16, 1945. Laurence wrote four press
releases before the blast to provide a believable cover story.
"If you blow off one corner of the United States, don't expect to keep it out of the newspapers," Price warned Groves
before the successful test. Groves released one of Laurence's
stories, attributing the flash and bang to the explosion of an
ammunition dump.

Laurence later accompanied the atomic raid on the Japanese city of Nagasaki and wrote follow-up stories. News
reports focusing on the long-range medical danger of fallout
remained censored for many months after the bombings—by
order of General Douglas MacArthur in Japan and by a postwar extension of the domestic voluntary censorship program, endorsed by President Harry S. Truman, dealing
strictly with atomic weapons. The War Department used
censorship to downplay discussion of the atomic bomb as an
inhumane weapon while simultaneously issuing press statements casting doubt on radiation casualty figures out of
Hiroshima and Nagasaki.

Chicago Daily News reporter George Weller defied military authorities to sneak into Nagasaki a month after the
bombing and gather information about the effects of atomic
attack on a city. His series of four reports would have given
America its first newspaper account of radiation sickness.
Instead, MacArthur spiked the stories. They vanished until
Weller's son found carbon copies in his father's papers after
Weller died in 2002. Only then did the stories appear in
print. Instead of Weller's account of Japanese civilians dying

of an undiagnosed, untreatable disease, Americans read reports prepared by Laurence for the Pentagon. Back at the *Times,* Laurence's reporting indicated his continuing identification with the Manhattan Project and its army overseers. "The Japanese are still continuing their propaganda aimed at creating the impression that we won the war unfairly, and thus attempting to create sympathy for themselves and milder terms, an examination of their present statements reveals," Laurence wrote in a commentary that began on the front page. "Thus, at the beginning, the Japanese described 'symptoms' that did not ring true."

THE GOSPEL, THE BISHOP, AND THE MISSIONARIES

The broad endorsement of domestic self-censorship resulted in part from the patriotism of a war in which America responded to attack, and in part from Price's administrative style. He called his manner "the Voice of the Dove." He demanded that censors be courteous and issue requests, not orders, to journalists. He also hammered at military officials not to make unreasonable censorship requests if they wanted journalists to heed them. Thus, the fabric of domestic censorship rested on a system of trust among journalists, the government, and the armed forces. Price acknowledged this faith-based system by creating a religious lexicon to describe his operations. Censors called their work "the gospel." Price was "the bishop," and his liaisons throughout the country took the title "missionaries." Missionaries were respected newspaper journalists who traveled the country, beginning in spring 1942, to ensure the nation's thousands of editors possessed and understood a copy of the *Code of Wartime Practices*. To guarantee fairness, Price wanted all publications, large and small, to follow the same code. As there were only 901 American AM radio stations, most of which could be contacted through networks, the censors saw no need to create a broadcasting missionary group.

Price gained respect by privately communicating with violators. Only once did the Office of Censorship make an example of a censorship bust. It issued a news release in May 1942 criticizing Jeff Keen of the *Philadelphia Daily News* for publicizing the visit of Soviet Foreign Minister V. M. Molotov to Washington. The paper's publisher, fearing a public backlash if Molotov came to harm as a result of the story, suspended Keen for three months. This single episode made American journalists realize how public pressure might be brought to bear if they refused to censor themselves. It also demonstrated that voluntary censorship had teeth.

Price had the authority to impose prior restraint on radio but refused to use it. In March 1942, Price had asked Biddle for a legal opinion about censoring radiotelegraphy—point-to-point communications that were essentially radioed telephone calls. Biddle's reply surprised Price. The attorney general noted that because radio waves did not respect international borders, they therefore fell under mandatory censorship, just as did letters that left the United States. Biddle's opinion invited Price to assume total control of not only the nation's radiotelegraph companies but also its commercial radio stations. Price declined the offer. Controlling radio would require the immediate training of thousands of radio censors. It would not only alienate the radio industry but also raise the suspicions of the print press. Price decided to keep

Biddle's opinion secret, like a "club in the closet," and bring it out only in an emergency. Meanwhile, he said he would see how well radio journalists censored themselves. His decision proved well-founded. Aside from the New Mexico broadcaster who balked at providing translations, radio was as cooperative as the print media were during World War II.

A handful of news topics proved especially difficult to censor during the war. Chief among them were stories about the president's travels, weather, and Japanese balloon-bomb attacks on the American mainland. Roosevelt, like Wilson and other wartime presidents, justified secrecy about his travels in his role as commander in chief. He invoked the censorship code to hide his frequent weekend travels between the White House and his estate on the Hudson River. Enemy agents, not knowing the route or time of his presidential train journeys, could not know when and where to plant bombs or booby traps. Critics accused the president of using censorship for political and personal gain. In fact, Roosevelt abused the secrecy to cover his secret meetings with former lover Lucy Mercer Rutherford, which his daughter Anna arranged.

The biggest challenge to the presidential section of the wartime code occurred in September 1942 when Roosevelt planned to tour wartime production facilities shortly before the midterm congressional elections. The president initially wanted to travel without any journalists accompanying him. He reasoned that they would falsely describe the journey as a politically motivated trip, which he vehemently denied. Price convinced Roosevelt that if he had nothing to hide, the press would convey that message to the public. The president approved a compromise. He agreed to travel with a representative of each of America's three major wire services if they would agree to withhold their stories until completion of the trip.

The Ferdinand Magellan, the president's steel-reinforced train car, traveled a counterclockwise journey through the industrial upper Midwest, down the Pacific Coast, and across the South. Roosevelt made unannounced inspection stops at a tank-manufacturing plant in Michigan, a naval training station in Chicago, a cartridge company in Minnesota, and other defense installations. He tested reporters' patience at the Puget Sound Navy Yard by addressing 5,000 workers and driving through downtown Seattle while insisting that his visit remain off the record. Newspapers and radio stations along the way privately grumbled, but they withheld coverage of the trip until Roosevelt returned safely to Washington on October 1. At that time, a group of reporters released a petition complaining about Roosevelt's secrecy. Most editorials, however, and the public supported the president. When the president's life was at stake, *United States News* editor David Lawrence said, "the customary rule is to err on the side of suppression." NBC's Blue Network conducted a call-in survey and found 91 percent of the public endorsing Roosevelt's need for secrecy about his wartime travels. The issue of censorship of presidential movements remained for the rest of the war, but it grew less significant both through a loosening of the rules as well as greater transparency by Roosevelt's successor in the White House.

The weather proved an awkward news story for the first half of the war. Radio's speed-of-light transmissions could provide the enemy with accurate, up-to-the-minute descriptions of the conditions over likely military targets. Furthermore, news about weather patterns over the United States, which moved eastward into the Atlantic, and short-range forecasts could be equally dangerous.

Price asked newspapers to limit severely the weather news they reported. The censorship code restricted radio even further, asking stations not to air any weather information unless it specifically was released for broadcast by the National Weather Bureau. This restriction took weather-news censorship to ludicrous heights in 1942, particularly when WGN broadcaster Bob Elson called the play-by-play for the annual *Chicago Tribune* charity football game between the National Football League champions and a team of college all-stars. Fog off Lake Michigan completely obscured the field during a live broadcast of the August 28 game. Elson kept broadcasting despite his inability to call the game or tell listeners why he could not see it. Similarly, sportscaster Hal Totten gave a ludicrous announcement during a Chicago White Sox–Philadelphia Phillies baseball game on July 3, 1943: "The umpires have called the game for reasons I cannot speak of, but whatever has caused the delay is also making the spectators go back for cover, and yes, here come the ground keepers with whatever is used to cover the ground so whatever is causing the delay won't affect the ground too much."

Weather news accounted for about half of all censorship code violations during the first two years of the war. As America's war fortunes improved, the Office of Censorship lifted most radio restrictions about weather stories on October 12, 1943. The rest were rescinded in May 1945, with Germany defeated and Japan on the defensive.

Domestic censorship about news of Japan's last-ditch

effort to attack America in the final months of the war may have contributed to the only civilian deaths from an assault on the mainland. Five children and the pregnant wife of a minister died during a picnic on Gearhart Mountain, Oregon, on May 5, 1945, when a balloon bomb launched from the Japanese home islands exploded. The pastor, Archie Mitchell, said the blast occurred when one of the children touched a downed balloon.

The Japanese military began launching the first of 9,300 high-explosive and incendiary balloon-bombs late in 1944. Prevailing winds carried at least 285 to North America, where they landed. They failed to cause the widespread panic Japan had desired. The War Department insisted on a news blackout about the bombs, hoping Japan would not discover their ineffectiveness and would continue to waste resources on their construction. Price fought the censorship request as an unreasonable restraint on journalists, who could see the bombs with their own eyes and report their existence authoritatively. The blackout fed ignorance and rumors, leaving vulnerable anyone unfortunate enough, like the Oregon picnickers, to stumble across a downed balloon. However, Price managed only to get the army to release a basic news story after the Oregon incident. Restrictions remained until war's end.

AMERICAN PROPAGANDA AND PUBLICITY

Although civilian journalists supported Price's censorship, they balked at government propaganda. The bad taste left by the CPI contributed to the disorganization and distrust in

America's war-information program in World War II. Roosevelt had little knowledge of the potential of wartime propaganda, but he knew the public feared a return of Creel's excesses. When advisers such as Stimson and Knox called for the creation of a government propaganda agency after the outbreak of the war in Europe, Roosevelt refused until he could minimize accusations of partisan manipulation.

By default, discussions of ways to counter Nazi propaganda at first fell to private organizations and cabinet members. Several put forward their own plans, which Roosevelt finally approved with the creation of the Office of the Coordinator of Information (OCI). Its director, William J. Donovan, viewed propaganda as a weapon to demoralize enemy troops and "soften up the civilian population." The first person Donovan hired after opening the agency July 11, 1941, was playwright Robert E. Sherwood, who had written many of Roosevelt's speeches. Sherwood understood the power of the spoken word and believed that America's strongest response to Nazi propaganda was "the power of truth." That December, Sherwood put his ideas to the test by inaugurating the Voice of America and hiring famed radio producer John Houseman to supervise it. First by relaying messages via the BBC, then by adding short-wave broadcasts, the Voice of America began speaking to Europe in January 1942. By April it had grown to a round-the-clock operation in multiple languages.

While the Voice of America targeted foreign audiences, another new propaganda agency aimed at the home front. Like the Office of the Coordinator of Information, it had a name that suggested a purely objective agenda: the Office of Facts and Figures (OFF). In the face of a growing Nazi threat and repeated calls from his advisers to fashion a domestic response, Roosevelt created the office by executive order in October 1941. He named Librarian of Congress Archibald MacLeish as director. MacLeish maintained that the agency limited its activities to spreading accurate information in order to promote understanding of the administration's policies, but the OFF actually disseminated propaganda—albeit the "white" or "gray" kind, based on selected facts, as opposed to the "black" variety that spread outright lies. The office followed "the 'strategy of truth' rather than the 'strategy of terror' . . . followed by the propaganda offices of the totalitarian states," MacLeish said. The principle of saturating audiences with accurate information remained the nation's official policy for the duration of the war. However, the definition of "truth" became subject to interpretation. MacLeish, an interventionist and liberal, upset conservative politicians and proved unable to get widespread support for a coherent propaganda policy for the home front. Many OFF staffers left out of frustration.

By early 1942, government officials demanded a stronger propaganda program for foreign audiences and a more open "information" system—the word *propaganda* being avoided for domestic consumption—at home. "It all seems to boil down to three bitter complaints," historian Allan M. Winkler quoted one observer as saying. "First, that there was too much information; second, that there wasn't enough of it; and third, that in any event it was confusing and inconsistent." The Bureau of the Budget began the push toward a consolidation of war-news agencies by asking Milton S. Eisenhower to survey the problem. He saw the need for greater coordination but balked at creating a version of World War I's Committee of Public Information. Meanwhile, the bureau drafted an executive order to blend the various federal information agencies. When Roosevelt received the bureau's and Eisenhower's plans, he discussed them with advisers for two months before making a decision. He let Nelson Rockefeller, who had directed all propaganda and information programs aimed at Latin America through the office of the Coordinator of Inter-American Affairs, keep control of his narrowly focused organization. Donovan maintained his secret intelligence operations but was forced to relinquish control of propaganda. Those functions of the Office of the Coordinator of Information, along with the Voice of America and the operations of the OFF and the news-gathering Office of Government Reports, were folded into the new Office of War Information (OWI), created by executive order on June 13, 1942. The OWI's birth through presidential order placed its budget under the control of Congress. That meant the administration's views of propaganda—and "truth"—could be challenged by lawmakers who did not share similar views.

In creating the agency, Roosevelt hesitated long enough to ensure that Elmer Davis, a radio journalist, would agree to direct it. Roosevelt said he wanted the radio commentator "with the funny voice. Elmer—Elmer something." Davis knew the problems that had plagued the nation's war-information agencies. During the early months of the war, before his appointment to head the OWI, he had complained about the government's chaotic news organization. "Under one head, with real power, they might get somewhere," he said. "Objection has been made that it might be hard to pick the man to head them. But almost anybody would be better than half a dozen heads."

The appointment met with broad approval in the press. *Time* magazine described Davis as "clear-headed, sensible" and "one of the best newsmen in the business." Davis had been a Rhodes scholar and worked for the *New York Times* in World War I before enjoying a freelance career and joining CBS in 1939. His flat Indiana voice seemed reassuringly believable to millions of listeners. However, he lacked the government background and passion of Sherwood and MacLeish. Likewise, never having run an organization of any size—at CBS, he had a single secretary—he lacked Price's administrative skills.

The president ordered the OWI to "formulate and carry out . . . information programs designed to facilitate the development of an informed and intelligent understanding, at home and abroad, of the status and progress of the war effort and of the war policies, activities, and aims of the Government." In practice, Davis could not force government agencies, each jealously guarding its territory, to release information. The War, Navy, and State departments, as well as other federal offices, went their own way. When Davis approached Stimson to complain that the armed forces kept too much information from the public, Davis got a lecture and what he called "the polite brush-off." Roosevelt could have stepped in to support the OWI in its interagency squabbles, but he remained aloof. Eventually, Davis worked through channels and gained a measure of cooperation from Stimson, including a candid assessment of the army's defeat at Kasserine Pass in North Africa in February 1943.

The navy proved even more intractable. Davis butted heads with Knox and Chief of Naval Operations Ernest King. Davis once said he "suspected that Admiral King's idea of War Information was that there should be just one communiqué. Some morning we would announce that the war was over and that we won it." Still, Davis's patience paid off. With Price's help, Davis managed to convince Roosevelt the navy had held back too much information about ship losses in 1942. Hanson Baldwin of the *New York Times* had learned about the navy's refusal to announce significant sinkings and had warned that his paper might violate the *Code of Wartime Practices* and publish the news. By the end of October, a week before national elections, Davis got the navy to release the names of all ships that had been sunk, including the devastating loss of the aircraft carrier *Hornet* a short time before. Baldwin backed off his threat.

The OWI did much more than just release news to the press and radio. It also attempted to influence public opinion, relying heavily on the popular media of radio and motion pictures. Radio offered the fastest, broadest medium of communication. Ninety percent of Americans listened to an average of four hours of radio programming each day during World War II. Radio executives voluntarily placed patriotic wartime messages on the air. Working with the Domestic Radio Bureau of the OFF and then with the Radio Division of the OWI, networks began weaving propaganda messages into popular shows. OWI Radio Director William B. Lewis established the Network Allocation Plan, which placed war messages about once a week into daily programs and twice a month into weekly programs. Audiences for popular programs heard plots in which the characters dealt with

OWI-suggested topics such as gas rationing, sugar substitutes, price controls, and scrap-metal roundups. On *The Jack Benny Show,* for example, Benny supported the October 1942 national scrap-metal drive by donating his broken-down Maxwell automobile to a salvage yard. The campaigns enjoyed some successes. When the OWI tested the effectiveness of its radio campaigns, it placed an appeal for merchant seamen exclusively on the program *Fibber McGee and Molly.* The next day's enlistments doubled.

Lewis had less success in shaping the lyrics of popular songs. He asked the Music War Committee, a citizens group of composers led by Oscar Hammerstein II, to put specific themes into songs. Few aired on the radio. Typical of the aesthetic failure of mixing propaganda with dance music was the song "Save the Grease" by Joe Sanders. It contained these lyrics:

> Save the grease from the potsy
> It's for peace!
> Make it hotsy
> And we'll pour it on the Nazi.

The OWI also had mixed success with Hollywood movies, which Roosevelt had identified as an "essential war industry." Early motion pictures about the war were "escapist and delusive," MacLeish said. Movies portrayed Allied troops as bravely fighting the enemy, but they did little to explain the principles the troops were fighting for. The OWI attempted to rectify this by suggesting five themes as national priorities: explaining why America fought; portraying the Allies and their citizens; encouraging war production; bolstering domestic morale; and showing the heroic efforts of

America's armed forces. The OWI's Bureau of Motion Pictures lacked the authority and budget to do more than observe and make suggestions. However, the Office of Censorship could deny an export license for any movie that gave an unapproved message. As foreign distribution often spelled the difference between an American movie showing a profit or loss, the threat of withholding an export permit carried great weight.

Hollywood remained defensive against any overt attempts to meddle with its craft, but it discovered that war-themed movies such as *Mrs. Miniver* could be artistic, propagandistic, and profitable. For every movie that seamlessly incorporated government-approved themes, many others brimmed with absurdities—Tarzan defeating "Nadzies" in *Tarzan Triumphs,* or *Mr. Winkle Goes to War,* in which Edward G. Robinson portrayed a middle-aged bank clerk who went through a holidaylike boot camp without ever having to get a haircut. Most early war films were antiseptic. Of the sixty-one fictional war movies Hollywood produced between May and November 1942, only five showed an American combat death.

Hollywood's greatest contribution to the national propaganda campaign may have been the documentary work performed by some of its top directors on behalf of the armed forces. These included John Ford (*The Battle of Midway*), John Huston (*The Battle of San Pietro*), William Wyler (*The Memphis Belle*), and Frank Capra (*Why We Fight*). Chief of Staff George C. Marshall personally asked Capra to make the *Why We Fight* series of seven films to explain the war. The War Department ordered them shown to all recruits, and Roosevelt released them to the public. They remain milestones of simple propaganda. To create the first film in the series, Capra took official Axis-power films and edited them to call attention to images portraying America's enemies as foolish and evil.

Davis had difficulties giving direction to the OWI's Domestic Branch. The office contained many brilliant propagandists, such as MacLeish, who wished to promote an activist agenda, laying out policies and promoting them aggressively to the public. Others, such as Domestic Branch director Gardiner Cowles, disdained any heavy-handed approach. Some staffers thought the Domestic Branch should be a conveyor belt for government information or a cheerleader for the president's policies. Caught in the middle, without taking charge, sat Davis. "We are in a sense an auxiliary to the armed forces," Davis had told a House committee late in 1942. Though pragmatic, his attitudes did little to provide clear guidance to his subordinates early in the war.

Conflict came to a head in spring 1943. The OWI prepared a pamphlet giving a grim view of the American food supply. The secretary of agriculture and head of the Office of Economic Stabilization complained that the report would help the farm bloc divert scarce resources to farm equipment. In the debate over whether to change the pamphlet before publication, the writers defended their principles and resigned. Other staffers followed, including historian Arthur M. Schlesinger Jr., who expressed dissatisfaction with slanted information in domestic propaganda.

"We are leaving because of our conviction that it is impossible for us, under those who now control our output, to tell the full truth," they said in a statement. "No one denies that promotional techniques have a proper and powerful function in telling the story of war. But as we see it, the activities of OWI on the home front are now dominated by high-pressure promoters who prefer slick salesmanship to honest information. . . . They are turning this Office of War Information into an Office of War Bally-Hoo."

Roosevelt's political critics, heartened by the defections, seized on the OWI's publication of *Victory* magazine as another weapon to use against him. The publication, intended for foreign audiences, glorified the president as "Champion of Liberty" and included his color photograph on the cover. Republican Senator Rufus C. Holman of Oregon assailed the magazine's description of Roosevelt as opposing "the toryism of the conservative reactionary." Presidential critics in Congress closed ranks against the OWI as a convenient target. Despite Davis's insistence that any description of the war effort for overseas audiences had to mention the president in some fashion, Congress expanded its critical examination of propaganda materials the members perceived as too liberal. Some lawmakers opposed the financial ideas in a pamphlet about taxation; others, particularly Southern Democrats, complained about the racial equality espoused in the OWI's "Negroes and the War" booklet.

As a result, Congress slashed the OWI's Domestic Branch budget to $2.75 million, forcing the closure of its motion picture and publication offices. No longer could OWI produce domestic propaganda; instead, it was reduced to being largely a liaison to other federal information-producing agencies. Roosevelt, reluctant to spend political capital, refused to intervene or use his veto. Davis carried on— "making bricks without straw," in the words of Interior

Secretary Harold Ickes—but the OWI had essentially become an information service for America's allies, content to follow the State Department's lead rather than its own.

Herbert Brucker, a historian who coined the phrase "freedom of information," viewed the different paths of World War II censorship and propaganda as defining the limits of America's trust in government information programs. Creel had been both censor and propagandist and failed. When the two functions were split, Davis struggled and Price flourished. "From this we can deduce that it is wartime propaganda, rather than wartime censorship, that sets ill with Americans," he wrote.

World War II demonstrated that the American home front would tolerate intelligent censorship but be less likely to embrace government propaganda, especially when it was clumsy and overt. It showed that despite the inherent conflict in press-military relations, the two sides could compromise and cooperate.

FOUR

ON THE TEAM: REPORTING, AND SUPPORTING, WORLD WAR II

"It matters a great deal what we say the purpose is. It makes all the difference in the world: indeed, it is for us to decide whether he died for the fulfillment of a purpose, like the boys of the American Revolution, or whether he died for the fulfillment of practically nothing, like the boys of World War I. The dead boys will become what we make them."
   —*Life* magazine, July 5, 1943, on printing the
   names of 12,987 Americans killed in combat

In the 1940s, for the first time, Americans on the home front received information of distant war in real time and experienced the emotional power of real combat photography. Popular magazines, motion pictures, radio, and even the nascent television industry that reached a few thousand TV sets expanded the impact of news coverage of World War II far beyond the staged images and sanitized prose of World War I.

The new potential worried the American government

and armed forces. A live radio broadcast might immediately give information to the enemy that compromised operational security. Photographs of the true horrors of combat, spread rapidly around the globe by electronic transmissions, could reach millions within days, if not hours, and cause Americans to rethink their views of the war. Yet preventing people from seeing and hearing the war could be equally dangerous. Civilians sheltered from bad news might grow complacent, scaling back their commitment to total war. They might have unrealistic expectations about the postwar world. Or they might treat exaggerated wartime rumors as facts.

Broadcasting posed the greatest threat, as evidenced by its larger list of censored topics in the domestic *Code of Wartime Practices.* The Office of Censorship worried not only about radio's ability to send messages at the speed of light, across any political or military border, but also about the impact of radio's immediacy and emotional power on a mass audience.

INFLUENCE OF RADIO AND PHOTOGRAPHY ON WARTIME REPORTING

By the 1940s, radio had outgrown its infancy as a point-to-point wireless telephone. It had matured, first into an entertainment industry spreading music, conversation, and scripted dramas and comedies, and then into the broadest and swiftest purveyor of information. In 1942, roughly 300 million people around the world listened to the radio. The United States alone had 55 million receivers, including at least one in 83 percent of American households. Tens of millions of listeners tuned in to hear the news and commentary of the NBC Blue Network's Drew Pearson and Walter Winchell, compared with less than a million people who subscribed to the *New York Times* or *New York Herald Tribune.*

Surveys underscored the rise of radio as a news medium. In 1938, most Americans considered the newspaper their primary source of news. By the start of the war, radio had become the preferred medium. It arrived cheaply—there was no subscription fee, as for a newspaper—and brought important and timely news more swiftly than any printing press.

CBS had demonstrated radio's potential for wartime coverage when Edward R. Murrow made his on-air debut as part of the first live, international news roundup. Before then, what passed for in-depth radio news was little more than commentary from dulcet-voiced personalities such as Lowell Thomas of NBC and Boake Carter of CBS, hired to read the news from the wire services and local newspapers and offer their own window dressing. The twenty-nine-year-old Murrow set precedent with his first broadcast March 13, 1938, by giving his eyewitness report of the German annexation of Austria. He noted the German storm troopers riding through Vienna in open trucks, "singing and tossing oranges out to the crowd," as well as a sense of expectation for the arrival of Adolf Hitler.

A network of land lines and shortwave transmitters sent his voice, and those of CBS correspondents in other capitals, across the ocean to a national audience, giving American listeners a broad array of news and opinion, independently gathered and shared live. According to Murrow biographer Joseph E. Persico, the technological success of the transatlantic broadcast paled in comparison with the new thrill of wartime journalism—"the listener's sensation of being on the scene, as though some knowledgeable friends had dropped by to explain what had happened."

Few people give much thought today to the miracle of intimate communication on a global scale. Yet, it revolutionized reporting in World War II and helped build support for the Allies. Murrow's broadcasts from the rooftops and streets of London during the Blitz of 1940 portrayed a hardy and determined people standing up to the German war machine. Listeners believed. Hearing a particular, familiar human voice carried credibility beyond the printed word. At the start of the Blitz, only 16 percent of Americans favored sending more aid to Britain. Within weeks, after a steady stream of Murrow's broadcasts detailing nightly poundings from German bombers, more than half of those surveyed wanted to do more to help.

Murrow went on Allied air raids to report the bombing of Germany during the war and marched into Buchenwald to document the horrors of the Holocaust at war's end. His just-the-facts treatment of what he saw and heard of the concentration camp—"more than five hundred men and boys lay there in two neat piles"—startled the world despite its deliberate understatement. "I pray you believe what I have said about Buchenwald," Murrow said at the conclusion of his broadcast. "I have reported what I saw and heard, but only part of it. For most of it, I have no words. Dead men are plentiful in war, but the living dead, more than twenty thousand of them in one camp. And the country round about was pleasing to the eye, and the Germans were well fed and well dressed. American trucks were rolling toward the rear filled with prisoners. Soon they would be eating American rations, as much for a meal as the men at Buchenwald received in four days. If I've offended you by this rather mild account of Buchenwald, I'm not in the least sorry." The story landed on front pages and on the BBC. The British news media, still smarting from the accusation of spreading false propaganda during World War I, apparently believed that a dispassionate account of Nazi mass murder by America's premier radio correspondent would be beyond reproach.

Photography also had taken a quantum leap since World War I. Moving pictures dominated American entertainment, especially after the addition of sound to film in the 1920s. Hollywood movies helped create the public's image of war, and newsreels such as the *March of Time*—which drew an audience of 15 million in the 1930s—did much to set the public's news agenda. By 1940, Americans went to movie theaters three times a week. They shared, with no distinctions among class, race, or region, the same photo stories produced by studios and the same news images from the *March of Time, Fox Movietone, News of the Day,* and other newsreels.

What they saw in the newsreels after 1939 was war, albeit heavily censored. A content analysis found that 73.9 percent of the stories in American newsreels in 1943 related to government news, defense news, political news, and combat news, much of it shot by military cameramen trained in the States by newsreel company photographers. Despite its ubiquity, film was a relatively slow medium of communication. Motion pictures had to be shot, developed, printed, and distributed, which took weeks. The printed still-camera photograph, however, could be shared much more quickly, thanks to the advent of new printing techniques, wire transmission of halftones starting in 1924, and transoceanic radio transmissions.

Starting in the 1930s, mass-audience photographic magazines began publishing weekly collections of news and feature photographs from around the world. The pioneer was *Life,* created in 1936 by Time Inc. Readers enamored of the magazine's large, artistic photographic reproductions pushed its circulation to 3 million and its readership to 17.3 million, out of 130 million Americans, by the end of the 1930s. Three years later, as America began to take the offensive in the Pacific and in North Africa, *Life* could boast that two of every three people in an American armed forces uniform read the magazine.

"Total war is fought with cameras as well as cannons," said *Movies at War,* a publication of the Motion Picture Industry's War Activities Committee. Indeed, World War II marked a crucial stage in the propaganda use of images. Military censors checked 35,000 still pictures and 100,000 feet of motion picture film every week during the Allied invasion of France in 1944, along with 3 million words from print journalists. The vast majority was cleared for release. Combat photographs, like printed words and radio broadcasts, thus impacted America's propaganda campaign in two ways—suppression, when officials believed they threatened to create or reinforce defeatism, and mass circulation, when those same officials intended to raise morale.

Faced with a huge demand for information during World War II, the United States government sent 1,646 accredited journalists into combat zones, including 127 women. Reporters saw more and reported more than they had in the

1917–1918 conflict. Permission to wander and report varied with the theater commander, but most accredited correspondents, especially in Europe and North Africa, enjoyed the freedom to live with combat units and interview whomever they pleased. Like the twenty-first-century practice of embedding, this close relationship contributed not only to journalists' ability to report and photograph the war in great detail but also to their identification with the units they covered.

ERNIE PYLE, REPORTER AND LEGEND

No journalist was, or is, as celebrated as Ernie Pyle. He loved the infantry—the "God-damned infantry," as he called it. He praised infantrymen in his syndicated newspaper column as the "mud-rain-frost-and-wind boys." Pyle mingled with riflemen, engineers, artillerymen, chaplains, medics, and just about anyone else willing to share his experience. Rather than write about strategy or tactics, Pyle focused on what he saw and heard. Each column presented the details of one person, place, or event. The practice became commonplace in later wars, but Pyle was the first to make a career out of telling the story of the soldier, not the army. "I haven't written anything about the 'Big Picture' because I don't know anything about it," Pyle once admitted. "I only know what we see from our worm's-eye view." That included combat-weary soldiers, foxholes, hospital tents, and "graves and graves and graves."

Readers assembled the big picture by putting the pieces together, as if they were colored threads in a tapestry. Observers likened Pyle's technique to having a friend or relative write letters from the front. Over time, they formed a favorite correspondence. The method proved so popular that Pyle had millions of readers and received thousands of letters, including many from the wives of men in uniform. Soldiers appreciated him too. General Omar Bradley said his men fought better with Pyle nearby, while General Mark Clark said Pyle "helped our soldiers to victory."

Achieving nearly universal popularity was a neat trick for the shy farm boy. Ernest Taylor Pyle was born in 1900 to a sharecropper family in a two-story house outside Dana, Indiana. An only child, he grew up reserved and sensitive, teased by the town kids for his awkwardness and country clothes. Looking for an escape from farm life, Pyle enrolled at Indiana University with no career goals. All he knew, he told a friend, was he wanted "to do things." He majored in economics, but he discovered a love for journalism on the campus newspaper, the *Daily Student*. He left school and took jobs with papers in Washington and New York before settling into a seven-year routine as roving correspondent for the Scripps-Howard newspaper chain. Pyle crisscrossed the continent twenty times, wearing out a Ford and a Dodge convertible coupe and three typewriters. The travels acquainted him with virtually every corner of America and gave him an excellent way to break the ice with soldiers overseas—when he learned where they were from, he could make small talk about their hometowns.

Pyle took a break from his domestic travels in late 1940 and early 1941 to visit Britain. He reported for an American audience about the German attempt to bomb London into submission. He watched for three hours as incendiary bombs touched off hundreds of fires around Saint Paul's Cathedral. Like a minimalist painter, Pyle sparingly applied words to his dispatches to re-create the night in print. The incendiary explosives bloomed as "white pinpoints" that "stabbed" the dark night. Pinkish-white smoke rose in a great balloon of cloud, out of which gradually emerged the shape of the cathedral dome. Amid his skillful reconstruction of the night, Pyle sprinkled his plain Indiana way of speaking. "There was to be no monkey business this night," he said by way of introducing his account of the attack.

Pyle's editors tried to convince him to return to his work as a stateside reporter to distract the public from the war. Pyle didn't want that. He flew to Ireland, planning to write about the buildup of Allied military camps in the British Isles and maybe stay to observe America's first combat against the Germans and Italians. He ended up covering the war on and off until his death. He was shelled and strafed in North Africa, faced a tank offensive at Kasserine, wandered the icy Italian mountains, walked the beaches of Normandy one day after the D-day invasion, survived a fierce bomber attack by friendly forces at Saint-Lô in northwestern France, and covered the Pacific war in spring 1945. He lived in foxholes, ate standard chow with the enlisted men, and slept wherever he could find shelter. Soldiers appreciated his willingness to live as they did.

Pyle identified with the dead and showed readers a war they had not seen before: individual, personal, and emotional. While in North Africa, as he watched surgeons operate on wounded GIs, he saw a chaplain run and kneel beside a dying man. "The chaplain said, 'John, I'm going to say a prayer for you,'" Pyle wrote. "Somehow this stark announcement hit me like a hammer. He didn't say, 'I'm going to pray for you to get well.'"

His columns occasionally personalized a combat death, an extreme rarity of reporting at that time. His most famous column, about how soldiers in the Thirty-sixth Division reacted to the death of their captain near San Pietro, Italy, described the hushed silence around the body and the tenderness with which soldiers and officers said their goodbyes. One soldier "squatted down, and he reached down and took the dead hand, and he sat there for a full five minutes, holding the dead hand in his own and looking intently into the dead face, and he never uttered a sound all the time he sat there," Pyle wrote. "Finally he put the hand down. He reached over and gently straightened the points of the captain's shirt collar, and then he sort of rearranged the tattered edges of the uniform around the wound, and then he got up and walked away down the road in the moonlight, all alone." The *Washington Daily News* devoted its entire front page to the column, printed in large type. The scene also became the climax of the Hollywood movie *The Story of G.I. Joe,* with Robert Mitchum playing the character of the doomed captain.

Pyle was killed April 18, 1945, on the Pacific island of Ie Shima, near Okinawa, while covering his last invasion. The jeep in which he was riding came under fire, and Pyle dived into a ditch. When he raised his head to look around, a Japanese machine gunner put a bullet through his skull. Soldiers erected a sign there to honor him: "At This Spot the 77th Infantry Division Lost a Buddy." All told, thirty-seven accredited American reporters and photographers died in

World War II, and 112 suffered injuries. That was four times the casualty rate for the American armed forces.

THE JOURNALIST AS "QUASI" OFFICER

The best reporters, besides Pyle and Murrow, included the *New York Herald Tribune*'s Homer Bigart; the *New Yorker*'s A. J. Liebling and John Hersey, who respectively reported the war in Europe and the devastation of Hiroshima; and Martha Gellhorn of *Collier's* magazine. Gellhorn refused to be held back because of her sex. She defied regulations to sneak aboard a hospital ship during the Normandy invasion; it was her only way to get close to the action. She gathered information for a story on the recovery of the wounded and then waded ashore. Her success at getting on the beach infuriated her husband, North American Newspaper Alliance reporter Ernest Hemingway, who had played by the rules and not been allowed off his ship.

When the army learned of Gellhorn's unapproved activities, she was arrested and confined to a training camp for nurses in England. She threw away her credentials, slipped out of camp, and hitched a ride on a military plane to Italy. She later regained her good standing and became one of three reporters invited to cover the Eighty-second Airborne's assault on the Netherlands. In the *Collier's* article "Death of a Dutch Town," Gellhorn described the devastation caused by Nazi occupation and directly addressed the wholesale deportation of Europe's Jews to face extermination in concentration camps.

Although World War II became the most thoroughly covered war to that time, civilians saw and heard little or no news that military censors considered too risky to release. Especially sensitive topics included friction with America's allies, racial tensions, and the most graphic photographs of American dead. Furthermore, news media in the United States, like the media of all World War II belligerent nations, did not publish news of a single atrocity committed by their own forces.

Censorship by the armed forces proved effective but often superfluous to journalists policing themselves. Public opinion closed ranks as a result of the sneak attack at Pearl Harbor, and combat journalists were no exception. Just as domestic journalists followed the *Code of Wartime Practices* partly out of patriotism and partly out of fears that failure to do so would lead to harsh laws, combat journalists censored themselves to avoid offending readers or the officials who provided them access to the front.

"We edited ourselves much more than we were edited," wrote John Steinbeck, who reported on combat in Europe for the *New York Herald Tribune.* "We felt responsible to what was called the home front. There was a general feeling that unless the home front was carefully protected from the whole account of what war was like, it might panic." He described self-censorship as patriotic and practical, noting that any reporter foolish enough to evade censorship "would be put out of the theater by the command, and a correspondent with no theater has no job."

The pervasiveness of self-censorship in the combat zones was evident in the three-month suppression of news about General George S. Patton's publicly slapping two soldiers in military hospitals. The first incident occurred August 10, 1943, as Patton interviewed men who had been wounded during the invasion of Sicily. When he came upon a shivering soldier who sobbed that he couldn't stand the shelling, Patton called him a "yellow bastard" and slapped his head so hard his helmet liner flew off. Five days later, the general executed a repeat performance, slapping another victim of shell shock with his gloves and kicking him.

Journalists Demaree Bess and Merrill Mueller of NBC learned of the assaults and gathered signed statements from doctors and patients. The story quickly spread throughout the press camp and beyond, yet nobody made a move to publish it. The two reporters, along with Quentin Reynolds of CBS, flew to General Dwight D. Eisenhower's headquarters to inform the general and seek his advice.

According to Reynolds, Eisenhower said, "You men have got yourselves good stories, and as you know, there's no question of censorship involved," because the news was factual and did not affect security. Bess then spoke up to say the press corps had decided to kill the story on its own initiative. "We're Americans first and correspondents second," he said. That pleased Eisenhower, who then revealed his own belief that publication would undercut the effectiveness of the Allies' top cavalry general and contribute to Axis propaganda. The journalists treated Eisenhower's statement as a request for self-censorship, and all agreed to suppress the story.

The story of Patton's slapping the two American soldiers remained out of the news until Pearson learned the details in Washington, D.C., and broadcast a summary November 21, 1943, over the NBC Blue Network. Pearson found no objections to broadcasting the Patton story either in the *Code of Wartime Practices* or among the staff members at the Office of Censorship. Furthermore, he was much less constrained by peer and military pressures; as an unaccredited home-front journalist, he operated outside army control and was virtually immune from retribution. Release of the story did not stop Patton from commanding an army during the invasion of northern Europe, however. Nor could it conceivably have given valuable information to the enemy, as Patton's irascible personality was already widely known to friend and foe alike.

Eisenhower considered journalists to be "quasi-staff officers . . . accredited to my headquarters." He avowed that opinion wins wars, observing in April 1945, "Public opinion must be honestly and fearlessly informed." Yet, after Pearson broke the news of Patton's assaults, Eisenhower and the War Department stonewalled reporters seeking confirmation. Only after two days of clamoring by the press corps in Washington did Eisenhower advise his chief of staff to "tell the full truth" and approve the release of the complete story.

The status of press members as "quasi" officers, at least in Eisenhower's estimation, mirrored their indefinite place in the bureaucracy of war. They were not exactly soldiers, not exactly civilians. To receive accreditation to cover the war, a journalist had to submit to an official examination of his or her background, opinions about the war, and reliability. "By the time you are accredited you have no secrets from the War Department and neither do your ancestors; but it is right that this should be so because as a war correspondent you have access to many sources of vital military information," photojournalist Margaret Bourke-White said in 1943. "You are in a position of great trust."

The armed forces demanded such trust because they could not discipline or control journalists as they did soldiers or sailors. Accreditation meant that the armed forces would feed, transport, and billet journalists with units in the war zones and relay their stories and photographs overseas. In return, the journalists had to submit their materials to official military censorship and follow a list of regulations. Failure to adhere to the accreditation rules could cause a journalist to lose his or her credentials, be expelled from the combat zone, or even court-martialed.

Combat journalists wore uniforms to prevent them from being shot as spies if captured, but they had no insignia of rank. Instead, they wore green armbands or patches identifying them as reporters or photographers. Journalists had the arbitrary rank of captain assigned to them to fit them into military regulations regarding transportation, shelter, and possible capture by the enemy.

Officially, journalists were supposed to report to the public relations officer of the unit to which they had been assigned. The PR officer "is to be regarded by the War Correspondent as their C[ommanding] O[fficer]," a military manual explained, "and all communications on official matters will be addressed to him. Senior Officers should not be approached in person or by letter except through the Senior PR Officer concerned, or present." In practice, most individual officers elected to cut the red tape. Eisenhower, for example, signed passes giving journalists the right to free movement. The passes declared the bearers should not be interfered with as they went about their work.

The press had greater liberty to report than in World War I, not only on what happened but what it meant. Eisenhower's censors passed a Pyle column, during the North African campaign in December 1942, complaining that

America's military policies allowed "soft-gloving of [collaborationist] snakes in our midst." The Associated Press's Drew Middleton wrote that German soldiers had severely beaten the American army and forced its retreat at Kasserine Pass; Eisenhower's censors also cleared that story. In Burma, General Joseph Stilwell told reporters the Allies took "a hell of a beating" from the Japanese, and the American press applauded his candor after the statement was released in the United States.

General Douglas MacArthur, in command in the southwest Pacific, was not so forthcoming. Like Eisenhower, he publicly said it was "essential" the public know the truth in order for democracy to succeed. However, MacArthur's definition of truth required journalists to slant their dispatches to play down the casualties inflicted on his forces and play up his role in his troops' successful offensives. Reports that failed to conform to these rules did not survive the censor's shears in MacArthur's press office. If journalists dared to interview one of MacArthur's soldiers without permission, the reporter risked expulsion, and the soldier a court-martial. Admiral Ernest King was equally reticent to relax the rules on journalists covering the navy. Not only was news of the sinking of American ships suppressed in early and mid-1942, but the press also underplayed the full story of the navy's unlikely, pivotal victory over the Japanese at the Battle of Midway in June 1942 because of the navy's excessive secrecy. Even the names of ordinary sailors were banned from news accounts until a journalists' rebellion reversed the policy in the final months of the war. King finally loosened up. As the war turned in America's favor, he began bringing groups of journalists into his confidence and sharing his analysis.

Some important stories remained unpublicized for the entire war despite widespread knowledge of their existence. Roy A. Roberts, president of the American Society of Newspaper Editors, complained in a letter to Major General Alexander D. Surles of the War Department's public relations office about the suppression of three widely known stories in the Sicilian and Italian campaigns. In addition to the Patton slapping incident, Roberts listed the loss of twenty-three Allied planes to friendly fire during the invasion of Sicily and the German air raid that caught the Allies off guard at Bari, Italy, sinking seventeen ships in the British-controlled harbor. Surles erroneously replied that only two ships filled with ammunition had been sunk at Bari. He also failed to mention that one of the vessels destroyed in the raid, the Liberty ship *John Harvey,* was carrying ten tons of mustard gas. Its 200 gas bombs had been intended for retaliatory strikes if the Germans ever initiated chemical attacks. However, the sensitive nature of blister agents aboard an American ship in an Italian harbor had prompted the army to keep the cargo a total secret. Thus, when the *John Harvey* exploded and spilled its deadly cargo into the water and air, medical personnel lacked the proper information to diagnose and treat the more than 600 known burn victims. The wounded received treatment for conventional, not chemical, burns, and sixty-nine died. While Allied civilians eventually learned of the "second Pearl Harbor" at Bari, the presence of mustard gas remained censored for political reasons. British Prime Minister Winston Churchill insisted on a cover-up, and the American government agreed.

Another example of political censorship kept Americans from knowing about the end of the war in Europe for twenty-four hours. Correspondents watched on May 7, 1945, as German General Alfred Jodl signed the papers of his nation's surrender at a schoolhouse in Reims, France, where Eisenhower had his headquarters. Yet the British and American armed forces, with President Harry S. Truman's endorsement, ordered reporters to hold the news for a day to allow the Soviets to run their own surrender ceremony in Berlin. The plan aimed to improve America's and Britain's already strained relations with the Soviets.

No security issues could be involved, as the war was over. Nevertheless, all reporters but one agreed to the censorship. Edward Kennedy of the Associated Press, who had reluctantly held the news of Patton's assault on two soldiers in Sicily, refused. He had heard a German-language radio announcement and knew the German people already had been informed of their surrender at Reims. Allied troops also had heard the news, and the Office of War Information's European broadcasting station had aired the news in twenty-four languages within an hour of the signing.

"The absurdity of trying to bottle up news of such magnitude was too apparent," Kennedy said. He found an uncensored phone line to London and put his scoop on the AP wire. American civilians celebrated. Kennedy's colleagues, however, complained and had the AP's accreditation to cover the war in Europe suspended. When Eisenhower lifted the ban after eight hours, fifty-four reporters from competing news organizations filed a protest. The AP fired Kennedy and apologized for breaking the news before the requested release time.

"I do not think Kennedy imperilled the lives of any Allied soldiers by sending the story, as some of his critics have charged," Liebling wrote in the *New Yorker*. "He probably saved a few, because by withholding the announcement of an armistice you prolong the shooting, and, conversely, by announcing it promptly you make the shooting stop."

A key operational rule intended to guide censorship was whether the enemy already knew the information the correspondent wished to publish or broadcast. Accredited correspondents could appeal military censorship rulings on that basis. Walter Cronkite, a United Press (UP) wire service reporter covering the air war in Britain, successfully overturned a censor's ruling over an important development in the American bombing campaign against Germany. General Ira Eaker had adopted the British "Pathfinder" technique of flying a few planes at low levels to illuminate a target for subsequent waves of high-altitude bombers. The method proved effective in pinpointing sites covered in clouds, which previously had stymied the American air force's daylight bombing raids. Cronkite learned of the development and wrote a story describing the Americans' initial Pathfinder mission that bombed the city of Emden in 1943 through a thick cloud blanket. A military censor spiked the story for revealing too much tactical information. Cronkite appealed to the chief censor.

"I pointed out that the Germans at Emden sure as the devil knew that there was complete cloud cover through which those bombs tumbled. Their fighters had flown over the clouds to attack the Americans, and their antiaircraft had fired through it," Cronkite recalled. "Who were we kidding? Who were we keeping the story from except the American people?" He won the argument and saw his story lead the military paper *Stars and Stripes* the next day.

The armed forces controlled not only the content of the correspondents' communication, but also its method of transmission from the war zone to the home front. Press reporters often had timely stories sent to the United States via a point-to-point shortwave radio connection operated by the Army Signal Corps. An army reader took the censored "voice-cast" copy and dictated it to a distant transcriber for distribution. During the invasion of France, the army's mobile radio transmitters, teletype circuits, and a commercial Press Wireless radio installation augmented speedboats and even carrier pigeons in getting the news across the English Channel and to America. A radio hookup with the call letters JESQ—"Jig Easy Sugar Queen" in the phonetic military alphabet—had enough power to send voice messages to London for splicing into transatlantic cable connections to New York. The Press Wireless radio hookup had the call letters SWIF—"Somewhere in France"—and relied on a portable diesel generator for power. It made its first transmissions, direct to Long Island, seven days after D-day. Stories after D-day moved from reporters' typewriters in the field to the desk of a New York editor in as little as twenty minutes.

With mailboxes and telephones being scarce in the middle of the ocean, reporters at sea had to rely completely on naval cooperation in getting their stories swiftly home. The alternative was to wait for ships to arrive in port, which could take days or weeks. Yet just such a slow method provided the *Chicago Tribune* with one of the biggest, and most controversial, scoops of the war. *Tribune* reporter Stanley Johnston witnessed the Battle of the Coral Sea on May 7 and 8, 1942, on board the aircraft carrier *Lexington*. The Japanese navy torpedoed and dive-bombed the ship, and over the next eight hours it burned and sank. Rescuers pulled Johnston from the surface of the Pacific and put him aboard a transport headed for California. During the slow journey home, Johnston befriended an unidentified officer. The man showed the reporter the most sensitive of secrets: a communiqué detailing a Japanese battle group steaming toward Midway Island. The list had been compiled from intercepted radio communications. They were sent in code, but the navy had managed to crack the cipher and read the enemy's messages.

Johnston kept a copy of the communiqué when he disembarked at San Diego and headed to Chicago. On June 6, he saw a wire report of the American victory at the Battle of Midway. He knew the victory resulted in part from the decoded messages and realized he had a scoop. Johnston's front-page story in the *Tribune*'s June 7 edition carried the headline "Navy Had Word of Jap Plan to Strike at Sea." Although it did not overtly state that the Japanese operational code had been broken, that fact would have been plain to any knowledgeable reader. "The strength of the Japanese forces with which the American navy is battling . . . was well known in American naval circles several days before the battle began," Johnston wrote. Insiders knew he had copied the secret communiqué because he had duplicated its unusual spellings of the Japanese ships.

The story touched a nerve in Washington, where the navy feared the news would reach Tokyo and cause the Japanese navy to change the code. Roosevelt initially wanted to have Marines occupy the *Tribune* building on Lake Michigan and possibly charge the paper's publisher with treason. The president had his attorney general, Francis Biddle, prepare to prosecute the *Tribune* on charges of violating the Espionage Act. At the last minute, however, after a grand jury already had begun meeting, the case was dropped. The code had remained readable despite the news leak; the government feared a public trial would certainly reveal the secret to Japan. Johnston personally avoided punishment on a technicality: he had never signed his accreditation papers, which would have required him to submit his story to navy censors before publication.

Military censorship of images rested on photographers' reliance on the armed forces to transport and sometimes develop and print their film. Furthermore, magazine layouts containing photographs received a second layer of military censorship, aimed at gauging the impact of the photographs' size, arrangement, and accompanying text. Knowing their work would be censored, combat photographers either policed themselves to follow the 200-page military censorship code or shot pictures with the confidence that the armed forces would withhold offending photographs, or black out sections that identified the dead or revealed battlefield secrets.

Bourke-White, one of the original *Life* photographers, carried a pass in Italy signed by the deputy theater commander that entitled her to "take pictures of any activities without regard to censorship, which will be exercised by proper authorities at the completion of her mission." The pass, citing her star status, gave her carte blanche to go where she wanted and photograph what she wanted, and requested that she be given any necessary air or ground transportation.

Bourke-White, born in 1904, enjoyed raising eyebrows. As a child, she took snakes to school; as a teen, she posed nude for an art class. She chose a job in photography—an unusual choice for a woman in the 1920s—after pondering and rejecting a career in herpetology. She earned a reputation as an industrial photographer in Cleveland and took up aerial photography for Trans-World Airlines in 1935. She shot for Time Inc.'s *Fortune* magazine and took the cover picture for the debut issue of *Life*. Eager to shoot pictures of the war in Europe, Bourke-White signed up to go with the army and became the first female accredited correspondent—an act that forced the army to approve a skirted variation of the official correspondent's uniform. She proved fearless in the face of combat, becoming the first woman on an air raid and a regular witness to artillery attacks.

In her chronicle *They Called It "Purple Heart Valley,"* Bourke-White described how the army handled her film of the Allied invasion of Italy. Film and caption material went by army pouch to the Pentagon. There, the Signal Corps, or *Life* technicians working under army supervision, made prints from the negatives. *Life* received only the approved photos. Censors reviewed Bourke-White's raw notes, which formed the basis for captions, as well as the completed layout before publication.

Accredited photographers had to represent one of four organizations: the AP, International News Photos, Acme Newspictures, or, as an indication of *Life* magazine's special status, its parent company, Time Inc. They provided all publications with civilian photographs of the war through a pool arrangement. (*Life* had special pictures held for simultaneous release in its weekly edition, to avoid being beaten by the daily competition with its own photographs.) The government had decided on a pool system as a matter of policy. War photos had to be equally available for all consumers. Likewise, print and radio journalists filed pool reports when a military action could not accommodate all coverage requests. Reporters filed pool reports to the OWI for national distribution during the first five days of the Normandy invasion. After that, they reverted to competition for the best and fastest news.

Military censors knew they would get in more trouble for releasing questionable photographs or bits of news stories than by withholding information of marginal sensitivity. In borderline cases, they chose secrecy. Photographs blocked from publication ended up in a secret Pentagon file called "the Chamber of Horrors" by its managers. The chamber's images ranged from serious wounds to dead Americans (enemy dead were routinely cleared for publication) to victims of psychological trauma and evidence of sexual activity by America's fighting forces.

The censorship began with the attack on Pearl Harbor. Presidential press secretary Stephen Early told reporters one American battleship had been capsized, several others damaged, one destroyer sunk, and a number of planes put out of commission. Actually, eight battleships and three light cruisers had been sunk or damaged, along with three destroyers and hundreds of military planes. The only photographs released immediately to the press were long-distance views of towers and smoke. A few photographs of greater detail appeared in February 1942, but it was not until that December the navy released more explicit pictures of the devastation. The photos portrayed flames, smoke, and battle damage, but the human cost in burned and twisted bodies remained censored.

The censorship fit a widespread mood. Many civilians remained unconvinced of the need for sacrifice, partly because war seemed so distant. Pearl Harbor was thousands of miles from most American homes, and civilians had no firsthand experience of war's impact. Military authorities shocked by the easy Japanese victory feared that too much candor about the war would demoralize the home front in early 1942. Combat photography historian Peter Maslowski suggested that military and civilian censorship, in weeding out the bad news, "nourished the prevalent complacency and fostered an optimistic outlook bordering on overconfidence."

Rumblings that too much censorship might be counterproductive first surfaced in June 1942, although it would take more than a year for substantial policy changes. That month, the army's adjutant general suggested overly censored news of the war failed to keep political and military leaders adequately informed. More news also would bring the benefit of "an enlightened people" more willing to sacrifice. Roosevelt endorsed the concept of more frankness in war coverage in order to unite the country for a long fight and decided in spring 1943 to expand civilians' view of the war. The timing was good. As the Allies took the offensive in the Pacific and the Mediterranean, government authorities foresaw a possible shift in public opinion, with the complacency of 1942 tilting toward overconfidence. Roosevelt hoped pictures and stories of soldiers and sailors facing grave reality would inspire noncombatants to equal sacrifice. Furthermore, polls showed that 39 percent of Americans that summer believed the government was making the situation look better than it was.

In May 1943, the army's combat camera units received a

memo outlining the president's desire for photographs that would show war's "grimness and hardness" to civilians. "I'm not arguing for stories that will chill the blood of a mother or sweetheart," an OWI official told newspaper executives in explaining the change, "but we do want to know what our sons are really enduring." After the policy was publicly announced, *Newsweek* published pictures of badly wounded Americans in the Pacific. However, the trickle of candid photos from military censors soon dried up. Army Signal Corps restrictions grew throughout the summer, and the marines and navy closed their files to the OWI. The OWI's Elmer Davis urged Roosevelt to release photos of dead Americans, and the president agreed. When opinions differed on releasing information, Roosevelt shifted the burden to the military to demonstrate why it should be withheld rather than requiring the OWI to prove the case for its release. The War Department agreed to dip into the Chamber of Horrors and released dozens of pictures.

Three of the first photos portrayed the stub of a soldier's amputated leg, the torn bodies of paratroopers in Sicily, and three dead soldiers lying in the sands of Buna Beach, New Guinea. *Life* published the Buna photo, by George Strock, on September 20, 1943. The image remains a touchstone of World War II censorship and publicity: The bodies lay intact and peacefully composed, as if asleep. No faces or identifying features were visible. The photograph suggested death without the blood-chilling gore the OWI had counseled against. While the deaths seemed close at hand, the dead still remained impersonal in their sacrifice.

"What shall we say of them?" *Life* asked its readers about the Americans in the seven-month-old photograph. "Shall we say that this is a noble sight? Shall we say that this is a fine thing, that they should give their lives for their country? Or shall we say that this is too horrible to look at?" It concluded that if soldiers had the fortitude to endure such horror, civilians had the fortitude to look at it. Five of six letters published by the magazine endorsed the photo's publication. A Louisiana dredge company worker's letter said employee participation in a payroll deduction plan to buy war bonds increased from 55 percent to 100 percent after he posted the Buna photograph.

With precedent set and positive reaction secured, the armed forces began routinely releasing photos of dead Americans, either composed to hide faces or with black bars inked across the eyes. Such publications became routine by D-day.

Some subjects remained censored. Photos of the worst insults to flesh—horrible shrapnel wounds, decapitations, shredded genitalia—remained off limits. The emotionally wounded also remained a casualty of truth not only throughout the war but also long after. Filmmaker John Huston, famous for directing *The Maltese Falcon,* created a film in 1945 about the treatment of psychologically disturbed soldiers at the army's Mason General Hospital. *Let There Be Light* portrayed the struggles of psychotics, paralytics, and other victims to regain a measure of normal life. Huston received permission to visit any part of the hospital and film anything he pleased. The access apparently became too free for the army's taste, once it learned of the film's content. When Huston tried to debut the film, military police confiscated it before the audience could see it. The army suppressed the film until 1980.

Huston said the army withheld *Let There Be Light* because "wounds that you can see—heroes without legs or arms—are acceptable, because it shows a love of country and patriotism and the right stuff." Emotional injuries, on the other hand, had to be covered up. "The authorities wanted to maintain the 'warrior' myth, which said that our American soldiers went to war and came back all the stronger for the experience."

If combat lost its glory in World War I, combat news lost its romance in World War II. Truth remained the stated goal of American coverage, but the government and armed forces feared too much truth—mutilation, friction among the Allies, soldiers gone mad from stress—would compromise the nation's desire and ability to conduct total war. The balancing point stood where news kept citizens informed enough to want to continue the war until gaining the enemy's unconditional surrender, but not so informed they shrank in horror and lost their enthusiasm.

The press of World War II expanded the view of combat available to the home front beyond that of previous wars. Americans did not recoil at what they saw. In the decades to come, a new mass medium, television, would push the door open wider still in Korea and Vietnam.

FIVE

THE GREAT
DIVORCE:
KOREA AND VIETNAM

*"Are you correspondents telling the people back home the truth?
Are you telling them that out of one platoon of twenty men, we
have three left? Are you telling them that we have nothing to
fight with, and that it is an utterly useless war?"*
— Lieutenant Edward James to
  New York Herald Tribune
  correspondent Marguerite Higgins,
  South Korea, July 1950

The wars in Korea and Vietnam matched nothing in American experience. The same could be said for their journalism. America entered both in defense of small, far-off democracies. South Korea and South Vietnam appeared to have little significance to American security until the clash of Cold War ideologies recast them as the front line of a new fight for global dominance. Despite its status as the world's strongest superpower, the United States fought both wars under restraints designed to keep the fighting from spreading to total conflict with China and the Soviet Union—to keep the Cold War from turning hot and igniting World War III.

Unlike previous American wars, both conflicts ended with something less than victory. The Korean War of 1950–1953 halted with a military stalemate approximating the status quo ante. The Vietnam War—which saw America's role gradually escalate from 1954 through 1969, decline until a pullout in 1973, and end with final defeat of South Vietnam by a combination of North Vietnamese regulars and Vietcong guerrillas in 1975—shook up America's beliefs in political and military superiority.

Both wars received unprecedented levels of coverage. Margaret Bourke-White considered the Korean War the most thoroughly documented and South Korea "the most consistently raked over news center in the world." Vietnam raised the bar even higher. The first to be reported extensively by television, it outpaced Korea to become what historian Clarence R. Wyatt described as the "most covered but least understood" war in American history.

The correlation of the wars' heightened levels of news coverage with their unsatisfactory conclusions has continued to spark debate. Did one cause the other? Did the news media act as handmaidens of doom by misrepresenting America's war aims? Or did they expose flaws in strategy and tactics that would have precluded victory no matter the circumstances of battlefield conflicts and public debate?

JOURNALISM IN THE CONTEXT OF
THE COLD WAR

The answers lie not only in the wars themselves but in the context in which they were played out. Concerns about national security reached extreme—even paranoid—levels after World War II. Eastern Europe fell under Soviet domination, and China turned communist. President Harry S. Truman redirected American foreign policy in 1947 with a pledge to help democratic nations, starting with Greece and Turkey, fighting to stave off communist takeovers. In 1949, the Soviet Union exploded its first atomic bomb. American foreign policy toward communism came to be embodied in a single word, "containment."

American diplomat George F. Kennan, the author of the containment doctrine, argued that nations around the rim of the Soviet sphere of influence had to be given a boost of confidence. Political, economic, and ultimately military force had to help the vulnerable nations push back, or "contain," communist expansive pressures. Under the containment doctrine, two things had to happen for communist nations to back off: Democracies had to intimidate, and communists had to agree to be intimidated.

In such a highly charged atmosphere, every nation gained significance as an outpost against communist expansion. If any nation fell, Western governments feared it would take neighboring nations with it. Unfortunately for the United States, insurgents in South Vietnam and the governments of North Vietnam, North Korea, China, and the Soviet Union were visibly intimidated neither by America's technological superiority nor by its possession of nuclear weapons.

In the Cold War atmosphere of danger and suspicion, the American government regularly classified routine information as secret. In the late 1940s and early 1950s, Truman disapproved of what he saw as recklessness by the news media, particularly in publicizing information about atomic installations that might make them targets for sabotage. Truman already had a classification system for military information, issued by President Franklin D. Roosevelt on March 22, 1940. It created presidential security classifications for "all official military or naval books, pamphlets, documents, reports, maps, charts, plans, designs, models, drawings, photographs, contracts or specifications."

Truman used his executive powers to expand the list in 1951, giving civilian agencies the authority to classify sensitive materials as top secret, secret, confidential, or restricted. When journalists protested, Truman replied, "The safety and welfare of the United States of America comes [*sic*] first with me." During the previous year, Truman had ordered the State Department to clear public statements on foreign policy by government employees, and the Defense Department to do the same for military pronouncements. In the ensuing decades, information related to national security during peacetime, particularly concerning atomic energy, received levels of scrutiny previously reserved for wartime defense.

The federal government pressured domestic journalists to fall in line during the Cold War. The Federal Bureau of Investigation spent hundreds of hours seeking the source of leaks to the press and investigated for potential prosecution any reporters who accepted leaks. Journalists who angered the White House during the Vietnam War might find their income tax returns repeatedly audited by the Internal Revenue Service, as did Marvin Kalb of CBS; their stories vetted by the Central Intelligence Agency, as occurred with David Halberstam of the *New York Times;* or their bosses threatened by the White House, as happened to CBS President Frank Stanton after a correspondent filed a report showing U.S. Marines torching a Vietnamese village. President Richard Nixon circulated lists of fifty of his "enemies" in the press.

One of the most influential documents of the Cold War was suppressed as top secret despite its key role in shaping international relations and expanding the defense budget. National Security Council document no. 68, or "NSC-68," guided basic defense policy for two decades. Received at the White House in April 1950, two months before the outbreak of the Korean War, NSC-68 offered the first integrated assessment of national security requirements in the atomic era.

The report made three key points. First, the Soviet Union sought world domination. Second, the United States needed a rapid buildup of political, economic, and military strength no later than 1954, the year of "maximum danger," when the document forecast the Soviets would have a strong atomic arsenal capable of reaching the United States. The buildup would make the United States too strong an adversary to confront. Third, America's defense would require abandoning tight military budgets. The government had to expand greatly what it spent on guns, bombs, planes, tanks, and especially atomic weapons, but not necessarily on people. This assumed that Soviet manpower would be difficult to match.

Truman signed a memo in September 1950 making NSC-68 a matter of policy. The document suggested the importance and difficulties of placing limits on free expression. "The democratic way is harder than the authoritarian way because, in seeking to protect and fulfill the individual, it demands of him understanding, judgment and positive participation in the increasingly complex and exacting problems of the modern world," NSC-68 said. "It demands that he exercise discrimination: that while pursuing through free inquiry the search for truth he knows when he should commit an act of faith; that he distinguish between the necessity for tolerance and the necessity for just suppression."

The document added that the government would be justified in bending or breaking the law, by taking "any measures, covert or overt, violent or non-violent," to frustrate the Kremlin. A key problem, NSC-68 said, was to avoid acting so harshly as to make new enemies in foreign nations that teetered between democracy and communism. Under such policy, ends justified most means. Officials could act in ways calculated to defend democracy while undermining its core principles of free speech and free press.

Advocates at the highest levels gave their support. A Pentagon spokesman told reporters in 1962 that every government had the right to lie in order to protect its vital interests. A decade later, Nixon told an interviewer, "When the president does it, that means it is not illegal."

NSC-68 led to the growth of America's atomic arsenal. But limited wars exposed the limited value of nuclear weapons. "Korea ripped away our complacency, our smug feeling that all we had to do for our safety was to build bigger atomic bombs," *New York Herald Tribune* reporter Marguerite

Higgins wrote in 1951. Using the atomic bomb against a small nation would cost the United States in the court of world opinion and possibly invite Chinese or Soviet retaliation.

KOREA

It was a measure of Americans' faith in their government during the Cold War that public opinion polls showed widespread support for the escalation of combat in the early years of the Korean and Vietnam wars. A few weeks into the Korean War, in summer 1950, more than 75 percent of Americans responding to a poll approved of sending military aid to South Korea, even though 43 percent predicted it would lead to atomic war.

At the time of the poll, there had been little time for Americans to form opinions about combat in Korea. Unlike World Wars I and II, which the United States entered after years of combat by foreign nations, the Korean War began without warning. On June 21, 1950, Higgins reported a statement by General Douglas MacArthur that there would be no war in Asia for at least ten years. Four days later, several North Korean infantry divisions, supported by Soviet tanks, crossed the border and headed south.

Journalists, led by a vanguard of wire service reporters, flocked to South Korea. Meanwhile, Truman dispatched MacArthur to the front to see if American air and sea power could halt the invasion. The general surveyed the South Koreans' retreat and concluded that only ground troops could stem the tide. America took his recommendation to the United Nations and won its approval for a multinational intervention.

Higgins arrived at the front July 5, along with photographer Carl Mydans. They watched as the first American combat troops, in two rifle companies, engaged the North Koreans for the first time. Higgins knew a rout when she saw it and reported it as such for the *New York Herald Tribune.* Untested American youths fled when their rifles and bazookas proved no match for the Soviet tanks, she said. Mydans told her, "My God, they look as if the ball game was over and it's time to go home."

The American troops fell back toward the southern tip of the Korean peninsula, buying time for reinforcements to arrive. During the chaotic retreat, Higgins heard Lieutenant Edward James describe the futility of fighting an "utterly useless" war against superior numbers with inferior weaponry. She repeatedly heard reluctant soldiers say, "Just give me a jeep and I'll know which direction I'll go in."

Higgins stayed close enough to the fighting to watch soldiers die, hear a general order his men to fight to the death rather than retreat, and survive nearby explosions. She never lacked for courage. Born in Hong Kong in 1920, Higgins took journalism classes at the University of California and got her master's degree at Columbia University in New York City. She spoke Cantonese and French in addition to English. Her academic credentials, along with her determination to get close to the news she covered, helped her dig out details that other reporters missed. She wrote on the Nazi death camps at the end of World War II as well as the communist takeover of Poland and Czechoslovakia. Her time in postwar Eastern Europe instilled in her a lifelong hatred of communism, manifest in her unquestioned support for the war in Korea and, later, Vietnam.

In addition to her skills, Higgins had luck. She groused about being transferred in 1950 from Europe to Tokyo to be Far East bureau chief for the *Herald Tribune*. The Korean War erupted twenty-five days later. Higgins took the first flight into Seoul, aboard a military transport full of artillery shells. She caught a ride in MacArthur's private plane. After she wrote about American troops' initial retreats, General Walton Walker banished her from Korea—on the pretense that there were no toilets for women at the front. MacArthur, charmed by Higgins, overruled his subordinate and ordered her back. "Ban on women in Korea being lifted," MacArthur cabled. "Marguerite Higgins held in highest professional esteem." That fall, she went ashore in the fifth wave during MacArthur's bold invasion of Inchon, which cut off the North Koreans and began a reversal of fortunes.

Higgins continued taking risks and miraculously surviving. Her determination helped make the *Herald Tribune*'s coverage the best of the war. It also pushed her colleague, Homer Bigart, to take similar chances. "This correspondent was one of three reporters who saw [a North Korean enveloping action], and was the only newsman to get out alive," Bigart wrote in the *Herald Tribune*. Enemy fire cut down the other two, Ray Richards of the International News Service and Ernie Peeler of *Stars and Stripes*. The war proved particularly dangerous for journalists. Nearly 300 received accreditation, with about a quarter of them covering the front at one time. Seventeen died, including ten Americans.

Higgins explained that the only way to cover the war with honesty was to see it at the platoon or company level or to join a patrol. Many correspondents took to carrying handguns. Despite this violation of military rules, the precaution seemed wise considering the number of civilians killed on both sides. Reporter Fred Sparks carried a gun, remarking on the futility of shouting "*Chicago Daily News!*" to any enemy soldier who might jump into his foxhole.

In addition to the physical danger, correspondents faced a multitude of logistical and communication difficulties. Many hitched hundred-mile rides to the front to gather the news, slept only three to four hours a night, and then hitchhiked back. In the first few months of the war, only one cable connected military headquarters with Tokyo, forcing reporters and photographers to file between midnight and 4 A.M., or 2 and 4 P.M. If the military claimed priority on the line, reports were delayed. Often, through the end of 1950, the surest way to get a story or photograph to the States involved a round-trip flight to Tokyo. As the war progressed, the armed forces added telephone and teletype lines to division headquarters and opened commercial lines. That allowed the news to reach Tokyo within a few hours.

At first, the press administered its own voluntary censorship system in conjunction with Defense Department rules ordering the armed forces not to release operational details of value to the enemy. Journalists were asked to avoid publicizing a list of topics including names and positions of military units, allied casualty figures, and reinforcement strength. In addition, the voluntary code requested nondisclosure of "any such information as may be of aid and comfort to the enemy." In other words, information that lacked operational security value would run afoul of the voluntary code if it raised the enemy's morale or lowered that of the U.N. forces.

Correspondents never disputed issues of purely military

security, Higgins said. She acknowledged that slipups occurred but attributed them to ignorance or confusion. However, many published stories angered officers during the early
months of the war because they exposed inexperience and
weakness. The AP's Tom Lambert and UP's Peter Kalischer
briefly were banned from the war zone over accusations of
"giving aid and comfort" to the communists.

MacArthur publicly endorsed self-censorship in Korea.
Even after three months of fighting, he considered war correspondents "essentially responsible individuals" who had
struck "the proper balance between public information and
military security." But the censorship system began to un-
ravel by late 1950. Military officials declined to share sensitive background information for fear it would leak. Meanwhile, competitive pressures kept journalists pushing for
more and more information. There were no press pools in
Korea, so each correspondent scrambled to avoid being
scooped.

Melvin Voorhees, chief censor of the Eighth Army, alleged "hundreds" of security violations of the voluntary
code. These included the landing and movements of the
First Cavalry Division, a premature announcement of the
invasion of Inchon, and the initial recovery of American
prisoners of war. None were shown to cause casualties.

Other stories fell victim to self-censorship. Killings of
civilians rarely made the news despite journalists' awareness
of the effects of aerial and artillery bombardments. Cold War
patriotism also prompted journalists to hide unpleasant details. Hal Boyle of the Associated Press and William H.
Lawrence of the *New York Times* (not the same as William
Laurence, who covered the Manhattan Project) learned that

refugees died by the score when American troops destroyed the Tuksong-dong bridge August 3, 1950, but that fact never appeared in their published accounts.

Likewise, when American soldiers slaughtered civilians at No Gun Ri out of fear of their having been infiltrated by guerrillas, the story received only a paragraph, two months later, in the *New York Times.* An Associated Press investigation into the tragedy won a Pulitzer Prize a half century later. Although details remained in dispute, the army found sufficient evidence during a fifteen-month investigation to determine that American soldiers had killed an unknown number of Korean refugees at No Gun Ri.

Edward R. Murrow of CBS had a Korean War report censored by his bosses in New York. Murrow flew into South Korea ten days into the fighting, aboard a transport plane filled with blood for the wounded. On the runway to greet the plane at Pusan was veteran correspondent Bill Downs, who waved and shouted to Murrow, "Go back! Go back! It ain't our kind of war!" Instead, Murrow toured the front and filed a bleak account raising serious questions about battlefield decisions and lack of reinforcements. He closed by saying, "When we start moving up through dead valleys, through villages to which we have put the torch by retreating, what then of the people who live there? . . . Will our reoccupation of that flea-bitten land lessen or increase the attraction of communism?" CBS executives spiked the story because it could be seen as raising enemy morale and might cause the network to lose its accreditation. Murrow protested furiously, but CBS held firm.

Reporters demanded an official form of censorship "to keep them clear of error," wrote Marshall Andrews of the

Washington Post. The Overseas Press Club agreed. Truman also expressed concern about news leaks in Korea after the Chinese intervened in fall 1950 to help the North Koreans. Defense Secretary George Marshall, responding to a request from MacArthur to sort out security issues after the press published news of General Walton Walker's death before it could be announced, met with a panel of journalists in December 1950. Their discussion cleared the way for military-run censorship. "It is indeed a screwy world . . . when a soldier fighting to preserve freedom of the press finds himself opposed by the press itself," MacArthur acknowledged.

In late December, the armed forces imposed a formal combat-zone censorship system much like the one in World War II. Stories censored by the military included exposés of South Korean corruption and POW camp disturbances, neither of which affected battlefield security.

Skepticism greeted officially approved statements. Robert C. Miller of the United Press pointed out that a photograph on display in Tokyo, of a bridge supposedly blown up by "pinpoint" aerial bombardment, actually had been demolished by army engineers. "Many of us who sent the stories knew they were false," Miller said, "but we had to write them for they were official releases from responsible military headquarters, and were released for publication even though the people responsible knew they were untrue."

One stateside reporter, investigative journalist Drew Pearson, repeatedly questioned the official version of the war. His aggressiveness prompted five FBI investigations in 1950 and 1951 aimed at intimidating his sources and building a case for prosecution. None ended in charges.

The first investigation occurred after Pearson published a

newspaper column in December 1950, based on "telecons" from Korea to the United States, regarding MacArthur's conduct of the war. Pearson reported that MacArthur's rosy assessments varied with the intelligence his staff was cabling to Washington. MacArthur said in late November there were not enough Chinese in Korea to interfere with getting his troops home by Christmas. On December 2, MacArthur said there were about 500,000 Chinese in Korea. Two days later he inflated that number to more than a million, and on December 15 he reported a "bottomless well of Chinese Communist manpower" on the peninsula. Yet, his intelligence chief was cabling far lower numbers to Washington— 285,000 Chinese and 150,000 North Koreans.

Pearson identified the actual units facing the U.N. troops and gave a list of the communist troops' usual equipment: rifles and hand grenades, mostly, with oxen and mule carts for carrying ammunition. Marshall asked the attorney general's office to investigate the source of the leak. FBI agents found no answers. They ended the inquiry after interviewing about 400 government employees who had access to the messages and discovering that 900 more had clearance to see the documents. Pearson never named his sources.

Pearson said his column about the Chinese army could not be considered a military secret of value to the enemy. The news already had appeared in the European press, and there was no reason Americans should not also know, he said. His reporting aimed to shed light on errors that led to costly casualties. Quoting from the cables also protected him from right-wing accusations of lying in order to create a good story.

Formal censorship lasted until after Truman fired

MacArthur in April 1951 for making unapproved foreign policy statements. MacArthur's successor, General Mathew Ridgway, reinstated the voluntary code.

Combat soon reached a stalemate along a front very near the original border between North and South Korea, as peace talks dragged on for two years. Correspondents covering the talks received secondhand briefings from officers who had not been at the negotiating table. A distorted picture of the two sides' bargaining positions emerged, with a Western briefing officer at one point flatly—and wrongly—denying the existence of a communist proposal to accept a political boundary along the existing front. Attempts to interview U.N. negotiators directly were forbidden. Some journalists got a more accurate picture of the talks' progress by interviewing Australian reporter Wilfred Burchett, a communist accredited to cover the delegation of North Koreans and Chinese for *Ce Soir* of Paris.

The Korean War was the last conflict in which print journalists, radio reporters, and still photographers reigned supreme. Television had worked its way into only a third of American households by 1952 but would reach 86 percent of homes by the end of the decade. Even though the technology existed to televise film shot in Korea over the airwaves, the war did not invade American living rooms in live, color-television broadcasts.

Murrow's most famous televised story of the war, a documentary about Christmas in Korea, appeared more like a holiday card from the front than an insider's view of combat—albeit a postcard fashioned out of nearly twenty miles of film shipped to New York. Television cameras and supporting equipment were bulky and heavy, making it impossible to film combat up close without inviting rifle fire. Instead of the boom of artillery, Murrow focused on the daily life of a company of infantry, including the digging of foxholes in the frozen ground.

VIETNAM

The war in Vietnam, which America entered in earnest a decade after the close of the Korean War, witnessed a leap in technology and media content. Television cameras, as well as still-picture versions, grew smaller and lighter, permitting coverage closer to the action. Full-color images gradually replaced black-and-white. And the reluctance to draw the curtain across war's darker images grew weaker as journalists revealed more brutal truths.

A new president, John F. Kennedy, retained his predecessors' commitment to the policy of containment. After a difficult negotiating session with Soviet Premier Nikita Khrushchev, Kennedy told the *New York Times*'s James Reston in an off-the-record talk that America needed to demonstrate its willingness to stand up to communist aggression. The place he picked was Vietnam, which had been partitioned, like Korea, after World War II. Kennedy tripled the number of military advisers in South Vietnam, which was struggling against pressure from North Vietnam as well as guerrillas known first as Vietminh and later as Vietcong (*cong* meaning "communist"). American officers began advising and training South Vietnamese soldiers and secretly leading air raids in which native fliers played little or no role. Meanwhile, Kennedy stepped back from serious consideration of massive atomic war. NSC-68 and atomic stockpiles had proved unusable in Korea, after all. Instead, Kennedy, Defense Secretary Robert McNamara, and their brain trust proposed greater flexibility in fighting limited wars. The new form of warfare aimed to inflict enough pain to make enemies decide to halt their aggression. The equation had one flaw: Enemies might respond emotionally rather than rationally. Warfare might steel their resolve to fight, just as the Blitz in World War II had galvanized rather than broken Britain's spirit. The enemy needed only patience and fortitude.

Both sides fighting the Vietnam War realized public opinion would be a key battlefield. "The war was fought on many fronts," said General Vo Nguyen Giap, architect of the Vietcong victory. During the Tet Offensive of 1968, he said, "The most important [front] was American public opinion." Giap's American counterpart, General William C. Westmoreland, reached a similar conclusion. In the summer after the Vietcong's Tet assault, he said, "In view of the impact of public opinion on the prosecution of the war, the accuracy and balance of the news coverage . . . attained an importance almost equal to the actual combat operations."

The difficulties of fighting limited war became apparent as the American presence expanded in the early 1960s. Guerrillas moving among the South Vietnamese public could not be distinguished from friendly civilians. Nor did they fight in convenient battle groups. Instead, they relied on surprise and stealth to attack when odds favored them and to slip into jungles when they did not. Fighting could erupt virtually anywhere, anytime. It would continue to do so unless the vast majority of South Vietnamese citizens found a reason to prefer their government to the communists. Thus, the war's political and economic fronts weighed as heavily as military engagements.

With no battle lines and no control over the eruption of violence, there could be no effective American restraint of the news media in Vietnam. Reporters could not be kept from the news. They could, however, be coerced and intimidated. South Vietnamese goons beat and evicted journalists whose reporting on ineptitude and corruption offended President Ngo Dinh Diem in the early 1960s. South Vietnam expelled *Newsweek*'s Francois Sully, NBC's Jim Robinson, and the AP's Peter Arnett, who also suffered repeated pummelings by Diem's secret police.

Shortly after Diem died in a coup, President Lyndon B. Johnson considered but rejected mandatory military censorship. Such censorship would have required the cooperation of a sympathetic South Vietnam, but Johnson refused to suffer any more public relations disasters by letting Saigon control American journalists. Formal press censorship also might have alienated Americans who had been told they were fighting for Western-style freedoms.

Once again, the armed forces asked journalists to follow voluntary censorship. Although the rules changed a bit throughout the war, they generally included the normal ban on news of troop movements, future operations, and spying. However, they added a new twist: Given the central role of bombing raids in Washington's strategy of trying to break the enemy's will, the military devoted extra attention to controlling information about air strikes.

Despite the lack of formal censorship, writers and photographers who wished to cover the war had to be accredited. First came the usually easy accreditation to the South Vietnamese government, based on possessing a passport, visa, evidence of news media employment, and proof of immunization. Then, to be accredited to the American military mission (Military Assistance Command–Vietnam), the applicant had to show a letter on news agency letterhead indicating work for hire and ensuring that the employer would take responsibility for the bearer's conduct and professional actions. The process proved so easy that as the number of accredited journalists swelled to nearly 700 at the height of the war, members of the press corps included writers for a college alumni magazine and *Ms.* magazine. The war was particularly dangerous, given the lack of a front to define combat zones. A total of forty-five journalists died; an additional eighteen disappeared and were presumed dead.

An accreditation card allowed a correspondent to grab a seat, if one was available and the operation wasn't secret, on a military helicopter, transport plane, or ground vehicle. Journalists also could eat in mess halls and bunk in military housing. Accreditation opened the door to attendance at the daily briefing at the military press office in Saigon. The briefing officer gave a summary of the day's news, including tactical operations and casualties. Journalists called the daily ritual "The Five O'Clock Follies." According to Halberstam of the *New York Times,* the briefing officer rarely had witnessed the events he described and could not personally vouch for the accuracy of the information he gave out. News collected through military observers in the field grew more inflated, and more optimistic, as it rose through the ranks, was synthesized by information officers, and presented at the Follies. Halberstam recalled that any corpse on a battlefield joined the enemy death toll, which, in the absence of battle lines, served as de facto scoreboard of the war's progress. "All of these battles were victories. At the daily briefing the American Army won the war a thousand times against the Vietcong and the North Vietnamese," he said.

Some journalists threw up their hands at their inability to reconcile the official version of the truth, which they often doubted, and the journalistic training that urged them to accurately report quotations from official sources. Michael Herr, a reporter for *Esquire* magazine, created some of the most powerful accounts of the war by abandoning the old rules of journalistic detachment. Just as conventional firepower could not produce victory, conventional reporting could not produce clarity, he said. Herr's style evolved into a free-flowing chaos that mirrored the conflict: "Rounding Le Loi there was a large group of correspondents coming back from the briefing, standard diurnal informational freak-o-rama, Five O'Clock Follies, Jive at Five, war stories; at the corner they broke formation and went to their offices to file, we watched them, the wasted clocking the wasted."

A credibility gap opened as journalists compared what they heard from military spokesmen and what they saw when accompanying troops into combat. United Press International reporter Neil Sheehan got a lesson in the importance of checking facts after he had been in South Vietnam for two weeks. He received a tip from an officer about a major battle at My Tho that had left hundreds of Vietcong dead. He rushed it onto the wire after verifying that a conflict had taken place at the specified time and place. Shortly after UPI sent the story to the United States, Sheehan awoke to a jarring phone call. Veteran correspondent Homer Bigart, covering the latest war, had called to complain that Sheehan's story had overshadowed his own dispatch. The senior reporter demanded that Sheehan get dressed and accompany him to the battle zone to count bodies. At My Tho, they found fifteen.

Sheehan took the lesson to heart. At the 1963 battle of Ap Bac, the communists fought in a sustained, coordinated attack for the first time. American-led South Vietnamese forces lost four helicopters in five minutes, took serious casualties, and refused to press an attack, allowing the vast majority of the outnumbered Vietcong to escape. Yet American military spokesmen portrayed the battle as a victory. Admiral Harry Felt criticized Sheehan's downbeat wire reports, saying, "You ought to go down and talk to some of the people who've got the facts." Sheehan replied, "You're right, Admiral. That's why I went down to Ap Bac every day during the fighting."

Similarly, Felt suggested at a press conference that Malcolm Browne, the AP's lead reporter in South Vietnam, had wandered out of the mainstream of official news. "Why can't you get on the team?" Felt asked.

Halberstam and Charlie Mohr of *Time* magazine fought to get their carefully reported accounts published intact despite the home front's tendency to lend more credence to official military versions than to the work of young war reporters. Mohr quit after *Time,* which had continually edited his stories to change their tone from negative to positive, criticized the press corps in Saigon. (Mohr accused the magazine of "shelling its own troops.")

Halberstam's paper took another tack. Instead of sanitizing

or spinning his reporting, the *New York Times* ran Halberstam's account of a series of mass arrests in South Vietnam next to a second version of the same story, attributed to CIA and U.S. embassy sources, that said the opposite. Within three days, the State Department admitted that the official version had been wrong.

Halberstam's reporting so infuriated President Kennedy that he ordered the CIA to analyze every story the reporter wrote, beginning in June 1963. The CIA checked the stories line by line and reported back: They were "by and large accurate" but "invariably pessimistic." Kennedy asked the *Times* in October 1963 to consider removing Halberstam from South Vietnam, but the paper refused. In the following years, Johnson spoke of Halberstam as a traitor when the president met with Washington reporters preparing to go to Saigon. However, an analysis of Halberstam's news reports by historian Daniel C. Hallin revealed they typically supported the American soldiers in the field. Ordinary troops usually welcomed reporters, who gave them a voice in Washington that often differed from their commanders' views. If Halberstam reported pessimism, particularly in analyzing the weaknesses of South Vietnamese troops, Hallin concluded it was an accurate distillation of opinion in the field.

An official American policy of downplaying the action of its armed forces in Vietnam during the Kennedy administration contributed to the growing credibility gap. The State Department and U.S. Information Agency (USIA) tried to shape favorable news coverage in 1962 by issuing secret rules for press relations in Saigon. The instructions, known as Cable 1006, underscored the need to portray the war as pri-

marily run by the South Vietnamese. The cable said it "is not
. . . in our interest . . . to have stories indicating that Americans are leading and directing combat missions against the
Vietcong." Negative stories drew criticism and made relations difficult; ergo, Cable 1006 urged the armed forces to
bar correspondents from accompanying missions that might
result in bad press for the United States or its allies. Officials
refused to acknowledge what journalists could see: Far from
being detached advisers, Americans flew combat missions
against the Vietcong.

Browne opposed the secrecy with which the war was
being fought, but he supported the fight against communism. "What worried me," he later wrote, "was the unwill-
ingness of the Kennedy administration to fight openly, pre-
ferring instead to wage a shadow war out of sight of the
American public. If we Americans had nothing to be
ashamed of, why not frankly acknowledge our role as bel-
ligerents?" The deception went all the way to the top. A
reporter asked Kennedy at a 1962 press conference, "Mr.
President, are American troops now in combat in Vietnam?"
The president answered, wrongly, "No."

The press began to enjoy a better relationship with the
armed forces in 1964. The State Department that summer
ordered the information officers in Saigon, led by Barry
Zorthian, to promote "maximum candor and disclosure
consistent with the requirements of security." In reaction to
earlier negative but truthful reporting, the military concluded it had to change its information policy to maintain
credibility.

Unfortunately for the military, the realities of war remained bleak. The South Vietnamese government still

inspired little confidence in the countryside, and the Vietcong continued to be resourceful, tenacious fighters. As the American government swiftly escalated the number of combat soldiers on the ground, beginning in 1965, it also boosted its public relations campaign to win hearts and minds. No amount of spin, however, could turn black into white—or bad into good.

Photographs and television images added to official suspicions about the press. Words could be nudged in a variety of ways by editors in America, but images resisted reinvention. One of the more controversial television reports, filed by Morley Safer of CBS, captured a U.S. Marine torching a South Vietnamese village with a cigarette lighter. Johnson, outraged at the broadcast, phoned the network president to accuse CBS of having "shat on the American flag." The Johnson administration tried to smear Safer as a communist and his report as a staged event, but CBS stood by the story.

Three of the most famous photographic images of the Vietnam War portrayed violence in the streets of South Vietnam. In the first, a Buddhist monk set himself on fire during a carefully planned demonstration to protest Diem's crackdown on religious freedom. Browne's photograph of the immolation, splashed across newspaper front pages around the world, caused President Kennedy to tell his ambassador to Saigon, "We're going to have to do something about that regime." Shortly after that, Diem died in a coup staged with the quiet approval of the American government. The second photograph, by Eddie Adams of the Associated Press, captured the summary execution of a Vietcong suspect in Saigon during the Tet offensive. Brigadier General Nguyen Ngoc Loan pulled his pistol and put a bullet in the man's brain while Adams and an NBC television film crew recorded the event. The third, by South Vietnamese photographer Nick Ut, showed a naked girl, burned by a misdirected napalm strike, running down a road and screaming in agony. Such images represented a quantum leap from the heroics and quiet deaths of World War II photographic recollection.

In the years since the Vietnam War, a legend has grown up linking the communist victory to the actions of the media in general, and television in particular. News from Vietnam, including a weekly body count, aired repeatedly on the three major television networks in the 1960s and early 1970s. It included violence in moving images, occasionally unlike anything Americans had seen before. A Marine major writing in 1987 in the army's *Military Review* journal blamed television for losing the war, claiming, "The power and impact of television was *the* deciding factor in turning American public opinion from one of supporting the U.S. defense of South Vietnam to one of opposing it."

Memory is a fickle thing. A content analysis of the television news reports on Vietnam from August 1965 to August 1970 revealed that only 76 out of more than 2,300 depicted heavy fighting. Commonly, what passed for combat actually depicted troops on patrol or firing their weapons at an invisible enemy. The impact of such images remains subject to debate, but evidence suggests they acted as a Rorschach test: Viewers saw things they could interpret in a variety of ways. For war hawks, violent images could reinforce commitment to sacrifice; for doves, the same images could emphasize the human costs of an unacceptable war.

"There is no empirical evidence that TV news 'shapes'

mass public opinion—or that any news medium does," wrote broadcasting historian Lawrence W. Lichty. His conclusion appeared to be supported by a Louis Harris poll in 1967, which found that 31 percent of respondents said television helped them decide to oppose the war. When asked if television made them more likely to "back up the boys in Vietnam," however, the same group said yes, by more than two to one.

Body counts mattered more than television. Studies of public opinion and casualties in the Korean and Vietnam wars revealed that regardless of the level of press coverage, public support fell 15 percentage points for every tenfold increase in casualties. In other words, when American casualties rose from 100 to 1,000, support declined by 15 percentage points.

Likewise, mythology surrounds the Tet Offensive of 1968, inflating the media's importance in covering the Vietcong uprising. In popular memory, Tet ranks as the most important event shaping American public opinion of the war. Peter Braestrup, a Vietnam War reporter for the *Washington Post,* argued that journalists' interest in sensation resulted in an overemphasis on images of dramatic action during Tet, at a cost of context and coherence. The result: a hyperbolic account of a battle that cost the Vietcong huge losses but that undermined American confidence.

Other scholars have studied the same archived news reports and reached different conclusions. Months before Tet, America's three major news magazines—*U.S. News & World Report, Time,* and *Newsweek,* representing a political spectrum from right to center to left, respectively—had concurred that stalemate seemed likely in Vietnam. After Tet, those same magazines accurately portrayed Tet as a setback for the Vietcong.

Coverage of Tet expanded preexisting doubts. Polls for the first time found a plurality of Americans considered sending troops to Vietnam "a mistake" in October 1967, more than three months before Tet. The surprising Vietcong offensive of early 1968, which briefly placed guerrillas in the U.S. embassy compound, also impacted some influential observers in the media. CBS anchor Walter Cronkite, convinced by earlier military pronouncements that the war was being won, decided to tour South Vietnam and see for himself after Tet shattered his complacency. Upon his return, he broadcast a clearly labeled personal editorial calling for a negotiated settlement of the war; he made public his opinions that it could not be won and should not be allowed to end in defeat. "To say that we are closer to victory today is to believe, in the face of the evidence, the optimists who have been wrong in the past," Cronkite said. "To suggest we are on the edge of defeat is to yield to unreasonable pessimism. To say that we are mired in stalemate seems the only realistic, yet unsatisfactory, conclusion. . . . It is increasingly clear to this reporter that the only rational way out, then, will be to negotiate, not as victors, but as an honorable people who lived up to their pledge to defend democracy, and did the best they could." A dejected Johnson told his aides, "If I've lost Cronkite, I've lost middle America." The president weighed the growing antiwar sentiment and chose not to seek reelection.

Richard Nixon, Johnson's successor, also had issues with press coverage. He ordered an unpublicized bombing campaign against communist bases in Cambodia in spring 1969, just as America prepared to begin gradually withdrawing its forces. He hoped the bombing and a cross-border invasion by American and South Vietnamese forces would pressure North Vietnam to seek a diplomatic end to the war. In the short term, however, revelations of the expansion of the war into Cambodia, coupled with reports by journalist Seymour Hersh of a massacre of civilians at My Lai, touched off rioting at American college campuses.

In 1971, Nixon attempted to prevent the *Washington Post* and *New York Times* from publishing a secret, government-commissioned history of the Vietnam War. He lost the case at the Supreme Court. The government failed to meet the heavy burden of proof, established in *Near v. Minnesota,* that publication of the so-called Pentagon Papers would violate national security. Similarly, no journalist in Vietnam ever jeopardized military operations, according to Zorthian.

An accord signed in Paris in 1973 allowed Nixon to claim "peace with honor" and bring the last American troops home. But no declaration of peace could speak as loudly as the communists' continuing desire for victory. Fighting continued until South Vietnam capitulated in 1975. Thus, the war's messy resolution mirrored its muddled conduct, in which every official pronouncement—the Vietcong were nearly defeated, the South Vietnamese government was winning public support—sparked equally believable statements, statistics, and observations asserting the opposite.

In the end, according to military historian William M. Hammond, no amount of public relations could have saved South Vietnam. Washington's political and military power brokers "forgot at least two common-sense rules of effective propaganda: that the truth has greater ultimate power than the most pleasing of bromides and that no amount of massaging will heal a broken limb or a fundamentally flawed strategy."

No change in coverage would have taken the initiative from the enemy. Casualty counts rose, and with them, public (and press) dissent did as well. America's military and government leaders explored ways to keep both manageably low in future conflicts.

SIX

SEE NO EVIL: CONTROLLING ACCESS IN THE 1980S AND 1990S

"I had more guns pointed at me by Americans or Saudis who were into controlling the press than in all my years of actual combat."

—Retired Colonel David Hackworth, on his attempts to report about the 1991 Persian Gulf War for *Newsweek*

The press and the military learned different things in Vietnam. Journalists developed a greater appreciation for the need to verify information independently. Military officers, however, came to distrust the press. Many of them, overlooking the flaws in strategy and tactics, attributed the loss of South Vietnam to unfettered reporting in general and to television in particular.

Patrick Bishop of London's *Daily Telegraph* noted that while he reported on the 1991 Persian Gulf War, he heard a recurring chorus of blame: "If there was one 'lesson' the U.S. military learned from the Vietnam war, it was that journalists lost it for them. It was a never-ending refrain from the General's office to the Mess Hall chow line," especially when talk turned to the television networks and the *New York Times*. Lieutenants and captains of the 1960s and 1970s had risen to become generals, admirals, and cabinet officials by the 1990s, giving them the power to apply their lessons in the field. And they did.

They took their cue from the Persian Gulf War commander in chief, General H. Norman Schwarzkopf. He had discovered the media's worst excesses as a child. His father, New Jersey State Police Superintendent Herbert Norman Schwarzkopf, led the investigation into the kidnapping of aviator Charles Lindbergh's son. The prosecution turned into a media circus, dominating the trial of kidnap and murder suspect Bruno Hauptmann. Some reporters accused the elder Schwarzkopf of botching the investigation, although the trial ultimately ended with a conviction. H. Norman Schwarzkopf was born two years later, but he grew up hearing the family's stories and eventually digging into the press clippings. As a soldier in Vietnam, he felt disgust toward the way the presence of the news media could dominate events; one of his commanders paid more attention to how the war looked on TV than how it was fought. In approving the rules for press coverage in the Persian Gulf, Schwarzkopf concerned himself with both reality and appearances. He kept the news media controlled without raising widespread public concern. He had learned, as had the rest of the armed forces, there were ways to have the cake and eat it too.

Military analysts in the United States had taken lessons in 1982 as Britain went to war with Argentina over the disputed Falklands in the South Atlantic. Britain launched an armada on an eight-thousand-mile voyage to reclaim the occupied islands, four hundred miles off the coast of South America. Along for the ride were twenty-nine accredited reporters, photographers, and technicians in a pool representing the British news media. Unusual circumstances allowed total control of the news. The journalists, who apparently had been screened in advance to keep out any who might be too critical of the war, had to rely on the armed forces for access to the war zone as well as transmission of their stories and pictures back home. Britain vowed to fire on any ships entering its exclusion zone around the Falklands, making independent reporting impossible. Six shipboard public relations officers censored the news. They told journalists to "help in leading and steadying public opinion in times of national stress or crisis."

Official statements in London supplemented the stories filed by the press, but thanks to censorship and a patriotic tone to the correspondents' accounts, the two versions looked and sounded much the same. Journalists found their reports of the "failure" of a British bombing raid had been changed by the censor's blue pencil to refer to the raid's "success." Censors also turned a description of British troops mistakenly firing on their comrades into a firefight with Argentines. News stories reached Britain as much as thirty-six hours after they had been filed.

American military observers seized on Britain's achieving a swift, popular victory while effectively controlling the media. An American naval public affairs specialist who studied the Falklands conflict suggested a new paradigm of war coverage in the *Naval War College Review*. Favorable press coverage, wrote Lieutenant Commander Arthur A. Humphries, required the military to "control access to the fighting, invoke censorship, and rally aid in the form of patriotism at home and in the battle zone." To achieve what Humphries called "favorable objectivity," he urged the exclusion of undesirable correspondents.

Humphries faulted the British Ministry of Defense in one area. Censorship was only part of a program of news management, he wrote. In the absence of information, the news media would seek to fill the vacuum with whatever they could find, including rumors and news from alternate sources. Superior news management must provide an abundance of military briefings and pictures, he said, flooding the media with information. In essence, the new paradigm called for the government to provide its own news, using the media as a direct pipeline to the public, instead of surrendering control of the stories to editors and reporters.

CENSORSHIP BY EXCLUSION

The American military's first opportunity to test this new version of press relations occurred a year after the Falklands war. In 1983, the United States invaded the Caribbean island of Grenada to extract American medical students believed to be held by a Marxist government allied with Cuba. Schwarzkopf served as deputy commander of the mission. The invasion was planned with great secrecy. Even the press offices of the White House and Pentagon were not informed about the invasion until one hour before it took place. The military excluded journalists from the island for the first two days of combat under the rationale of preserving secrecy and keeping them from danger. The navy blockaded the island, saying it wanted to keep out any Cuban reinforcements and to try to catch the government's leader if he should try to flee.

The operation's commander in chief, Admiral Joseph Metcalf, defended the island's isolation. He said, "I did not want the press around where they would start second-guessing what I was doing." Two reporters who actually reached Grenada during the early stages of the attack wound up being detained on an American warship. When other journalists hired a speedboat to try to get to the island, the navy ordered a fighter pilot to fire warning shots across its bow. The boat turned back. One of the reporters later asked Metcalf what he would have done if the speedboat hadn't reversed course. "We would have blown your ass right out of the water," Metcalf responded.

Until fifteen journalists came ashore on the third day, details of the invasion remained out of the public eye. Whereas the military had said 1,100 Cuban "professional soldiers" occupied the island, combatants actually numbered about 100. Early reports of pinpoint attacks that spared civilians also proved false; a navy jet's bombing raid killed at least seventeen people at a mental hospital. Fourteen of the eighteen Americans killed in the invasion died because of accidents or friendly fire. "What really happened in Grenada was a case study in military incompetence and poor execution," two former military intelligence officers declared in the *Boston Globe.*

Complaints about being excluded from an American war for the first time in the nation's history led to a postwar press-military conference. Discussion centered on how to grant access to journalists in the early stages of future wars yet provide for operational security. General John W. Vessey Jr., chairman of the Joint Chiefs of Staff, asked retired army General Winant Sidle to chair the panel of journalists and military public affairs officers. Sidle had been the chief of information for the army for four years during the Vietnam War and thus was familiar with the military and journalistic points of view.

The so-called Sidle Commission met early in 1984. It skirted the topic of censorship, making its main recommendation the creation of a National Media Pool to be called up when swift military action precluded broad coverage. The pool harked back to the Russo-Japanese War nearly a century earlier, in which Japan restricted access to the front and forced Western journalists to share officially released information. Pool membership consisted of a small group of seasoned military affairs journalists who would rotate in and out regularly. They were expected to quickly answer the call to join American troops anywhere in the world as hostilities broke out. The plan called for them to share their information with the rest of the press corps until the pools could be replaced with open, expanded coverage.

In a letter to Vessey, Sidle "emphatically" expressed the view that "reporters and editors alike must exercise responsibility in covering military operations. As one of the senior editors who appeared before us said, 'The media must cover military operations comprehensively, intelligently, and objectively.' The American people deserve news coverage of this quality and nothing less. It goes without saying, of course, that the military also has a concurrent responsibility, that of making it possible for the media to provide such coverage."

The Joint Chiefs and secretary of defense approved the

report, making it official military policy in April 1985. The
National Media Pool received ten tests in the following four
years. Pool members covered military exercises, the protec-
tion of Kuwaiti oil tankers during the Iran–Iraq conflict, and
the deployment of parts of two army divisions to Honduras
in 1988 after Nicaraguan troops crossed the border.

The American invasion of Panama in December 1989
provided the first test of the pool in combat. Although it was
the largest American military action in a foreign country
since the Vietnam War, the effort to capture Panamanian
President Manuel Noriega, who was implicated in international drug trafficking, received little combat coverage other
than images officially released by the Pentagon. The press
pool of sixteen journalists flew to Panama within hours of
the invasion. Upon arrival, the journalists itching to cover
street fighting were taken first to a room to watch a CNN
television broadcast, and then to a lecture by an American
diplomat about the history of Panama. While combat raged
outside, the press pool spent four days removed from the
heaviest fighting. Only when a sector had been secured were
journalists allowed to visit it.

"We missed what could have been some great stories, including stuff which, ironically, Southern Command brass
should have been scrambling to let us see," one pool member said. "A case in point was the U.S. Military's entrance
into Colon, the port city at the Atlantic end of the canal, in
response to uncontrolled looting. This was . . . more than
two full days after the initial invasion. We were only a short
helicopter ride away, but they kept us away from the operation until evening, when it was nearly over."

The denial of access created the illusion of a swift and

nearly bloodless operation. Television played and replayed pictures of troops in helicopters but avoided images of civilian casualties and dead Americans. The military's official death toll counted 314 Panamanian military and 202 civilian deaths, along with twenty-three American troops. Other sources in Latin America later numbered civilian casualties in the thousands. Dozens of civilians were shot to death when mistaken for soldiers. One American lawyer represented thirty-two cases in which American troops killed civilians—"none of them armed, none of them dangerous," he said. Civilian victims included a woman in labor, shot on her way to the hospital while in a car marked with a white flag.

FROM DESERT SHIELD TO DESERT STORM

While the fog of war makes such tragedies all too common, restrictions on American press coverage ensured the majority occurred beyond the ability of journalists to witness or report them. Such restrictions continued during the Persian Gulf War in the early 1990s, when limitations on what pool correspondents could see and hear, along with an aggressive attempt by the military to promote its own view of combat, once again left Americans with a distorted view of the fighting. Despite Sidle's recommendations, the media failed to report "comprehensively, intelligently, and objectively" in the Middle East. A comprehensive account proved impossible to obtain, as the military allowed journalists only a narrow view of combat. Intelligence suffered too, as journalists with little or no military training or knowledge pitched questions at generals in live television broadcasts. The stupidity of certain inquiries—such as those seeking sensitive details about America's war plans—led to a parody of the press on NBC's *Saturday Night Live*. The comedy skit reportedly erased any doubts in the White House that the press restrictions had gone too far. Objectivity also took a hit as press coverage paid almost no attention to war opponents, and television networks hired prowar analysts who had retired from the armed forces to shape their coverage.

Iraqi President Saddam Hussein began the hostilities. Hussein alleged that Kuwait had violated international oil production accords, costing Iraq billions of dollars as it was trying to recover economically from its eight-year war with Iran. He also raised old questions about Kuwaiti sovereignty and vowed to turn the nation into Iraq's nineteenth province. In early summer 1990, Iraq positioned several divisions along the Kuwaiti border and demanded a ransom in exchange for what *Boston Globe* and *New Republic* journalist Michael Kelly called "the privilege of remaining uninvaded." When Kuwait refused to pay, Hussein's tanks and troops crossed the northern border on August 2.

Hussein gambled that America's historical hands-off policy toward inter-Arab conflicts, as well as its tilt toward Iraq during its war with Iran, would leave him free to operate. He was wrong. President George H. W. Bush opted to counter the invasion in order to protect Saudi Arabia from further Iraqi aggression and to expel Iraqi forces from Kuwait.

Bush committed American troops to Saudi Arabia on August 7 and began putting together an international wartime coalition. At the same time, high-ranking officials in the Bush administration began crafting a plan for America's information policy. Their bedrock concern: Avoid the perceived mistakes of Vietnam. That war so haunted the government and military that after the Persian Gulf War ended, a Freedom Forum study of 66,000 news stories about the crisis in Kuwait determined that the word "Vietnam" had been used 7,299 times, "more than any other word or term." Bush referred to Vietnam during his opening and closing statements on the war, vowing to avoid that war's errors and to exorcise its ghosts.

The first manifestation of the military's new press policy came from a navy captain working in the U.S. Central Command headquarters in Tampa, Florida. Ron Wildermuth, General Schwarzkopf's chief aide for public affairs, spent the first twelve days after the Iraqi invasion of Kuwait hammering out a blueprint for media coverage of the conflict in the Middle East. Known as Annex Foxtrot, the document declared, "News media representatives will be escorted at all times. Repeat, at all times." Military escorts were essential, Wildermuth said. "You needed an escort to provide a liaison with the units. That military guy speaks military. It's just smart."

While Wildermuth was developing Annex Foxtrot, the Pentagon secured permission from the xenophobic Saudi Arabian government August 10 to allow Western pool reporters into the kingdom to cover the American troop buildup, known as Operation Desert Shield. That evening, members of the National Media Pool got the alert to prepare for deployment. Assistant Defense Secretary Pete Williams took the pool members to the Saudi embassy in Washington August 11 to obtain the necessary visas. The pool reporters next flew to Tampa for a visit with Schwarzkopf, then on to Dhahran, Saudi Arabia, where they arrived August 13. The original pool consisted of seventeen people representing the Associated Press, United Press International, Reuters, CNN, National Public Radio, *Time,* the Scripps-Howard newspaper chain, the *Los Angeles Times,* and the *Milwaukee Journal.* For their first two weeks in Saudi Arabia, they shared their reports with all media. After that, the Saudi government began issuing visas to more journalists, and the military allowed independent filing of exclusives. The press corps swelled to nearly 800 by December.

Reporters struggled to find news they could use during the long buildup to war. Ground rules laid down by the military asked journalists not to publicize troops' names, units, or numbers. The military also balked at identification of planes, tanks, and other weapons. Even specific locations were forbidden, making the standard newspaper dateline, "Somewhere in Saudi Arabia," something of a standing joke among reporters.

Restrictions aimed to prevent Iraqi intelligence from realizing the only news of real significance: The Pentagon's initial portrayal of a swift and powerful troop buildup to protect the Saudis relied on smoke and mirrors. The early deployment lacked the numbers and weapons to defend Saudi Arabia if the Iraqis chose to invade their western neighbor in force. "We're just speed bumps," a Marine informed *Washington Post* reporter Molly Moore. Moore and the rest of the press corps accepted such information to help them better understand the situation on the ground, but they did not divulge it in their stories.

Diplomatic and military briefings in Washington dominated the news, as press restrictions in the Middle East led to the creation of vague and lightweight news accounts from

American bases in eastern Saudi Arabia. Journalists on the scene focused on the same small set of stories over and over: the heat, the loneliness, the expansion of the military presence, and the Saudis' patriarchal culture. The *Washington Post* found reporters grumbling about doing little more than watching soldiers "change the oil" or "dig foxholes" and occasionally chase tanks and camels in search of photographs that fit American stereotypes of desert war.

Reporters and photographers also signed up to visit troops through arrangements with the Joint Information Bureau, or JIB. The Central Command established the JIB in Dhahran "to facilitate media coverage of U.S. forces in Saudi Arabia." A second bureau later opened in Riyadh. Visiting journalists registered with the Saudi government and American armed forces at the JIB, made arrangements for tours, and received their escorts. A popular tour stopped at "Breakfast at Tiffany's," a field kitchen near a runway that offered the treat of real bacon, forbidden by Islamic dietary law. Reporters wanted to see and do more but were frustrated by the long wait for the limited seats on military helicopters and vans. Women journalists had the added difficulty of complying with Saudi laws requiring them to wear long sleeves and skirts and to hire men to drive them. "We wanted to eat sand in the desert with soldiers, crouch in foxholes with Marines, bounce across the dunes on tanks," Moore said.

Meanwhile, a huge public relations operation got under way to build support for war against Iraq. Bush painted Hussein as worse than Adolf Hitler and compared the Iraqi invasion of Kuwait to the Nazis' domination of Europe. Atrocity stories fanned the flames of hatred. Amnesty International reported in December that Iraqis had tortured and killed hundreds of Kuwaitis. The agency cited "widespread abuses of human rights." These included "the arbitrary arrest and detention without trial of thousands of civilians and military personnel; the widespread torture of such persons in custody; the imposition of the death penalty, and the extra-judicial execution of hundreds of unarmed civilians, including children." In addition, Amnesty International noted rumors that Iraqi occupation forces had allowed 300 premature babies to die in Kuwait City hospitals.

Some allegations were true. However, the baby incubator story, widely accepted at the time, lacked solid evidence. A variation of the story apparently first had surfaced in September 1990, when the London *Daily Telegraph* gave sketchy details from Kuwait's exiled housing minister. The story then jumped the Atlantic, appearing in the *Los Angeles Times.* It quoted two women recently evacuated from Kuwait, whom it identified only as "Cindy" and "Rudi," as saying Iraqis had taken babies out of incubators and left them to die.

Despite the lack of full identification for the witnesses, as well as any way to verify the story independently, the baby incubator story spread through the media. It received a boost in October when Bush referred to the "sickening" reports of babies being "heaved" out of incubators, and the congressional Human Rights Caucus provided a forum for details. A tearful teenage girl, who gave her name only as "Nayirah," testified to the caucus about what she said she had seen as a hospital worker: "I volunteered at the al-Addan hospital. . . . While I was there, I saw the Iraqi soldiers come into the hospital with guns, and go into the room where fifteen babies were in incubators," she said. "They took the babies out of the incubators, took the incubators, and left the babies on the cold floor to die." Months later, *Harper's Magazine* publisher John MacArthur identified the teenage girl as the daughter of the Kuwaiti ambassador to the United States. Her testimony had been arranged and coached by the public relations firm of Hill & Knowlton, which the Kuwaitis had hired to press their case against Iraq.

Most pediatricians in Kuwait were foreigners, who rebutted Nayirah's testimony as untrue in the *Seattle Times* and *USA Today*. Amnesty International later retreated from its claims of infanticide, saying "although its team was shown alleged mass graves of babies, it was not established how they had died and the team found no reliable evidence that Iraqi forces had caused the deaths of babies by removing them or ordering their removal from incubators." MacArthur acknowledged the existence of human rights abuses during the Kuwaiti occupation but said only a thorough investigation could sort true from false. Kuwaiti sources such as "Nayirah" would have been taken less seriously if their conflicts of interest had been revealed. All doubts, however, were suspended for the duration. "None of this could have occurred without the media's overwhelming credulity and willingness to repeat again and again the Hitler analogy," MacArthur said.

Negotiators sought throughout fall 1990 to persuade Hussein of the inevitability of war if he refused to back down. The United States demanded the withdrawal of troops, the restoration of Kuwait's government, and assurances of continued peace. A troop-withdrawal deadline was set for January 15, after which the American-led coalition promised to fight. A week before the deadline, the Defense Department's Williams sent the Washington bureau chiefs of

America's major media outlets the "ground rules and guide-lines" for covering combat in the Persian Gulf. The rules followed the standard formulas defining news that would aid the Iraqis, such as details about future operations and strikes and the size and specific location of coalition units. Addi-tional regulations included Annex Foxtrot's public affairs es-corts for journalists at Saudi and American bases. Journalists would be given the opportunity to join Central Command pools organized by category of news medium—there were pools for television, radio, wire services, news magazines, newspapers, photo, Saudi, international, and "pencil," a catch-all category for print reporters.

"News media personnel who are not members of the official CENTCOM media pools will not be permitted into forward areas," Williams wrote. "Reporters are strongly dis-couraged from attempting to link up on their own with com-bat units. U.S. commanders will maintain extremely tight security throughout the operational area and will exclude from the area of operations all unauthorized individuals."

Representatives of each medium decided who got slots in their pool. Major newspapers that had covered the defensive Desert Shield reserved slots for themselves, at the expense of smaller papers with fewer resources, as operations headed to-ward the offensive of Desert Storm. Hard feelings flourished among journalists excluded from the pools by their peers. Slots were relatively rare—130 initial pool memberships that expanded to 192, to be divided among 1,200 correspondents on hand on January 15—making them highly desirable. Those who had pool credentials from the JIB tended to re-inforce the system from which they benefited. Thus, the Pentagon's plan pitted media members against one another, making those who possessed the coveted pool slots work to keep them and support the JIB.

If war broke out, Williams told reporters in the final weeks of Operation Desert Shield, pooled media reports and photographs would receive military review before being released. "Material will be examined solely for its conformance to the attached ground rules, not for its potential to express criticism or cause embarrassment," he said. Each journalist's military escort would conduct the initial review. If the journalist and escort could not resolve disagreements about possible security violations, the story or picture would be sent to the JIB office in Dhahran for further review and, ultimately, to the Pentagon. If the Pentagon and the journalist's home office still disagreed, the originating reporter's news organization would have the final decision on publication.

REAL-TIME REPORTING OF WAR

Americans learned of the start of war not from their government but from their televisions. ABC correspondent Gary Shepard, stationed at the al-Rashid Hotel in Baghdad, heard antiaircraft guns firing into the air at 6:34 P.M.. Washington time, January 16. Shepard was on the air live, his voice paired with a map of the Middle East, when he interrupted his report to say, "Something is definitely under way here, something is definitely going on. . . . Obviously an attack is under way of some sort." Within moments, an American missile destroyed a communications center in the Iraqi capital, cutting transmissions by ABC and nearly all other broadcast networks. Only CNN remained on the air, thanks to a

$30,000-a-month "four-wire" connection to the outside world independent of Iraqi phone lines. As the bombs and missiles began hammering Baghdad, CNN's Bernard Shaw phoned the network's home office in Atlanta and said, "Get me on. Get me on." Two minutes after ABC broke the story, Shaw and CNN correspondents Peter Arnett and John Holliman went live on the air and stayed there for the next seventeen hours. From their room on the ninth floor of the al-Rashid, they described the explosions around Baghdad. As CNN had the unique ability to broadcast live from the Iraqi capital, albeit in sound only, it became a magnet for viewers. More than 200 American affiliates of other television networks temporarily switched their feed to CNN.

"The skies over Baghdad have been illuminated," Shaw began. "We're seeing bright flashes going off all over the sky." He passed the microphone to Arnett, who remarked on "tremendous lightning in the sky, lightninglike effects."

Nothing like it had been heard since Edward R. Murrow had broadcast from the rooftops of London during the Blitz of World War II. The difference was that Murrow reported from an allied city, while the CNN team spoke from the heart of the enemy's capital. By describing the fires and explosions caused by incoming coalition missiles and bombs, they acted, in effect, as forward spotters providing intelligence about damage. Lieutenant General Charles Horner, commander of the air attack on Iraq, used CNN to verify that his raids began on time and hit their targets. Bush declared he learned more from CNN than from the Central Intelligence Agency.

The Pentagon press office in Saudi Arabia announced the start of the war nearly a half hour after CNN had gone on-air with the news. The CNN trio went off the air when an Iraqi press liaison officer arrived at their hotel room and dragged a finger across his throat.

The Iraqi government permitted CNN to stay in the capital. The network provided a communication link directly to Washington and other centers of world opinion. However, Iraq forced representatives of other television networks to leave the country. The decision simplified censorship and propaganda by reducing the size of the Western press corps in Baghdad. Hussein, operating under the logic of Vietnam, apparently believed any security leaks would be more than offset by images of suffering and their likely impact on American public opinion.

Arnett, later joined by correspondent Christiane Amanpour, upgraded CNN's equipment with a portable satellite system to feed live video and audio to the world. Arnett received permission to visit bombing sites and interview Hussein. He dealt with Iraqi censorship but believed his stories merited the consequences of allowing the enemy a measure of control over CNN's news accounts of the war.

PETER ARNETT, MAGNET FOR CONTROVERSY

Arnett, born in 1934, had a face of worn leather, the resourcefulness of an Eagle Scout, and the temperament of a prizefighter. He had been covering wars since an uprising in Laos and the outbreak of the communist rebellion in South Vietnam. He once swam the Mekong River, carrying his typed dispatch in his teeth, to reach a telegraph office in Thailand. Later he won a Pulitzer Prize while working for the Associated Press in Vietnam. His most famous report quoted an unnamed major explaining an air strike on a population center during the Vietcong's Tet Offensive of 1968: "It became necessary to destroy the town to save it." President Lyndon B. Johnson demanded to know the major's name, but Arnett had guaranteed the officer anonymity in exchange for a candid interview.

Arnett proved a magnet for praise and criticism for his coverage from Baghdad. "I was in Baghdad for the people who watch CNN," not on behalf of the American government, he told CNN's Larry King. His presence gave Americans information they would not have otherwise received. Many did not appreciate it. When he reported about the destruction of buildings he identified as a baby-milk plant and a civilian air raid shelter, presidential spokesman Marlin Fitzwater accused CNN of being "a conduit for Iraqi disinformation" and identified the milk factory as a "production facility for biological weapons." Arnett said he would not know what a biological weapons site looked like. However, he found vats of white powder labeled "al-Ban Sweetened Milk" at the ruined building. He scooped up samples and carried them away in plastic bags. He gave some away and watched children and a companion consume the powder—the latter by stirring it into his coffee.

Arnett's report from the Amiriya district, where precision-guided missiles killed hundreds of civilians, provided some of the most powerful video of the war. Although CNN refused to run images of body parts, the smoking ruin and the fear and chaos surrounding the rescue effort gave Western viewers a rare look at the human cost of the war. Civilians had crowded into a building identified as

"Department of Civilian Defense Public Shelter No. 25." Witnesses interviewed at the scene said they had been staying there for weeks. After CNN aired video of the ruined building, however, the United States command in Riyadh said the shelter actually had served as a command-and-control bunker.

"It was not my job to argue with the U.S. government; it had an array of spy technology and special sources of information beyond my reach," Arnett said. "I did not for a moment believe the Iraqi claim that the shelter had been targeted by the Pentagon to kill civilians. The whole bombing campaign up to that time indicated otherwise." The Amiriya shelter could have been used by both civilians and soldiers, he said. It was also possible the missiles had somehow missed a legitimate target nearby, or that intelligence identifying the building as a military target had erred. No matter. After the images of dead civilians aired from Amiriya, fewer American raids targeted Baghdad.

High-profile officials attacked Arnett and CNN for what they considered unpatriotic actions. Senator Alan Simpson of Wyoming called Arnett a "sympathizer" to the Iraqi cause and alleged, falsely, that his brother-in-law had served with the Vietcong. Simpson later offered a left-handed apology in a letter to the *Washington Post*. He retracted the Vietcong allegation "in the absence of concrete evidence" and recast Arnett as a "dupe" or "tool" of Iraq instead of its supporter. In addition, thirty-four members of the House of Representatives signed a letter calling Arnett a "propaganda mouthpiece." After the war, Schwarzkopf questioned "the public's right to know" and accused Arnett's network of "aiding and abetting" Hussein by relaying Iraqi television images of captured coalition pilots.

But not even the Amiriya bombing could shake public support for the war or for CNN's coverage from inside Iraq. A Gallup poll conducted shortly after the bombing found 69 percent of Americans agreeing that the media should carry reports from Arnett and other journalists in Baghdad. Overall, the public approved of the news media's war coverage. According to *Times Mirror* polls conducted over the course of the war, 78 percent to 80 percent of Americans gave the media a "good" or "excellent" grade.

Television viewers voted with their remote controls. During the weeks surrounding the start of the air war, ratings for ABC, NBC, CBS, and CNN news programs ranked higher than ratings in the same weeks of the previous year. CNN recorded its highest ratings ever.

Americans polled in mid-February said they believed, by a two-to-one ratio, that their military had been holding back information about the war. Yet, when asked whether they preferred to give the military more control over releasing information or to let news organizations decide what to publish or broadcast, 57 percent chose the military and 34 percent the media. Thus, the public endorsed military secrecy as well as the performance of the news media during the Persian Gulf War. One way to explain the poll numbers is that the public did not know what it did not know. Attitudes about television coverage had developed during overwhelmingly supportive and antiseptic coverage. Before the war, one count by a media-monitoring group in New York found less than 1 percent of the three major networks' air time of news from August 8, 1990, through January 3, 1991, devoted to opponents of Bush's military policies in the Gulf.

Once the air strikes began, aside from the CNN images in Baghdad, television's view of war remained upbeat and nearly bloodless. TV relied heavily on military briefings, studio analysis featuring commentary by former generals and admirals, and video footage of high-tech weapons selected by the armed forces. The Pentagon released nose-camera video from laser-guided "smart" bombs destroying targets in Iraq with "pinpoint" accuracy. Bridges, buildings, and weapons blew up on camera, but military control over the images given to the media kept pain to a minimum.

The face of the enemy virtually vanished. American military officials spooked by the legacy of Vietnam declined to give Iraqi body counts or dwell on injuries and death. The military refused to release vivid video of Iraqi soldiers blown to pieces by American Apache helicopter gunships. A commander excited about the new technology of war let John Balzar of the *Los Angeles Times* view the video when he arrived at a forward unit ahead of his escort. "A guy was hit and you could see him drop and he struggled up," Balzar said. "They fired again and the body next to him exploded." After Balzar wrote about the video, press officers never allowed him back into an Apache unit, nor did they allow any other reporters near the tape. Not until after the war did Western audiences see close-up pictures of charred Iraqi bodies or learn that many enemy soldiers—perhaps thousands of them, according to an American colonel leading the operation—had been buried alive during combat by tanks fitted with bulldozer blades.

Also after the war, the U.S. Air Force announced only 7

percent of bombs dropped on Iraq and Kuwait had been the "smart" type, guided by lasers or radar and repeatedly featured in military-supplied video clips. Of the 93 percent that were conventional "dumb" bombs, 75 percent missed their targets. Reporters asked to see footage of bombs that missed their targets, similar to video clips released by the British, but Williams and Defense Secretary Dick Cheney ignored the requests.

America's Patriot missiles underwent a reassessment of their reputation. Schwarzkopf at one point announced the Patriots were "100 percent" effective at destroying incoming Iraqi Scud missiles. The Patriots' reputation suffered, however, when a computer software glitch prevented a battery from firing, allowing a Scud to hit an American barracks in Dhahran and kill twenty-eight. After the war, a professor at the Massachusetts Institute of Technology told the House Armed Services Committee that firing a Patriot at a Scud apparently caused more damage on the ground than allowing the Scud to land unhindered. Debris from the exploding Patriots and Scuds spread damage over a wider area, he speculated. The military defended the Patriots but backed off original claims. Army officers told House investigators that Patriots intercepted 70 percent of the Scuds fired against Saudi Arabia and 40 percent of those fired at Israel, targeted by Hussein in an attempt to bring the Jewish state into the war for propaganda purposes.

For the war's first five weeks, pools placed journalists aboard ships and at airfield runways. They got no closer to combat than to gain interviews with pilots and crewmen. Correspondents were denied available seats aboard bombers and other aircraft, where they could have witnessed combat for themselves. Since World War II, when Murrow and Cronkite flew in bombing raids against Germany, American correspondents had accompanied air strikes against the enemy. Only one journalist apparently flew on a bombing raid during Desert Storm, when Forrest Sawyer of ABC, frustrated by pool restrictions, talked his way aboard a Saudi-piloted bomber. Pool members came to realize escorted tours went only where the military agreed to go. Sites where stories might reveal controversy or danger ranked lower on the military list of priorities than places where the stories and photos were safe. Journalists in a pool who asked to visit a Patriot antimissile battery wound up visiting a garage where mechanics repaired trucks.

Some escorts allowed journalists the freedom to ask questions as they saw fit. Others attempted to shape respondents' answers. "You could get an angel or a devil," said National Public Radio's Deborah Amos. The Defense Department's official report to Congress on the conduct of the war acknowledged incidents in which escorts stepped in front of cameras to halt interviews, told journalists not to ask questions likely to result in unfavorable answers, and altered news reports.

In one case, an escort/public affairs officer attempted to intimidate soldiers being interviewed by NBC's Gary Matsumoto at a Patriot battery. Recalled Matsumoto, "Whenever I began interviewing a soldier, this PAO would stand right behind me, stare into the eyes of the [soldier], stretch out a hand holding a cassette recorder, and click it on in the soldier's face. This was patent intimidation . . . which was clear from the soldiers' reactions. After virtually every interview, the soldier would let out a deep breath, turn to the PAO, and ask [something like], 'Can I keep my job?'"

"I never saw any organized efforts at censorship," pool escort Lieutenant Charles E. Hoskinson Jr. said. "All I saw was the natural tendency in the military to keep things under control."

News coverage also suffered from breakdowns in the front lines once the hundred-hour ground war started on February 23. During and immediately after the offensive into Kuwait and southern Iraq, the JIB in Dhahran reviewed 343 pool reports. While 21 percent traveled from the front to the JIB in less than twelve hours, 69 percent took up to two days and 10 percent took more than three days. In a competitive business in which hours, or even minutes, can spell the difference between a scoop and a story nobody will read, delays sometimes kept news from reaching the United States while the conflict was still under way. Laurence Jolidon of *USA Today* traveled with an army unit, cranking out story after story about the ground war and handing them to his escort for transport to Dhahran. Not one made it into print before war's end.

Some pool members tried to thwart their colleagues' independent coverage of the war. Pool members covering a battle in the Saudi border town at Khafji blew the whistle when Robert Fisk, a nonpool reporter from a British paper, arrived to gather news without an escort. An NBC reporter yelled an obscenity at Fisk and shouted, "You'll prevent us from working. You're not allowed here. Get out. Go back to Dharhan." The NBC reporter then summoned his escort, who told Fisk, "You're not allowed to talk to U.S. Marines, and they're not allowed to talk to you."

In addition to escorts and pools, "security review" shaped the news in subtle ways. Censors changed a *Detroit Free Press* report that described American pilots as "giddy" after a raid, substituting the word "proud" instead. When reporter Frank Bruni objected, they compromised on "pumped up." Then the censors sent the report not to American readers but to the Thirty-seventh Fighter Wing in Tonopah, Nevada, which sat on the story until it was too stale for publication. Veteran war reporter Malcolm Browne of the *New York Times* learned from pilots that Stealth bombers attacked Iraqi sites possibly linked to the production of nuclear weapons. Censors argued that the news violated security and got Browne to agree to delete it. Within hours, the French news agency Agence France-Presse released the same news by quoting a source in the U.S. Senate; after that, Schwarzkopf announced the details of the raid.

To the military's credit, censorship challenges resulted in only five of the 1,351 print pool stories submitted to the JIB during the war being referred to the Pentagon. Four were cleared, as was the fifth after the paper's editor agreed to make changes. However, such tallies do not take into account stories lost or delayed, or news that never got reported in the first place because of limited access and escorts' control.

The most significant act of censorship came not from any public affairs officer but from Dick Cheney. He ordered a forty-eight-hour news blackout when the ground war began. Cheney suspended briefings in Dhahran and Riyadh, refused to release news in Washington, and held up pool reports from the front. Fitzwater and Schwarzkopf got him to lift the blackout within a few hours as the success of the ground campaign became apparent. The blackout stood in stark contrast to the D-day invasion of Normandy, when the military helped speed journalists' reports from the beaches as quickly as possible to London for distribution to the Allied nations.

THE PURSUIT OF INDEPENDENT COVERAGE

A few correspondents struck out on their own. The military called them "unilaterals." Bob McKeown of CBS beat the pool into Kuwait City by a day and made the first live television broadcast from the liberated capital. Unilateral Michael Kelly also entered the city before the pools. He discovered a party on every street corner and the endless honking of car horns amid a smashed downtown looking as if it had been "worked over by a gang of teenage vandals, drunk on Saturday night." When the JIB escorted the accredited press corps into Kuwait City a short time later, reporters saw civilians waving hundreds of tiny American flags to greet the arriving troops. Not until five years later did public relations consultant John W. Rendon reveal that he had arranged to distribute the flags to stage-manage the images beamed to American audiences.

Unilaterals found stories the military had tried to hide or spin. Bob Simon of CBS discovered a Marine unit under attack, abandoned Saudi defenses, and a burning oil refinery at the border town of Khafji before the ground war broke out. Reporters at the press briefings in Dhahran were told, falsely, the fighting at Khafji had involved a brave Saudi defense instead of Marines fighting street by street. Simon's curiosity to see the war for himself unfortunately led to his capture by Iraqi soldiers, imprisonment, and torture.

Coalition troops detained or threatened to detain more than twenty unilaterals. One of them, photographer Wesley Boxce of *Time* magazine, spent thirty hours under National Guard detention. The guardsmen searched and blindfolded him. Marines pulled their guns and threatened to shoot another unilateral journalist after they found and detained him. One Marine said, "We have orders from above to make this pool system work."

Bush halted the ground war after the Iraqis evacuated Kuwait. TV reporters had abandoned their pools and escorts in Kuwait and captured images of bombed vehicles and incinerated Iraqis on Highway 6 out of Kuwait City. Joint Chiefs of Staff Chairman Colin Powell called Schwarzkopf to tell him the pictures made the White House nervous. "The reports make it look like wanton killing," Powell said. In his memoirs, Schwarzkopf recalled, "I thought, but didn't say, that the best thing the White House could do would be to turn off the damned TV in the situation room."

As the war ended, a court case to decide the validity of the military press pools moved forward in New York. A group of small publications led by *The Nation* had filed suit in January 1991 against the Defense Department. Plaintiffs argued they sought not to establish the right of press access to a battlefield but to preserve a right that had always existed. Military press pools constituted a prior restraint, they argued, and carried a "heavy presumption" against their constitutional validity—a reference to the Supreme Court's Pentagon Papers decision. In response, the Pentagon's lawyers moved to dismiss the lawsuit. Pools, they argued, did not abridge *The*

Nation's First Amendment rights. The government cannot hinder the press, they said, but it is not obligated to help it.

Judge Leonard B. Sand of United States District Court in Manhattan handed down his ruling April 16—the same day, by coincidence, veteran combat reporter Homer Bigart died of cancer. Sand dismissed the suit, proclaiming the matter too "abstract and conjectural," especially since the conditions protested by the press no longer existed. He expressed confidence, however, that restrictions on "time, place, and manner"—constitutionally supported limitations on free speech—would be acceptable on the battlefield.

Sand expected press-military conflicts to occur again, but he also predicted changes in military regulations. "Who can say that during the next American overseas military operation some restriction on the number of journalists granted access at a particular time to a particular battlefield may not be a reasonable time, place, and manner restriction?" Sand wrote. "Who today can even predict the manner in which the next war may be fought?"

SEVEN

THE VELVET GLOVE: PRESS-MILITARY ACCOMMODATION IN THE TWENTY-FIRST CENTURY

"When did we become friends?"
—An astonished Lieutenant Colonel David Pere,
to the *Washington Post*'s Peter Baker in the
Marine war room in Iraq, 2003

"I am not one of them."
—Suggestion by Newhouse News Service war
correspondent David Wood that embedded
journalists write on their notebook covers

Warfare at the dawn of the twenty-first century emphasized speed, mobility, and technology. It took only three weeks in spring 2003 for American and British forces to subdue the army of Iraq, a country as large as California. The advance from Kuwait into the heart of Baghdad, which drove Saddam Hussein and his Baath Party from power, included the fastest sustained march in American military history, with troops covering 437 miles in one two-week stretch. Yet despite its short duration, the Iraq war was one of the most thoroughly reported in history. Six hundred accredited journalists covered combat from inside air, land, and sea units. Hundreds more attended military briefings at Central Command headquarters in Doha, Qatar. An additional 2,100 "unilaterals"—the unaccredited, and unprotected, independent journalists—wandered in search of news.

Journalists covering Operation Iraqi Freedom filed live video and telephone reports from the battlefield to television networks, radio stations, print publications, and the latest mass communication medium, the World Wide Web. The proliferation of cable television since the Persian Gulf War twelve years earlier meant Americans had more choices for coverage, including options with unabashedly pro-American slants. Ordinary citizens and soldiers also took on some of the roles of journalists, posting their own views to Web logs—or "blogs"—and further broadening the public discussion of war. In a totally new twist, one of the most popular blogs in the West originated from the keyboard of "Salam Pax," an Iraqi citizen in Baghdad.

Taken as a whole, these changes in mass communication created a new way of seeing America's latest kind of combat. "This is going to be a weird war," Major Hugh Cate III, public affairs officer for the 101st Airborne Division, said at the start of the invasion. "We're going to live it and watch it at the same time."

EXPANSION OF NEWS OUTLETS

Live reports of the terrorist attacks of September 11, 2001, and the war in Iraq intoxicated news junkies in America.

They watched much of the violence unfold, as it happened, on their TV and computer screens. They appreciated the scope of coverage in a war that initially enjoyed broad support. Almost nine in ten rated press reports on the terrorist attacks as "excellent" or "good," an unprecedented level of approval, according to the Pew Research Center for the People and the Press. Support remained high during the invasion of Iraq a year and a half later, when a poll by the Pew Center found 81 percent of Americans expressing a "great deal" or a "fair amount" of confidence in the accuracy of news reports, as well as three-quarters rating the quality of coverage as excellent or good.

Conversely, for all the breadth of war news from Iraq, Americans failed to get much depth. For example, a Pew Center poll during the war's final days found three in ten Americans saying the news media had paid too little attention to civilian casualties and the war's cost. Critics singled out TV reports from the combat zone as long on style and short on substance.

News consumers seeking a well-rounded picture of war turned to multiple sources, and Web sites in particular, for more information. Seventeen percent of Web users considered it a primary source of news—not a high percentage, but nevertheless significant considering America didn't get its first Web server until December 1991. The most popular Web site during the war was CNN.com, which had 26 million unique users, followed by MSNBC.com. Most such sites run by established news agencies gave viewers much of the same information available on television or in print. However, alternative Web sites provided news available nowhere else. Iraq Body Count, a volunteer organization based in the United Kingdom and United States, began keeping a civilian death toll in Iraq after General Tommy Franks of the U.S. Central Command announced, "We don't do body counts." Iraqbodycount.net, the organization's Web site, became a crucial, independent source of civilian casualty figures for antiwar activists as well as the *Washington Post,* United Press International, and other news organizations.

The new method of war coverage little resembled the pools, escorts, and censorship of the Persian Gulf War of 1991. Neither the military nor the media had been satisfied with those arrangements. Assistant Defense Secretary Victoria Clarke acknowledged that while the Pentagon had done a good job of putting journalists where they could produce a story during Operation Desert Storm, they had failed to help them send it home adequately. In the run-up to the next war against Iraq, she said, the Defense Department chose to give the press greater access. "We are not just taking the Persian Gulf War plan off the shelf and just tweaking it," she told journalists in October 2002. "It is in your interest to be out there getting as much news and information as possible about what might transpire; it's [also] in our interest."

The pool system, although remaining an option, vanished with the start of Operation Iraqi Freedom. Some observers saw its demise as inevitable, as neither the military, which wanted public understanding, nor the press, which wanted to provide the public with military news, supported the narrow focus of pool coverage. The 101st Airborne's Major Cate, in an essay for a college textbook published between the two Persian Gulf wars, said pools served "only to increase the lack of trust between the two institutions." Anticipating the Defense Department's new emphasis on access, Cate endorsed "embedding" journalists in military units as a way not only to help spread important news, but also to build trust between soldiers and journalists. Many observers expected embedding to impart a positive spin to news from the front, as journalists began to identify with their units.

EMBEDDING, PRO AND CON

The potential for security risks also was forecast to decrease, as few journalists would choose to disclose information that could put their own lives in jeopardy. War correspondent Joseph L. Galloway received a clear explanation of embedding's impact on security during the Persian Gulf War. The commander of an infantry division invited Galloway to join him during an attack on Iraqi troops and to cover the combat as an embedded reporter. "He pulled the cover off his battle map and he said, 'Here's where we're going,'" Galloway recalled. "And I'm looking up there counting Republican Guard divisions and we're going behind them, and the hair is standing up on the back of my neck. And he said, 'I trust you because Schwarzkopf trusts you, but more than that, I trust you because you're coming with me.' And it is the most cogent argument for operational security I've ever heard in my life."

Although it was a new word, *embedding* had old roots. Journalists had lived and traveled with military units during the Mexican-American and Civil wars, and during World War II Ernie Pyle had built a career on recording the details of life in front-line units. More recently, reporters had embedded with American military units during a humanitarian intervention in Somalia in the early 1990s and the conflicts in the Balkans a few years later. In those cases, the journalists usually stayed with their units for a short time, then moved out to file pictures and stories. Journalists covering the war in Kosovo, for example, stayed embedded for a week to ten days.

The Pentagon also embedded journalists with military units during the war that ousted the Taliban rulers of Afghanistan, who sheltered the al-Qaeda terrorists behind the September 11 attacks. Journalists grumbled, however, that embedding in ground units was delayed until combat had already been under way for six weeks. Until then, the only journalists on the ground gathered news without military assistance. Correspondents in Afghanistan had less access to American forces than they had in any previous war. The nature of the conflict—primarily fighting by special forces working with Afghan rebels in extremely rugged terrain—minimized opportunities for journalists to reach the most remote fighting as well as to report without compromising covert operations. Even so, they were denied contact with special forces until December and did not have access to the Tenth Mountain Division's base in neighboring Uzbekistan and the aircraft carrier where many of the raids began. "We had greater freedom of coverage of Soviet military operations in Afghanistan," CNN's Walter Rodgers said. After three American soldiers died in a friendly-fire accident, reporters found themselves locked inside a warehouse, far from the witnesses and the wounded. "The journalists were incensed, and they were right," said Clarke.

Frustrated at the limits of coverage when playing by the

military's rules, many journalists struck out on their own. That made them easy targets. Between the start of combat in October 2001 and the end of the year, deaths among journalists in Afghanistan outnumbered those of American soldiers. An Italian, a Spaniard, a Pakistani, and an Australian died in a Taliban ambush on a highway between Jalalabad and Kabul. An ABC reporter and crew would have died had they not stopped to film a half dozen camels alongside the road. Journalists could not predict where they might find danger. American Danny Pearl of the *Wall Street Journal* declined an assignment in Afghanistan because of the obvious risk. Nevertheless, he came to a violent end in Pakistan, executed by Muslim extremists.

Unembedded journalists found themselves frozen out by military news sources. Peter Baker of the *Washington Post* spent six months in Afghanistan without speaking to an American soldier. When Baker attempted to enter an American base south of Kabul to escape from a shelling, soldiers refused to let him inside.

Restricted coverage of the war in Afghanistan, coupled with lingering complaints about Operation Desert Storm, helped persuade the Pentagon to propose an expansion of the embedding program as America prepared to wage war in Iraq in 2003. The Defense Department agreed to provide embedded reporters with "minimally restrictive" access to the war zone if correspondents were willing to make long-term commitments to particular units.

Journalists' presence throughout the war zone would serve strategic purposes. They would be on hand to verify the discovery of any weapons of mass destruction, whose purported existence had been a main justification for the invasion. And they would offer an independent voice to counter any false claims. "We're supposed to be the anti–al-Jazeera," a reporter for a major American paper said in reference to an Arab cable news network that the White House accused of being overly pro-Arab. Another embedded reporter, Rick Atkinson of the *Washington Post,* said he considered embedding to have been "quite shrewd. I think [the Pentagon] wanted people to bear witness to the fact that there weren't atrocities, on the assumption that Saddam was going to use the propaganda ploy of claiming American atrocities."

The Pentagon's guidance to its public affairs officers on the rules of embedding emphasized the need to cooperate with the press. "Our ultimate strategic success in bringing peace and security to this region will come in our long-term commitment to supporting our democratic ideals," the embedding policy statement said. "We need to tell the factual story—good and bad—before others seed the media with disinformation and distortions." The instructions defined an *embed* as "a media representative remaining with a unit on an extended basis—perhaps a period of weeks or even months. Commanders will provide billeting, rations and medical attention, if needed, to the embedded media . . . as well as access to military transportation and assistance with filing/transmitting media products, if required."

The military's escort and censorship policy survived, at least on paper. The embedding guidelines stated that escorts could be assigned at the discretion of the unit commander, but their absence would not block a journalist's access to combat. "Bearer must be escorted at all times," said Atkinson's credentials, but he said the warning was "immediately and universally ignored."

As for censorship, the Pentagon stated its preference for "security at the source." Embedded correspondents no doubt would see and hear things that would benefit the enemy if published. In such cases, the embedding guidelines urged officers to brief the journalists about the sensitive information and ask them to remove classified items from their reports or delay publication until the danger had passed. Cosmetic and frivolous editorial changes were forbidden; journalists who disputed censors' decisions about removing news that might have concrete value to the enemy could appeal up the chain of command to the secretary of defense. Beyond these limits, "media products will not be subject to security review or censorship," the guidelines said. Furthermore, "media products will not be confiscated or otherwise impounded."

Censorship at the source took on added importance because of improvements in communication technology since Desert Storm. Technologically savvy journalists—and ordinary citizens and soldiers, for that matter—could publish or transmit information from the war zone to the world. Satellite communication gear, for example, had become cheap enough that nearly any news-gathering organization could afford it. The cost of such gear had dropped from about $100,000 in the early 1990s to about $20,000 by 2003. The gear also became smaller, shrinking from an ensemble so large it required a truck for transport to the size of a fifteen-pound briefcase. Satellite time became affordable, putting live video from anywhere in the world within reach of virtually any media outlet.

Equipment to capture video images likewise had grown smaller. The Pentagon encouraged journalists to use "lipstick" cameras, so named for their size and shape, as well as varieties mounted on helmets. NBC's David Bloom repeatedly checked with military sources to confirm their support for his creating a system that would beam live images from the Third Infantry Division while it moved through Iraq. Bloom combined mobile video cameras and satellite technology to report from a refurbished tank recovery vehicle in an armored convoy, often traveling at fifty miles per hour toward Baghdad. The images from his vehicle were microwaved two miles to a converted Ford crew-cab truck equipped with a gyroscope and an uplinked satellite dish inside a dome. The dish sent the images via satellite to NBC, which streamed them live on its MSNBC.com Web site. Bloom did not live to see live broadcasts of war's end; he died, at age thirty-nine, of a pulmonary embolism on the outskirts of Baghdad.

In the years since the first Gulf War, still-photography completed the transition from film to digital imaging. Any journalist could shoot with simple, automatic cameras. Digital transmission equipment could send color photographs from the middle of the Iraqi desert directly to the United States, via a laptop's Internet connection, within minutes of the pictures being taken. Text moved even faster. Journalists took advantage of the new medium of computers and data-transmission links to send stories not only to Web pages produced by news organizations but also to personal Web logs. CNN unilateral reporter Kevin Sites, for example, won an audience of millions for his personal blog about the fighting in northern Iraq but was forced by his home office to suspend it to concentrate on covering the war for his network. Sites eventually became a freelancer to pursue his preferred style of multimedia journalism. Other bloggers came from the ranks of amateurs. Web freelancer Christopher Allbritton, a former Associated Press and *New York Daily News* reporter, collected donations from his readers to send him to Iraq; after he arrived, he e-mailed his reports home and posted observations to his blog.

Bloggers and Internet correspondents could post nearly anything to the Web, ranging from valuable and truthful information to rumors, lies, and propaganda. Without editors to evaluate the news for them, Web surfers decided for themselves which Internet sites to visit and which versions of the news deserved attention. Myriad new voices, from both sides of the war, competed in cyberspace. Salam Pax, the pen name of a twenty-nine-year-old Iraqi citizen, filed uncensored Web reports about the attack on Baghdad from the vantage point of his home in the city. Reporting on the bombing campaign, he wrote, "The whole city looked as if it were on fire. The only thing I could think of was 'Why does this have to happen to Baghdad?'" When the city lost electrical power, Salam Pax became a regular columnist for *The Guardian,* a British newspaper.

Military families opened their own blogs, as did an American officer in the thick of the fighting who identified himself as "L. T. Smash." Other "milblogs" ranged from the sophomoric to the profane. Nevertheless, they allowed military personnel in the field to publish their own accounts of war anonymously and without censorship. Officers tolerated them at first but began cracking down as the blogs posted sensitive information or challenged authority. In 2004, an army infantryman using the Web name CBFTW found himself confined to base after his account of a firefight in Iraq conflicted with the official Pentagon version. Soldiers also posted dispatches to the Web about their ordinary lives, becoming their own worm's-eye-view correspondents for readers in the United States. News organizations embraced the virtually infinite realm of cyberspace to publish greater detail, analysis, and commentary to Web pages and blogs than could be published or broadcast in traditional formats. In addition, stories and photos deemed too graphic for general television or print-publication audiences could be shunted to the Web and flagged with warnings to potential viewers.

Some news agencies, such as the Associated Press, sent reporters into the war with two or more uplinked phones to avoid satellite congestion and provide backup if one system fell victim to breakdowns or interference. The AP's caution paid off when the Pentagon banned war-zone use of a satellite phone system owned by an Arab company. The phones' built-in global positioning system could help Iraqi missile batteries pinpoint troop locations, military officials said. Reporters switched to other systems, including one that had the Department of Defense as a client.

As predicted, embedding allowed journalists and military personnel to experience one another's culture and point of view, with the goal of promoting better understanding. "Whether you're a hawk or a dove, once you deal with people who do it, there's a new level of appreciation for them," said Byron Pitts of CBS News, who covered the war in Afghanistan. "It's one thing to view a victory or a mistake by the military from a distance. It's another when you can give some context to it, when you understand how it came about."

The Pentagon urged journalists to prepare for embedding by participating in media "boot camps." These short courses in military life exposed journalists to the basics of survival on the battlefield. The first camps opened in November and December 2002. *San Francisco Chronicle* reporter John Koopman, who had undergone Marine boot camp training at Parris Island in 1976, found the media version a bit like summer camp. Participants mainly sat in classrooms to learn about terrorism and infantry tactics and get a primer in chemical, biological, and nuclear weapons. Then the journalists received lessons in the field, including how to take cover. For many who had never served in the military, the experience proved enlightening; journalists realized the wide range of skills soldiers had to master before entering combat. *Milwaukee Journal Sentinel* reporter Katherine Skiba learned how to treat serious wounds, applying field dressings, a tourniquet, and a splint to another reporter pretending to be a combat victim.

The basic courses aimed to help correspondents know the risks of being embedded, a Pentagon spokesman told *USA Today.* "The less time soldiers spend taking care of reporters, the more they have to get on with their mission."

A similar, privately run camp conducted classes in northern Virginia to prepare journalists for the rigors of being taken hostage by terrorist organizations. Participants included journalists from the *New York Times,* the *Washington Post,* the Associated Press, *USA Today,* and ABC News.

Conversely, soldiers and officers preparing to serve in Iraq received instruction on how to talk to journalists. Troops at

Fort Bragg, North Carolina, got a refresher course on how to give an interview that would meet with official approval. A public affairs officer handed out plastic cards with talking points on one side—"We are not an occupying force. Goal is to help Iraqis secure their country"—and tips for interviews on the other, such as "Avoid using acronyms or profane language."

"If you don't tell your story, they will tell their own, and all they will have to go on is their own thoughts and opinions," the Fort Bragg briefing officer said, underscoring an unspoken subtext to emphasize good news over bad. "If we don't share with them what we do, the good things we do, they can't report it."

During the invasion, unit commanders in the field received a twenty-seven-page document essentially ordering them to cooperate with correspondents. The 101st Airborne Division prepared an orientation guide to Iraq containing an eight-step section on how to talk to the media. It included "Step 4—answer the question." The *Post's* Atkinson, who was embedded with the 101st, whimsically noted that the chapter immediately after the section on media relations provided guidance on Iraq's poisonous snakes.

Embedded journalists joined their units in mid-March 2003, just before the opening of the war. Central Command, which assumed control of combat journalism during the war, offered 920 embedding slots with the army, navy, air force, and marines. Only about 600 journalists actually were embedded, and 527 moved with troops into Iraq—nearly as many as covered the 1944 invasion of Normandy. One in five came from another country.

Unilaterals covered the war from both sides; many large

organizations had embeds and unilaterals to broaden their coverage. An additional phalanx of journalists, totaling more than 700, covered the press briefings at the Coalition Media Center in Qatar. There, reporters watched video clips and heard a one-star general, Vincent Brooks, summarize military news from a $250,000 stage set designed to create attractive television images.

The rules worked smoothly. Official censorship never emerged as a major issue. Most embedded journalists filed their stories and pictures without having them reviewed first. "Go wherever you want, ask whatever you want, and you understand what the security issues are," Marine Colonel Bryan McCoy told the *Chronicle's* Koopman when he arrived at his unit in the Fourth Marine Division. "As long as you know that and I know that you're not going to abuse that trust, do whatever you want; talk to whoever you want; write whatever story you want." Not until the Marines had entered Baghdad at the end of the invasion did McCoy ask to read the stories Koopman had filed during the previous weeks.

RICK ATKINSON, EMBEDDED OBSERVER

Other journalists reported receiving similar access and similar freedom, especially as officers and soldiers became accustomed to their presence and gave their trust. Atkinson traveled extensively with Major General David Petraeus of the 101st Airborne. He received access to Petraeus's briefings on attack plans, including PowerPoint presentations in the division's tactical operations center detailing Iraqi defenses. Atkinson reported immediately on a "fragging" incident by an American soldier who rolled two grenades into a battalion tactical operational center, killing one of his own officers and wounding fifteen additional troops. Atkinson got perilously close to battle, riding with Petraeus when a machine gun opened fire on their jeep. He also witnessed Lieutenant General William S. Wallace chew out his two-star generals in a profanity-laced tirade over a perceived lapse of security, a conflict that likely would have been shielded from outsiders' eyes or kept from publication in previous wars. And he reported Wallace's pessimistic assessment that because of the appearance of Arab paramilitary forces, the war would last longer than anticipated. The comment ran counter to the Pentagon's effort to portray the invasion as swift and sure.

"It cost Wallace his career," Atkinson said months after the war. "That was against the party line. . . . There was a big uproar over it, even though what Wallace was saying was first of all true. It was evident to anybody who was there." Atkinson pointed out that Wallace never said the coalition forces were losing the war. He merely said the conditions were difficult—sand, heat, wind—and that the enemy combatants were not the Republican Guards the Americans had been trained to fight.

Atkinson brought a background in history and literature to the battlefield. He had considered careers as an army officer, fiction writer, and an English professor at a university. Flat broke after getting a master's degree in English at the University of Chicago, with no serious job prospects, he took a job in the mid-1970s as a reporter at a newspaper in Pittsburg, Kansas. He discovered he had a knack for journalism. While in Pittsburg, he attended a screening of *All the*

President's Men at the town's small movie theater and identified his growing commitment to journalism. After eighteen
months, Atkinson moved on to a newspaper in Kansas City,
where he stayed until making the jump to Washington, D.C.
His first assignment for the *Post* required him to fly to Savan-
nah, Georgia, to hear General H. Norman Schwarzkopf
give a three-hour briefing on the Grenada invasion in 1983.

Although Atkinson maintained a love for newspapers, he
found the short narratives of daily journalism constraining.
While working at the *Post,* he took leave to write books
about the first Gulf War and the 1966 graduating class at
West Point. He left the paper again in 1999 to work on a
World War II book, *An Army at Dawn,* which won the
Pulitzer Prize for history while he was in Iraq with the 101st.
He put his continuing World War II research on hold to answer the *Post*'s call to return to the front lines. His understanding of twentieth-century wars, along with his personal
experiences, made him a keen observer of the changes in
media covering war.

"In 20 years of writing about the military—including two
previous stints as an embedded reporter, in Bosnia and Somalia—I had never seen a more intimate arrangement between journalists and soldiers," Atkinson told *Post* readers. As
a historian, he noted that reporters often traveled with military units during World War II, and yet "their dispatches
were heavily censored to the point that controversial, critical
and even mildly sensitive material was suppressed." In Iraq,
however, journalists mainly censored themselves, particularly
on details that might help Iraqi troops prepare for a coming
attack.

In relating his level of access, Atkinson recalled two events as particularly significant examples of the military's commitment to transparency. In the first, Apache attack helicopter pilots participated in a conference call with their counterparts just back from a disappointing mission, which had left only eight of thirty-five helicopters operational. Atkinson called the remarkable candor "a riveting—and revealing—exchange between aviators who had just been shot to pieces and others who were about to undertake their first combat mission toward Baghdad." In the second, during an assault on the city of Karbala, Atkinson stayed by Petraeus as he made decision after decision. "The sequence at times was ragged—particularly when two laser-guided bombs 'went stupid' and, in one case, detonated behind us—but it also provided a palpable sense of the relentless responsibilities of command," he wrote. Such access, available only when journalists agreed to share the lives of front-line soldiers, allowed Americans to see war closer than they had in decades. Atkinson called embedding a calculated risk, and "a fair gamble for both sides."

Karl Zinsmeister, the embedded editor of *American Enterprise* magazine, echoed Atkinson's enthusiasm for the new media access. "No major corporation, no educational institution, no other agency of government has ever invited me and other reporters into their war councils (literally), let me read their secret memos, given me unfettered twenty-four-hour access to their workplaces and employees," he wrote. "It's a tremendously brave gamble on the part of our Defense Department."

David Zucchino, a *Los Angeles Times* reporter embedded with the army, observed that journalists had not worked so closely with the armed forces in combat since the Vietnam

War. In all, he found the experience terrifying and exhilarating. "I slept in fighting holes and armored vehicles, on a rooftop, a garage floor and in lumbering troop trucks," he wrote. "For days at a time, I didn't sleep. I ate with the troops, choking down processed meals of 'meat, chunked and formed,' that came out of brown plastic bags. I rode with them in loud, claustrophobic and disorienting Bradley fighting vehicles. I complained with them about the choking dust, the lack of water, our foul-smelling bodies and our scaly, rotting feet."

The shared living arrangements let Zucchino write stories he could not have gotten from a distance: the battle for Baghdad, including the ferocious suicide attacks in cars and trucks; the performance of individual soldiers in combat; the hunt for souvenirs by the victors; and the uncovering of a cache of more than $750 million in a posh neighborhood where some of Hussein's top officials had lived.

TOO CLOSE FOR COMFORT

Not all the news was good for the American-led coalition. The embedding system and liberal censorship rules allowed some of the darker truths about war to emerge, starting with the fragging incident March 23. Six days later, the *Washington Post* reported the deaths of four American soldiers resulting from a suicide bomber driving a taxi full of explosives into a checkpoint near Najaf. It was the first such attack of the war. The *Post* quoted American reaction that branded the attack as an act of terrorism, as well as an ominous—and accurate—prediction from the Iraqi vice president: "This is just the beginning."

In another incident, Dexter Filkins of the *New York Times* described two marines discussing the difficulties of distinguishing civilians from combatants. They expressed frustration at Iraqi soldiers using women and children as shields. The marines said they sometimes declined to fire at Iraqi gunmen in order to avoid accidentally shooting civilians. At other times, snap decisions during firefights led to Americans killing noncombatants. Filkins quoted one of the marines as saying, "We dropped a few civilians, but what do you do? . . . I'm sorry, but the chick was in the way."

William Branigin of the *Washington Post* reported critically about the death of ten Iraqi civilians mistaken for more suicide bombers. Army Captain Ronny Johnson told his platoon to fire a warning shot at an approaching sport utility vehicle packed with Iraqis; when he heard no such warning and the car grew closer, he ordered the platoon's Bradley vehicles to shoot it. "That order was immediately followed by the loud reports of 25mm cannon fire from one or more of the platoon's Bradleys," Branigin wrote. "About half a dozen shots were heard in all. 'Cease fire!' Johnson yelled over the radio. Then, as he peered into his binoculars from the intersection on Highway 9, he roared at the platoon leader, 'You just [expletive] killed a family because you didn't fire a warning shot soon enough!'" Significantly, Branigin's eyewitness account contradicted the official version of the events, which reported a warning shot and only seven deaths.

Cate, the public affairs director, applauded Branigin's work. The "beauty" of embedding, Cate said, appeared in the completeness of his story. "He also reported . . . exactly how bad those soldiers felt about what had just happened, and how it was the darkest day in their lives, and how they brought so much to bear on themselves for this tragic accident to happen. So you got the full news package, as opposed to some sterile account from the Pentagon or spokesman saying, 'Today, yes, we had an incident and some civilians were killed at a checkpoint when they failed to stop.'"

If such details distinguished the embedded print reporters' work, they were lacking in much of the televised images of war. TV came under broad criticism from media analysts for three forms of distortion. The first distortion was deliberate. In the patriotic atmosphere following the 2001 terrorist attacks on New York City and Washington, D.C., some television news operations shifted from attempts to report objectively. One study, conducted by the media analysis group Fairness and Accuracy in Reporting, found that in the first three weeks of the Iraq war, prowar American sources outnumbered antiwar American sources on the evening newscasts of six networks by a ratio of twenty-five to one. On CBS's evening broadcast with Dan Rather, the ratio rose to nearly one hundred to one.

In a bid for ratings, Fox News flavored its broadcasts with overt boosterism. Fox News, created in 1996, compensated for its initially small staff and inexperience by emphasizing bright graphics, conservative commentators, and tabloid style. The format drew a niche audience mainly on the right side of the political spectrum. After the 9/11 terrorist attacks, Fox's formula further boosted viewership, leading it to overtake CNN in the cable ratings by January 2002. Its reporting of the Iraq war supported President George W. Bush, marginalized voices of the opposition, and steeped its coverage of combat in patriotic rhetoric. Bill O'Reilly, host of Fox's popular *The O'Reilly Factor,* told

America in February 2003, "Once the war . . . begins, we expect every American to support our military, and if they can't do that, to shut up."

Fox's success in attracting and keeping viewers to its war coverage influenced other television networks, with MSNBC shifting its lineup of talk show hosts to the right and CNN deciding to censor its reporters in the field. Atlanta-based CNN distributed a document before the war requiring all reporters to submit scripts to the home office for approval before they could air. According to Robert Fisk, a British journalist who obtained a copy, editors at the Atlanta home office could insist on changes or "balances" in dispatches. CNN toned down its coverage of the war for Americans and created a separate, more balanced broadcast for its international audience. Veteran CNN correspondent Christiane Amanpour decried TV journalists in Iraq for having "self-muzzled," telling CNBC that her network had been "intimidated by the administration and its foot soldiers at Fox News." Journalists avoided asking critical questions and created a positive tone, she said.

Boosterism contributed to, or reinforced, gross misunderstandings by American civilians. An audience survey conducted by the Program on International Policy Attitudes at the University of Maryland found Fox News's audience to be more misinformed than viewers of other broadcast news programs. In the survey, 80 percent of Fox's regular news viewers believed one or more false statements about the war in Iraq: that weapons of mass destruction had been found, that evidence had established al-Qaeda links in Iraq (none of the September 11, 2001, terrorists was an Iraqi), or that world opinion favored the war. At the other extreme, only

23 percent of audiences for National Public Radio and PBS television held such erroneous views. The researchers did not explore the issue of whether exposure to a particular broadcast caused the distorted views, or whether people who already held such views sought out broadcasts that reinforced them.

The second distortion occurred as a result of the speed with which information from the war zone circled the globe. The ability to send live video, audio, and text from Iraq to the United States accelerated the news cycle. The editor's traditional role of mediating the message—checking for accuracy, providing context, raising questions, all for the benefit of the audience—contracted as news outlets competed to scoop their rivals. Journalists on live television sometimes jumped to wrong conclusions and spread them before they could be refuted.

For example, in Fox's quick coverage of the fragging incident, the network said terrorists "apparently" were to blame and may have arrived in camp from across the Iraqi border. Fox then gave air time to a British television reporter who traced the attack to two Kuwaiti or Arab nationals, possibly working as translators for the Americans and wearing camouflage. The *Post's* initial story about the Iraqis' capture of Jessica Lynch, a teenage private first class, read like the plot of a made-for-television movie, guaranteed to raise morale. The *Post* said Lynch "was fighting to the death" even after sustaining multiple gunshot wounds. In fact, Lynch suffered all of her wounds during the crash of her Humvee and had not been stabbed or shot. The army later said her injuries caused unconsciousness, making it impossible for her to have fought to avoid capture.

Speed contributed to journalists' overreaction to a pause in the armed forces' advance on Baghdad. Supplies had run low and pockets of Iraqi resistance remained active, forcing the Third Infantry Division to halt short of the Karbala Gap. Some analysts suggested comparisons to the "quagmire" of Vietnam. Defense Secretary Donald Rumsfeld reacted by decrying the media's "mood swings" from optimism to pessimism, and back again, sometimes within a single day. While correspondents defended their reports, citing legitimate concerns among officers—including General Wallace—about strategy, supplies, and troop strength, the University of Maryland's college of journalism criticized the press's impatience. College Dean Thomas Kunkel said, "How can you intelligently discuss military strategy four days into a war as complex as the invasion of Iraq?"

Atlantic Monthly correspondent Mark Bowden suggested context as an antidote to the rush to judgment. He urged journalists to counter their desire to make snap judgments by offering alternative explanations for swiftly unfolding events. During the invasion's halt, he said, journalists could have told their audiences, "Yes, at the moment it looks like supply lines are overextended because the advance has been so rapid. That could mean that troops could be strung out and could become vulnerable. It also could mean that we are on the verge of an amazingly rapid success."

The third distortion occurred as the news media made choices of what to cover and what to ignore. The allure of live battlefield images led TV producers often to choose them over taped reports and studio interviews. Such selections, intended to attract viewers and advertisers, generated more excitement than understanding. Rumsfeld referred to the embedded journalists' reports as "slices of war." Others likened their impact as viewing the war through six hundred soda straws. An analysis of the embedded reports that aired on television during three of the war's first six days found six of ten were live and unedited; that reporters (and not soldiers) provided the only voices in eight of ten; that 47 percent described military action or its results; and that none depicted people being hit by the discharge of a weapon. In other words, the typical television report from an embed showed the journalist talking about, but not illustrating, the violence of war. "The most common criticism of the embedded reports is that they are only isolated pieces of a larger mosaic," researchers at the Project for Excellence in Journalism concluded, "and that relying too heavily on them would thus skew the picture viewers get."

The most famous image of the war, of Iraqis pulling down a statue of Saddam Hussein in Baghdad's Firdos Square, illustrated how a particular vantage point could lead to false conclusions. Marines diverted an M-88 tank recovery vehicle to the square, conveniently close to the Palestine Hotel, where most foreign journalists were staying. Television cameras recorded the Iraqis struggling to pull down the statue and calling on U.S. Marines to help. TV coverage gave the impression of a large crowd, joyful at Iraq's liberation. Still-camera pictures taken from a distance, however, revealed the square nearly empty—containing no more than 200 people, most of them international journalists. Of the handful of Iraqis in the square—out of a city of millions—observers identified some as supporters of Ahmed Chalabi, the man favored by the Pentagon to head a new Iraqi government. Arab observers as well as American critics of the war suggested the event had been stage-managed, an assertion denied by the military. In any event, a variety of television angles would have suggested alternative explanations to television viewers. Phillip Knightley, a historian of combat journalism, noted that television announcers witnessing the statue come down told viewers they were seeing history. "But whose history?" Knightley asked.

The researchers at the Project for Excellence argued that the evidence pointed toward a general distortion in television news. Their report quoted a network executive as describing broadcasts as "inundated" with close-ups and in dire need of perspective. Another journalist, ABC Pentagon correspondent John McWethy, told the *Washington Post,* "Riding around in a tank is fun, but you don't know [expletive] about what's going on."

The closeness of embedded reporters to the subjects they covered raised questions of whether they could remain detached observers. The issue is not unique to war; journalists who cover city hall or the police station need to balance their close working relationships with their sources against their duty to report objectively to their audiences. Two studies of the possible prowar bias of embedding suggested opposite conclusions. A study of four major newspapers' coverage of Desert Storm, the war in Afghanistan, and Operation Iraqi Freedom by the Department of Defense and the University of Oklahoma found the tone of embedded reports to be more positive than those written by nonembedded journalists. However, another study, a content analysis of war stories printed in the *New York Times* and *Washington Post,* found the papers had a more negative or neutral tone in their news coverage of 2003 as compared with 1991, challenging the notion that the Pentagon's emphasis on access would necessarily lead to positive spin. The papers also relied more on lower-ranking officers and less on top brass as sources in the war in Iraq than in Desert Storm, reflecting the embedding program's effect of putting journalists closer to the action.

According to the Pentagon's rules, embedded journalists could not leave their units. They were stuck for as long as they chose to remain unless they violated their agreements or opted out. The army briefly expelled Fox News correspondent Geraldo Rivera for describing future operations and drawing a map in the sand to show his unit's location, a violation of operational security. Thirty-five members of the news media, including about twelve embeds, were asked to leave the combat zone or were escorted out by the armed forces. The army tolerated al-Jazeera's embedded reports although officials grumbled about the coverage the network devoted to civilian casualties. The network's embedded correspondent, Amr el-Kakhy, found both Iraqi and American sources reluctant to talk. "You know, guys, you are a station with a reputation," an American colonel explained to el-Kakhy after al-Jazeera failed to get an invitation to a press briefing. Frustrated, el-Kakhy and his network decided to disembed the day Baghdad fell.

Unilaterals obviously did not have to stick with one particular military unit; however, their freedom came at a price. Journalists who wandered the battlefields or reported from the Iraqi side ran higher risks of being killed or wounded. An American tank crew fired on the unilaterals' main headquarters in Baghdad's Palestine Hotel after hearing their unit had been taking sniper fire and rocket-propelled grenades. The tank's single shell killed a Reuters cameraman and a Spanish cameraman and wounded three other correspondents. An investigation by the Committee to Protect Journalists determined the shelling, though "not deliberate, was avoidable." The Pentagon and commanders on the ground knew the hotel housed dozens of journalists, but that information didn't reach the tank commander in time. Journalists in the hotel reported not hearing any shots fired from the building before the attack.

During the period of major combat, which Bush declared at an end on May 1, 2003, journalists were ten times more likely to die in Iraq than any of the quarter million British and American soldiers. By August 2005, two and a half years after the invasion of Iraq, the war and continued insurgency had cost the lives of as many as eighty journalists and other media workers, most of them unilaterals.

The unilaterals accepted extra risks to report the kinds of stories they could only get from being unattached. They sometimes could not verify information they received from official Iraqi sources, but they nevertheless unearthed details beyond those reported by the embeds. One of them, the *Post*'s Anthony Shadid, received the Pulitzer Prize for reporting the war from the perspective of ordinary Iraqi citizens. Shadid, fluent in Arabic, wrote of how Ali Kadhim Subhi had to bury ten members of his family after an American bombing destroyed his home. In a poignant dispatch, Shadid described a mosque caretaker preparing the corpse of a fourteen-year-old boy for burial and asking, "What's the sin of the children? What have they done?" His reports of widespread Iraqi anger and ambivalence foreshadowed the difficulties of the continued American presence.

Another unilateral reporting from inside Iraq, Anne Garrels of National Public Radio, waded into a bombing scene and encountered a teenager who thrust a can at reporters. "He said it contained the brains of one of the victims," she reported. "Others showed off a severed hand. 'Is that what you call human rights?' scoffed one young man. 'Is that what you call liberation?' asked another."

Both embedded journalists and unilaterals presented new dimensions in war coverage—details, often in real time, that Americans had not seen in previous war coverage. Each kind of coverage had its strengths and weaknesses; both added to audiences' understanding. The ideal coverage for an informed American audience therefore required news consumers to seek out both kinds of reports—those that originated inside military units, and those that did not. Journalists in Iraq, along with civilians and soldiers who posted to the Web, created a richer tapestry of information than had been available in any previous war.

To become well-informed citizens, however, Americans actively had to seek out the news. Watching only one television station, scrolling only one Web site, or reading only one newspaper or magazine failed to provide the balance and the nuance of the full spectrum of media. Whether Americans would take advantage of the new choices offered them by technological advances in order to become intelligent news consumers—not to mention participants in representative democracy—would remain a key question in years to come.

EIGHT

THE FUTURE: THE QUEST FOR MORE LIGHT

"Bomb it and they will come."
   —Marquette University journalism professor
   Philip Seib

"Why are we here? Why should we stay?"
   —*New York Magazine* media critic Michael Wolff,
   to General Vincent Brooks at CENTCOM
   media center, Doha, Qatar

When Richard Harding Davis set off to cover combat a century ago, he preferred to travel "light." He ranked a folding cot, cooking kit, and folding chair as the three most important articles to pack into a war zone. After those, he wrote in one of his many memoirs, he liked to carry two collapsible water buckets, two collapsible brass lanterns, two boxes of sick-room candles, a dozen boxes of safety matches, an ax, a medicine chest, a toilet case, a folding rubber bathtub, a revolver with six cartridges, and twenty-five other carefully selected items—the underpants had to be silk, and his flannel shirt had to be gray. He noted about his handgun, "Except to impress guides and mule drivers, it is not an essential article. In six campaigns I have carried one, and never used it, nor needed it but once, and then while I was dodging behind the foremast it lay under tons of luggage in the hold. The number of cartridges I have limited to six, on the theory that if in six shots you haven't hit the other fellow, he will have hit you, and you will not require another six." To record information for his audience in the United States, he needed only a pad of writing paper, a self-filling fountain pen, a bottle of ink, a dozen envelopes, sealing wax, and stamps.

Fast-forward a century. The army's embedding invitation to Rick Atkinson of the *Washington Post,* successor in a line of war correspondents stretching from Davis through Ernie Pyle to the journalists in the Persian Gulf, suggested packing for "austere" conditions in Iraq. Items to avoid included curling irons, hair dryers, pornography, alcohol, "colorful news jackets," and guns. However, Atkinson's baggage included things Davis would have recognized: notebooks, clothing for hot and cold weather, shaving kit, and sleeping bag.

In addition, the modern war correspondent carries enough electronics to stock a small store. Atkinson had three satellite phones, three digital cameras, an array of batteries and cables, a tape recorder, tapes, and two laptops, "including one variant encased in a metal box that supposedly could withstand being run over by a Humvee." And, just in case, he carried a gas mask and chemical suit. "Whatever happened, I wondered, to the doughty war correspondent with a pencil, a pad, and a battered Underwood?" Atkinson asked himself.

The sun has long set on the era when war correspondents had time to write with fountain pens and post their dispatches. Speed is the new mantra of war journalism, just as the invasion of Iraq demonstrated it to be the new paradigm of war itself. The electronics that connect twenty-first-century journalists with their audiences have made the military's traditional controls of information obsolete. No longer is the war correspondent, like Pyle in the middle of the battlefields of World War II, forced to rely on military assistance to communicate. Gone, too, is the military's ability to impose absolute censorship. The World Wide Web, the satellite phone, and other jinns of modern technology can turn virtually anyone, including civilians and soldiers, into wartime journalists. They also vault nearly every obstacle to mass communication. While America's National Security Agency can intercept such messages, to expect any government office to screen them all and react to the risky ones in real time strains the imagination.

Instead of trying to impose difficult controls, the armed forces have adopted the wisdom of the schoolyard: If you can't beat 'em, join 'em. The result, the large-scale embedding program of Operation Iraqi Freedom, has reenergized the relationship between the military and the media. Journalists accepted the access they always wanted, while the armed forces received war coverage that, by virtue of having reporters living close to soldiers and officers, provided more war news without compromising operations.

Still, the media and the military face many issues. Striking the right balance would provide Americans with enough news to make informed decisions about military and political operations. It would empower American words and pictures to better serve the nation's interests—as well as the public's.

The foremost challenge is to use the new technology intelligently. Just as the computer and streamed video have replaced the handwritten dispatch, so have the demands of instant communication substituted snap judgments for the prose of bygone journalists who had time to think before acting. The media must decide whether having the ability to report a story of military consequence means they necessarily *should* report it before verifying it.

Americans have the right to know the news, whether on the battlefield or in the Pentagon. The issue is whether they need to know it imperfectly, and in real time. The media's continual cycle of publication and broadcast provides a mechanism to rectify mistakes, but corrections never spread as far as the error. And they are of little value to anyone who might be hurt by the media's haste. "When stressing speed, news organizations may be tempted to cut corners in what should be a deliberative process of judging newsworthiness and determining accuracy," observed Marquette University journalism professor Philip Seib. In Iraq, the competition to be first with the news led to erroneous reports on more than one occasion. That did not cost lives, but the same may not be true in future wars.

Because of the explosion of media outlets, coupled with the competitive twenty-four-hour news cycle they have created, the media can alter political and military actions even as they are being carried out. Generals and presidents often learn of developments on the battlefield from television networks before the news reaches them through official channels. Savvy combatants adapt instant communication to the demands of war, targeting global public opinion as a component of strategy.

Both aspects of the media's newfound power became apparent during the humanitarian intervention in Somalia in the early 1990s. Navy SEALs waded ashore on the beaches of East Africa to find American television cameras already in place, transmitting their arrival to world capitals. Months later, galvanized by images of street fighting and the body of an American soldier being dragged through the Somali capital, public opinion pressured President Bill Clinton to end the operation.

During the wars in the Persian Gulf, images of civilian suffering altered outcomes. A British news producer observed in the 2004 battle for control of Fallujah, a rebel center, that Western coalition forces withdrew from downtown because of concerns over how their intervention might appear to the Arab world. "We allowed a bonanza of hundreds of terrorists and insurgents to escape us—despite promising that we would bring them to justice," the BBC's Ralph Peters wrote. "We stopped because we were worried about what already hostile populations might think of us. The global media disrupted the US and Coalition chains of command. . . . We could have won militarily. Instead, we surrendered politically and called it a success. Our enemies won the information war."

Peters concluded that one way to counter the effects of instant communication is to "speed the kill"—to fight to such a swift conclusion that news has no opportunity to influence a battle in progress. Another option, of course, would be to attempt to prohibit cameras from the battlefield entirely. Given the ubiquitous nature of modern communication, the only way to carry out such a fight likely would be to choose the most isolated turf imaginable—the rugged crags of Afghanistan, for example—and try to achieve victory before the media arrived. That may happen again, but the military and government won't always be able to fight at times and places they control. Instead, their war plans must incorporate the presence of globally connected news correspondents and technologically sophisticated civilians.

Military and government officials are considering their options. The embedding process, coupled with speed-of-light communication, has convinced the front-line officer of the futility of trying to spin the news in real time. As a result, combat units now know their decisions will be swiftly made public. "The media were in our decision cycle," army Colonel Guy Shields, a public affairs officer, said after the Iraq war. "There was absolutely no way to place any spin control. The media were right there. . . . So don't even think about trying to BS them. You could not put spin on what the embeds were putting out."

At high-level press briefings in Washington and at command centers close to the battlefield, however, spin has remained healthy. Investigative reporter Seymour Hersh revealed in 2002 that the Central Intelligence Agency paid nearly $100 million to the Rendon Group public relations firm in the 1990s to handle press issues related to Iraqi opponents of Saddam Hussein's regime. The Defense Department later hired the same agency to advise it on ways to deal with "disinformation" arising out of the war against the Taliban in Afghanistan. The Rendon Group briefly took on the Pentagon's Office of Strategic Influence (OSI) as a client.

The Pentagon shut down that office after the *New York Times* reported its plans to "provide news items, possibly even false ones, to unwitting foreign journalists to influence public sentiment abroad." Internal documents obtained by the *Times* said the OSI debated finding ways to "coerce" foreign journalists and opinion makers and "punish" those who conveyed messages the American government opposed.

One key problem with circulating lies abroad as an American form of propaganda rests in the interconnectedness of modern media. Faked news items planted overseas will find audiences in the United States via the Web and satellite television. American citizens then might form political opinions based on lies.

In spring 2005, a congressional committee objected, rightly, to such muddied waters. The representatives endorsed sharp separation of fact from fancy, urging the Defense Department to keep "a clear, functional distinction between information operations that attempt to affect potential adversaries' information-collection efforts and public affairs activities that are designed to release timely, reliable, and accurate information to American and allied audiences."

It should go without saying that knowledgeable citizens, informed with the truth about their world, are the foundation of a healthy republic. On the other hand, lies have played an important role in warfare at least since the fifth century B.C.E., when Themistocles, an Athenian naval commander, fooled the Persians into poorly deploying their forces at the Battle of Salamis.

To what extent deception of the media remains an option in wartime is unknown. The army's field manual continues to advocate deception as a "fundamental instrument of the military art," but its unclassified text does not specify whether the news media are fair game.

Some government agencies apparently have reached that conclusion. A variety of federal offices now spin the news by creating their own news clips and passing them off as the work of objective, independent journalists. NBC reported in March 2005 the Bush administration had spent a quarter billion dollars on public relations, most of it financing the creation and distribution of video news releases. The video clips, first created in the Clinton administration, purported to be objective news but provided a proadministration slant, extolling President Bush's policies and affirming the wisdom of waging war in Iraq.

That wisdom came into question when invading forces failed to find weapons of mass destruction or al-Qaeda terror cells in Iraq in 2003. Journalists relearned the value of healthy skepticism and the danger of overreliance on high-ranking official sources. The *New York Times* apologized to its readers in 2004 for "coverage that was not as rigorous as it should have been" regarding the rationale for war in Iraq. The *Times* said it had failed to provide readers with sufficient qualification, did not air enough challenges from alternative voices, and placed too much emphasis on sources who acted primarily out of self-interest. In addition, the paper's editors admitted, the placement of news favored one side of the debate over the other.

A better model for investigative reporting came from the Knight Ridder chain of thirty-one newspapers. It stood virtually alone among the major media in 2002 in reporting serious doubts about Bush's rationale for war among career officers in the military, intelligence community, and diplomatic corps. Blunting the chain's influence was its lack of a paper in Washington or New York.

Another challenge to improved war reporting is the media's short attention span. Futurists Alvin and Heidi Toffler correctly have described the media as focusing on one crisis after another—"Abortion today. Corruption tomorrow." Political actions hasten to keep pace, they said, accelerating the need for decisions about increasingly complex matters. In military affairs, the media's addiction to fresh stories containing drama and sensation resulted in maximum attention to wars in Iraq and Afghanistan but relatively little on rebuilding those countries. Part of the problem is the media's tendency to focus more on what's going wrong than on what's going right.

"We have gotten a very empty view of what is happening in Afghanistan, and it is a dangerous view, because you get the impression that all America is about is bombing and high tech and bulldozing," said CNN's Christiane Amanpour. "I think America needs to have its other side shown to the world—its human side, the good things, the constructive things it is doing." She blamed the military's restrictions on access to Afghanistan for America's limited knowledge of that country.

However, operational security cannot explain the steep decline in attention paid to Afghanistan after 2001's invasion. The war there rated as the most-covered news story of 2001 on CBS, ABC, and NBC. By 2003, the country received only eighty minutes of coverage from the three networks, less than 20 percent of what it got the previous year and not enough to place it on the list of twenty most-covered stories. "If Afghanistan stays forgotten, it won't forget," the *Atlanta Journal-Constitution* editorialized after the war in Iraq. "Remember Afghanistan?"

Peter Arnett remembered. He had flown to Afghanistan after terrorists made their first attack on the World Trade Center in February 1993. American investigators discovered connections between the suspects in that bombing and Muslim radicals in Afghanistan, where the United States had previously backed an insurgency against Soviet occupation. While waiting in Pakistan for a plane into Kabul, Arnett chatted with a local newspaper editor. "The chickens are just going home to roost," the editor told him. "All you cared about was destroying communism, and you welcomed extremists to the struggle and trained them to kill. But many of those people don't like you either, and you're the next target."

Stability had failed to take hold in Afghanistan, he said, and the country was on its way to becoming a center of international drug trade and terrorist training. Arnett concluded, in 1993, he probably would have to return to Afghanistan because the story there was not over. It took eight years for him to be proved right.

After the end of major combat in Iraq, former CNN Washington bureau chief Frank Sesno believed Americans remained curious. They're asking, he said, "Is anything getting rebuilt [in Iraq]? Are they really democrats over there? . . . Could I see an interview with any of the founding fathers and founding mothers of this new, emerging country?"

They would have a hard time finding such stories, he concluded.

Talking heads make less compelling video than bombs exploding in marketplaces and at checkpoints. Yet the video of a bomb has no inherent meaning. Understanding comes from context that explains what is being bombed, why, to what effect, and what might happen after that. It is not the kind of simple, sound-bite story that media prefer. Television coverage of the war in Iraq made for compelling viewing, but it failed to meet the first duty of a socially responsible press as described by the influential 1947 *Report of the Commission on Freedom of the Press,* also known as the Hutchins Commission report: To provide "a truthful, comprehensive and intelligent account of the day's events in a context which gives them meaning."

War correspondence would benefit not only from reporters who seek to place combat stories into a broader context of politics, economics, religion, and culture, but also from those whose work promotes peace and stability after the shooting stops. It is a difficult task that runs counter to the long-term trends, particularly in television journalism.

"It is the businesspeople, the bosses who are in charge of our organizations, who have decided—for commercial reasons, mostly—that Americans don't need to know about international news, that they don't need to know anything other than business news, tabloid trivia, titillating stuff," said Amanpour. But the attacks of September 11 showed the dangers of complacency. Americans do care, she said. "People want to know what is going on, but our corporations have relied on what I call 'hocus pocus focus groups' that tell them essentially what they want to hear and fit their business plan. The net result is you get to a situation like September 11 and the whole country is saying, 'Why didn't we know more about this?'"

Amanpour has not shied away from difficult questions and provocative statements. Born in 1958 in London, she grew up in Iran, the daughter of an Iranian father and British mother. After studying journalism at the University of Rhode Island, she took a job as a graphics designer at a television station in Providence. She then worked briefly as a reporter, anchor, and producer for a Rhode Island radio station before joining CNN in 1983. Her reporting career took her to many hot spots, including Kuwait, Iraq, the former Soviet republic of Georgia, Somalia, and Afghanistan.

Her best-known reporting, however, occurred during the ethnic fighting in the Balkans after the breakup of Yugoslavia. Her focus on the war's impact on civilians led some viewers to question whether she had let her passions slant her reporting. Responding to criticism, Amanpour endorsed advocacy over neutrality if the former would serve the oppressed in wartime. For example, Bosnians suffered during what many obervers called a "humanitarian catastrophe" in the 1900s. Amanpour suggested that in extreme circumstances, neutral journalism can be an accomplice to suffering.

The government and the military have their own, powerful voices. Journalism, if it speaks for anyone, should speak for the silent and the powerless. However, asking tough questions on the public's behalf comes at a price. After Amanpour claimed the Bush administration and its cheerleaders among the media created "a climate of fear and self-censorship" and helped spread "disinformation" during the war in Iraq, Fox News called her "a spokeswoman for al-Qaeda." Similarly, Atkinson received "Dear Traitor" e-mails from some readers, and *New York Magazine's* Michael Wolff got 3,000 venomous e-mails, orchestrated by conservative television and radio hosts, after he questioned the value of press briefings during the war in Iraq. Clearly, the modern war journalist must have a thick skin.

Such may be the tenor of the times in a post-9/11 world. Or, it may be evidence of a new paradigm of journalism, in which all media are seen as the tools of political interests and no correspondent is safe from charges of bias. Nevertheless, Amanpour prefers a nation with a free press acting for the public's benefit, to one that automatically supports one political position over another. "If you didn't have an independent and free press, you'd have propaganda—ours, theirs, whoever's," Amanpour said. "You need a free press to sift through the propaganda and tell the story of what's going on, whether it's going well or badly. We are brokers of information, and if we don't exist, a nation, a civil society, a democracy is poorer."

The public wants wartime reporters who hide their opinions. A Pew Research Center poll in April 2003 found 69 percent of Americans saying they prefer neutral coverage of war, while only 23 percent wanted coverage to be overtly pro-American. Most—62 percent—felt the war coverage was handled properly, while 23 percent considered it too critical of the military and 9 percent not critical enough. The results indicate strong support for an objective, balanced media by a majority of Americans, with audiences on both extremes dissatisfied. Given the splintering of the media on the Web and cable TV, news consumers are sure to find some version of events that supports their view of conflict.

Unfortunately for a republic in wartime, public consensus also splintered as the fighting in Iraq moved from warfare to ongoing guerrilla tactics. Voters may no longer choose to visit the vast marketplace of ideas and become exposed to information that challenges their opinions. That attitude is bad for democracy. If Americans cannot agree about the relevant facts of military affairs—witness the substantial percentage of Fox News viewers who held demonstrably false views about the war in Iraq—they have no hope of forming a consensus on how best to conduct them.

What can the press and the military do?

The press can continue to demand access to the front lines. Not just as embeds but also as unilaterals granted a minimum of security—or even benign neglect. Unilaterals who volunteer for the dangerous job of reporting from the other side of the front lines, or from the unsecured areas of combat, deserve to not be treated like agents of the enemy. "What's the difference between the Iraqi army and the American army?" was the first line of a joke journalists told in the Iraq war. The punchline: "The Americans shoot at you."

As for the embedding program of Iraq, it generally won approval of journalists and soldiers, but there is no guarantee of continuation. The Pentagon controls the battle zone; what it gives it and the president can take away. Journalists must push for the right to cover future wars from as many angles and as many levels as possible—from the front lines to the operational headquarters to the Pentagon and White House—in order to act as proxies for the public.

When they do decide to embed, war correspondents must remember whom they work for: the American public, which, through its elected officials, sent the military into war to do its bidding. And they must not be afraid to ask tough questions about war, on the public's behalf. "It is not the journalist's job to be patriotic," Walter Cronkite told the U.S. secretary of defense during the Vietnam War. "How can patriotism be determined anyway? Is patriotism simply agreeing unquestioningly with every action of one's government? Or might we define patriotism as having the courage to speak and act on those principles one thinks are best for the country, whether they are in accordance with the wishes of the government or not?"

Embedding would benefit from adjustments, however. The military should attempt to embed reporters from the media with the most national clout—such as the top magazines, newspapers, television networks—in units most likely to see crucial action. That way, experienced military reporters would record war's biggest developments. Small media outlets likely would object to such arrangements, as they did when major papers got key assignments during Desert Storm. Nevertheless, it makes sense to ensure a front-row seat for the *New York Times,* the *Washington Post,* and a handful of broadcast networks.

Rick Atkinson also suggested allowing a small percentage of embedded reporters to move from unit to unit, in order to avoid getting stuck in a unit that ends up far from action. The military balked at shifting embeds among units during combat for logistical and safety reasons; wholesale shuffling likely would bring chaos. However, a small degree of shifting would guarantee that the most experienced, credible correspondents are on hand to observe the most important battlefield events. The fog of war otherwise would ensure that any detailed arrangements for placing veteran journalists in the right place at the right time would break down. Atkinson also endorsed placing a small number of experienced combat journalists with special forces. With proper guidelines against identifying secret operatives, they could report on sensitive operations without compromising security.

A return to long-term reporting commitments overseas also would help shape world opinion before crises erupt. So would efforts to educate Americans about the value of foreign news during interwar periods. Unfortunately, crisis-driven coverage remained the norm in Iraq three years after the invasion, as continued bombings and the abduction and captivity of American freelance journalist Jill Carroll dominated the news. Carroll, who wrote for the *Christian Science Monitor,* moved to Jordan before the 2003 invasion of Iraq "to learn as much about the region as possible before the fighting began." She spoke some Arabic and appreciated Iraqi culture. Despite her empathy for ordinary Iraqis who suffered as a result of the fighting, Carroll became one of hundreds of foreigners taken hostage after the war. She was held for eighty-two days before being freed in March 2006. "Somebody with her sensibilities, willing to take risks, is just the kind of reporter that is needed to explain the turbulence in Iraq to Americans," the *Boston Globe* editorialized shortly after she was kidnapped. The paper added that Iraqis who seize foreigners such as Carroll hurt the flow of information that otherwise would help the world better understand their troubled country.

"All of us together will have to learn how to reassemble

our broken world into a pattern so firm and so fair that another great war cannot be possible," Ernie Pyle wrote while sitting under an apple tree somewhere in France in August 1944, as combat in Europe turned irrevocably against the Germans. "To tell the simple truth, most of us over in France don't pretend to know the right answer. Submersion in war does not necessarily qualify a man to be the master of peace. All we can do is fumble and try once more—try out of the memory of our anguish—and be as tolerant with each other as we can."

As media analyst Walter Lippmann observed in his groundbreaking book *Public Opinion* more than eight decades ago, the news media are not substitutes for governments and institutions. Instead, he compared the press to the focused beam of a searchlight swinging around in the night, lighting one episode after another. "Men cannot do the work of the world by this light alone," he wrote. "They cannot govern by episodes, incidents, and eruptions. It is only when they work by a steady light of their own, that the press, when it is turned upon them, reveals a situation intelligible enough for a popular decision."

The military cannot, and should not, expect the media to switch off the beam when it happens across the ugliness of war or the errors of those who fight it. As the world grows ever more complex through communication, the prescription for democracy remains the same as it was during the Revolutionary War and Civil War, when the newspaper and magazine were the only mass media: More light, and less heat, upon the issues and actions of war and peace.

More light.

CHAPTER ONE

1   *"After reading this"*: Charles Belmont Davis, ed., *Adventures and Letters of Richard Harding Davis* (New York: Charles Scribner's Sons, 1917), 252.

Seven civilian journalists per publication: Susan D. Moeller, *Shooting War: Photography and the American Experience in Combat* (New York: Basic Books, 1989), 47–48.

2   *"Make myself rich"*: Charles Belmont Davis, ed., 232.

"Roosevelt, mounted": Arthur Lubow, *The Reporter Who Would Be King: A Biography of Richard Harding Davis* (New York: Charles Scribner's Sons, 1992), 185.

"I recognize that": William R. Shafter, "The Capture of Santiago de Cuba," *The Century Illustrated Monthly Magazine,* February 1899, 615.

3   *The navy cut:* Jeffery A. Smith, *War and Press Freedom: The Problem of Prerogative Power* (New York: Oxford University Press, 1999), 122.

"Right in the thick": Jack London, "Japanese Officers Consider Everything a Military Secret," *San Francisco Examiner,* 26 June 1904, 1.

Within four miles: Richard Harding Davis, *Notes of a War Correspondent* (New York: Charles Scribner's Sons, 1911), 220.

4   *By leaking news: Regulations for Press Correspondents,* n.p., 1904, box 20, folder 1, Jack and Charmian London Papers, Special Collections, Utah State University, Logan.

"Like standing outside": Frederick Palmer, *With Kuroki in Manchuria* (New York: Charles Scribner's Sons, 1906), 221.

"Prisoner and suspected spy": Lubow, 239.

8 *Benjamin Harris wrote:* Margaret A. Blanchard, ed., *History of the Mass Media in the United States: An Encyclopedia* (Chicago: Fitzroy Dearborn, 1998), 544.

"Their peril": Jack A. Gottschalk, "'Consistent with Security' . . . A History of American Military Press Censorship," *Communications and the Law* 5, Summer 1983, 35.

9 *"By influencing":* Carol Sue Humphrey, "The Vagaries of Original Intent," paper presented to American Journalism Historians Association conference, October 2000, 4.

"On the nineteenth": Nathaniel Lande, *Dispatches from the Front: News Accounts of American Wars, 1776–1991* (New York: Henry Holt, 1995), 8–9.

10 *Paine's "Crisis" essays:* Carol Sue Humphrey, *The Revolutionary Era: Primary Documents on Events from 1776 to 1800* (Westport, Conn.: Greenwood, 2003), 36–57.

John Mein, who published: Blanchard, ed., 38.

As delegates debated: Jeffery A. Smith, 28–29.

11 *"What is the liberty":* Alexander Hamilton, James Madison, and John Jay, *The Federalist: A Commentary on the Constitution of the United States* (New York: Tudor, 1937), 156–57.

"Few of us": Humphrey, "Vagaries," 17.

12 *Forbidding "prior restraint":* Jeffery A. Smith, 31.

"Clear and present danger": Schenck v. United States, 249 U.S. 47 (1919), 52.

"Both the government's ability": Jeffery A. Smith, 35.

13 *"False, scandalous and malicious":* Mitchell Stephens, *A History of News: From the Drum to the Satellite* (New York: Penguin, 1988), 199.

"The president's posterior": Humphrey, *Revolutionary Era,* 323, 330.

15 *4,000 pages an hour:* Stephens, 204.

100,000 copies: Brayton Harris, *Blue and Gray in Black and White: Newspapers in the Civil War* (Washington: Brassey's, 1999), 11–12.

"Of time and space": Martha A. Sandweiss et al., *Eyewitness to War: Prints and Daguerreotypes of the Mexican War, 1846–1848* (Fort Worth, Texas: Amon Carter Museum, 1989), 16.

American papers quadrupled: Harris, 9.

Meanwhile, literacy rates: Blanchard, ed., 315.

16   *"The organ of no faction":* Richard Kluger, *The Paper: The Life and Death of the* New York Herald Tribune (New York: Alfred A. Knopf, 1986), 34.

Bennett hired: George Wilkins Kendall, *Dispatches from the Mexican War* (Norman: University of Oklahoma Press, 1999), 11.

Rely on steamships: Blanchard, ed., 389.

17   *More than a dozen:* Kendall, 8, 12, 16.

Three celebrated reporters: Sandweiss et al., 6.

Worth cited Kendall: Kendall, 19.

18   *Killed a Mexican officer:* Michael S. Sweeney, *From the Front: The Story of War Featuring Correspondents' Chronicles* (Washington: National Geographic Press, 2002), 26–27.

"Contend that no result": Lande, 75, 78.

He documented: Kendall, 19.

Polk's official newspaper: Jeffery A. Smith, 94–95.

Thirteen years after: Phillip Knightley, *The First Casualty: From the Crimea to Vietnam—The War Correspondent as Hero, Propagandist, and Myth Maker* (New York: Harcourt Brace Jovanovich, 1975), 20.

19   *Confederate Congress forbade:* M. L. Stein, *Under Fire: The Story of American War Correspondents* (New York: Julian Messner, 1968), 19.

Condemned drunkenness: Ford Risley, "Peter Alexander: Confederate Chronicler and Conscience," *American Journalism* 15:1 (Winter 1998), 35–50.

Editors censored: J. Cutler Andrews, *The South Reports the Civil War* (Pittsburgh: University of Pittsburgh Press, 1985), 439–40.

20 *Congress authorized Lincoln:* Jeffery A. Smith, 99–100.
Fifty-seventh article of war: Ibid., 105.
He regularly scanned: Stein, 17.

21 *He jailed reporters:* Jeffery A. Smith, 100–102.
One recent study: David T. Z. Mindich, *Just the Facts: How "Objectivity" Came to Define American Journalism* (New York: New York University Press, 1998), 64–94.
"Relics of history": Jeffery A. Smith, 104, 110.
"They come into camp": Stein, 18.
Shuttered for two days: Gottschalk, 36.

22 *"Sensationalism and exaggeration":* J. Cutler Andrews, *The North Reports the Civil War* (Pittsburgh: University of Pittsburgh Press, 1955), 640.
"More harm": "Army Correspondents," *New York Times,* 25 August 1862, 4.
Ready market arose: William A. Frassanito, *Antietam: The Photographic Legacy of America's Bloodiest Day* (New York: Charles Scribner's Sons, 1976), 25.

23 *3,000 Civil War sketches:* Knightley, *Crimea to Vietnam,* 20.
"Mr. Brady has done": "Brady's Photographs," *New York Times,* 20 October 1862, 5.

24 *Wicked traitors:* Alexander Gardner, *Gardner's Photographic Sketch Book of the Civil War* (New York: Dover, 1959), plates 35, 94.
Gardner also repositioned: William A. Frassanito, *Gettysburg: A Journey in Time* (New York: Charles Scribner's Sons, 1975), passim.
"Only the press": Hazel Dicken-Garcia, *Journalistic Standards in Nineteenth-Century America* (Madison: University of Wisconsin Press, 1989), 51.
"Herein lies a danger": Ibid., 9.

25 *American newspapers competed:* Ibid., 54.

26 *"Amazon" warriors:* Joyce Milton, *The Yellow Kids: Foreign Correspondence in the Heyday of Yellow Journalism* (New York: Harper and Row, 1989), 89–90.

Newsreels also were faked: Raymond Fielding, *The American Newsreel, 1911–1967* (Norman: University of Oklahoma Press, 1972), 31–33.

27   *Watched the body of:* Moeller, 59–60.
   "I could go on": Charles Belmont Davis, ed., 243–44.

28   *"The People's War":* Moeller, 30.
   "The Great Reporter": Milton, 58.

29   *Moving to New York:* Lubow, 7–12, 40–47.
   "To sleep in the wet": Richard Harding Davis, *Notes,* 13–14.

30   *"Seriously apologized":* Lubow, 147–48.
   Journalists ran guns: Moeller, 49.
   "A splendid fight": James Creelman, *On the Great Highway* (Boston: Lothrop, 1901), 212.
   "Can't you mind": David Nasaw, *The Chief: The Life of William Randolph Hearst* (Boston: Houghton Mifflin, 2000), 139.
   Davis directed: Lubow, 175–78.
   "I thought": Charles Belmont Davis, ed., 225.
   Davis entered the town: Richard Harding Davis, *Notes,* 108–12.
   "Merry war": Charles Belmont Davis, ed., 246.

31   *"Nobody dares":* Milton, 279.
   Too inflammatory: Ibid., 334.
   Public opinion swung: Jeffery A. Smith, 122.

CHAPTER TWO

35   *"If people really":* Knightley, *Crimea to Vietnam,* 109.

36   *"First press agents' war":* "The Press Agents' War," *New York Times,* 9 September 1914, 8.

37   *"Efforts to curtail":* James R. Mock, *Censorship 1917* (New York: Da Capo Press, 1972), 24.
   Slipped out of port: Stewart Halsey Ross, *Propaganda for War: How the United States Was Conditioned to Fight the Great War of 1914–1918* (Jefferson, N.C.: McFarland, 1996), 27–28.
   "It all turns on": Ibid., 29.

38 *Poll in November:* H. C. Peterson, *Propaganda for War: The Campaign against American Neutrality, 1914–1917* (Norman: University of Oklahoma Press, 1939), 167.

Papered the United States: Ibid., 16.

Lists of names: Philip M. Taylor, *Munitions of the Mind: A History of Propaganda from the Ancient World to the Present Era* (Manchester, England: Manchester University Press, 1995), 177–78.

"The pro-Ally": Peterson, 16, 24.

39 *Dispatched a British officer:* Knightley, *Crimea to Vietnam,* 86–88.

To guarantee fluency: Emmet Crozier, *American Reporters on the Western Front, 1914–1918* (New York: Oxford University Press, 1959), 57.

"Only real war news": Nathan A. Haverstock, *Fifty Years at the Front: The Life of War Correspondent Frederick Palmer* (Washington: Brassey's, 1996), 164, 174.

40 *Three main topics:* James Morgan Read, *Atrocity Propaganda 1914–1919* (New Haven, Conn.: Yale University Press, 1941), 3, 199–214.

41 *Deliberately switched the captions:* Harold D. Lasswell, *Propaganda Technique in the World War* (New York: Peter Smith, 1938), 207.

Kadaververwertungsanstalt: Knightley, *Crimea to Vietnam,* 105–6.

42 *"After spending two weeks":* Peterson, 49.

"As for Uhlans": Irvin S. Cobb, *Paths of Glory: Impressions of War Written at and near the Front* (New York: George H. Doran Company, 1915), 111–12.

43 *1,200 statements:* Knightley, *Crimea to Vietnam,* 83–84.

Headline "German Atrocities": "German Atrocities Are Proved, Finds Bryce Committee," *New York Times,* 13 May 1915, 6.

Conveniently disappeared: Knightley, *Crimea to Vietnam,* 84.

44 *"The Proper Relationship":* Jeffery A. Smith, 131.

"Furnish information": Michael L. Carlebach, *American Photojournalism Comes of Age* (Washington, D.C.: Smithsonian Institution Press, 1997), 84–85.

45 *"Systematic falsification":* Stephen Vaughn, *Holding Fast the Inner Lines* (Chapel Hill: University of North Carolina Press, 1980), 9–10.

46 *"Verdict of mankind":* Josephus Daniels, *The Wilson Era: Years of War and After, 1917–1923* (Chapel Hill: University of North Carolina Press, 1946), 224–25.

Pamphlet "The German Whisper": Vaughn, 26.

Only 73,000: Knightley, *Crimea to Vietnam,* 122.

"No part of the great war": George Creel, *The Creel Report: Complete Report of the Chairman of the Committee on Public Information* (New York: Da Capo Press, 1972), 2.

75 million copies: George Creel, *Rebel at Large: Recollections of Fifty Crowded Years* (New York: G. P. Putnam's Sons, 1947), 164.

Coordinated and released: Creel, *Creel Report,* 2–6.

47 *First daily newspaper:* Ross, 230.

An average of six pounds: Vaughn, 194.

Accuracy of only four: George Creel, *How We Advertised America* (New York: Harper and Brothers, 1920), 50.

"Mr. Citizen": Committee on Public Information, "The Kaiserite in America," n.d., Special Collections, Harold B. Lee Library, Brigham Young University, Provo, Utah.

48 *Creel sent a letter:* Ross, 240–41.

"Has been guilty of atrocities": Harvey O'Higgins, "The Daily German Lie," n.d., CPI-1CI, entry 15, box 1, "Propaganda Reports" folder, Committee on Public Information, Record Group 63, National Archives, College Park, Md.

49 *Edited by Wilson:* Jeffery A. Smith, 139.

"It was not servants": Creel, *How We Advertised,* 17.

50 *"Above all, I wish":* Ross, 227.

Creel also roared: Jeffery A. Smith, 140.

Espionage Act of 1917: United States, *Laws, etc. (United States Statutes at Large)* (Washington, D.C.: Government Printing Office, 1937–) 40:1, 291 (hereafter *Laws*).

The "Big Stick": Daniels, 224.

50 *Many lost:* Lindsay Rogers, "Freedom of the Press in the United States," *Contemporary Review* 114 (August 1918): 177–83.

Among the victims: Jeffery A. Smith, 132.

51 *"Clear and present danger":* Schenck v. United States, 249 U.S. 47 (1919), 52.

The Sedition Act: Laws 40:1, 553.

Justice Department prosecuted: Zechariah Chafee Jr., *Free Speech in the United States* (New York: Atheneum, 1969), 79.

Trading with the Enemy: Laws 40:1, 413, 426.

52 *Failure to translate:* John D. Stevens, *Shaping the First Amendment: The Development of Free Expression* (Beverly Hills, Calif.: Sage Publications, 1982), 49.

"Constitution was adopted": Milwaukee Social Democratic Publishing Co. v. Burleson, 255 U.S. 407 (1921), 414.

"Convey the truth": Knightley, *Crimea to Vietnam,* 124.

Without military escorts: Moeller, 112.

Sam Browne belts: Crozier, 140.

53 *"As make a snapshot":* Moeller, 106, 110.

Pershing decided to allow: Ibid., 113–15.

"Unnecessary and unwarranted": Carlebach, 97.

54 *Not one photograph:* Moeller, 136.

House recommended Palmer: Haverstock, 192–96.

55 *"Some new way of killing":* Frederick Palmer, *My Second Year of the War* (New York: Dodd, Mead, 1917), 44.

"More and more": Frederick Palmer, *The Folly of Nations* (New York: Dodd, Mead, 1921), 312, 307.

Palmer's background: Haverstock, 3–12, 276.

56 *"You can't wrestle":* Ibid., 66, 62.

"Let nothing go": Jeffery A. Smith, 122–23.

"Following the same ratio": Haverstock, 198.

57 *Listed more than thirty:* Crozier, 279–81.

Had their credentials suspended: Ibid., 191–93.

58 *"Supply Blunders":* Knightley, *Crimea to Vietnam,* 130.

58   *Grateful French civilians:* Crozier, 190, 276.

59   *"The inculcation of hate":* Palmer, *Folly of Nations,* 316–22.
His last official act: Haverstock, 199–201.

60   *"If the angel":* George Seldes, *Witness to a Century: Encounters with the Noted, the Notorious, and the Three SOBs* (New York: Ballantine Books, 1987), 97.
Hindenburg answered: Crozier, 273–74.
"The American infantry": Seldes, 98–99.

61   *Hindenburg's frank admission:* Crozier, 277.

CHAPTER THREE

63   *"Principal battle":* Gerd Horten, *Radio Goes to War: The Cultural Politics of Propaganda during World War II* (Berkeley: University of California Press, 2002), 52.
"Secrecy is essential": George Creel, "The Plight of the Last Censor," *Collier's,* 24 May 1941, 13.
"Almost no issues": American Civil Liberties Union, *Liberty on the Home Front in the Fourth Year of the War* (New York: ACLU, 1945), 45.

64   *"Best-run bureau":* "U.S., British Censors in Harmony," *Editor and Publisher,* 15 April 1944, 10.
Roosevelt "liked conflict": Doris Kearns Goodwin, *No Ordinary Time: Franklin and Eleanor Roosevelt: The Home Front in World War II* (New York: Simon and Schuster, 1994), 24.
"I am a juggler": Ibid., 137.
Exposés of Britain's: Allan M. Winkler, *The Politics of Propaganda: The Office of War Information 1942–1945* (New Haven, Conn.: Yale University Press, 1978), 4.

65   *Institute for Propaganda:* Garth S. Jowett and Victoria O'Donnell, *Propaganda and Persuasion* (Thousand Oaks, Calif.: Sage Publications, 1999), 231–33.
Roosevelt decided to split: Betty Houchin Winfield, *FDR and the News Media* (New York: Columbia University Press, 1994), 155.

66   *Blurred lines of authority:* Frederick S. Voss, *Reporting the War: The Journalistic Coverage of World War II* (Washington, D.C.: Smithsonian Institution Press, 1994), 20–21.

"If anything, he thought": Francis Biddle, *In Brief Authority* (New York: Doubleday, 1962), 226.

"The constant free flow": Winfield, 231–33.

67   *War Department began limiting:* "Virtual News Censorship Set by War Department," *New York Times,* 14 June 1940, 12.

Knox issued 5,000: Michael S. Sweeney, *Secrets of Victory: The Office of Censorship and the American Press and Radio in World War II* (Chapel Hill: University of North Carolina Press, 2001), 23–26.

It sent Roosevelt: Ibid., 28.

68   *"I told Edgar":* Drew Pearson, *Drew Pearson Diaries* (New York: Holt, Rinehart, and Winston, 1974), 93.

69   *Chief on the list:* Sweeney, *Secrets,* 76–78.

More than 17,000: Patrick S. Washburn, *A Question of Sedition: The Federal Government's Investigation of the Black Press during World War II* (New York: Oxford University Press, 1986), 60.

70   *"A rare day" in 1942:* Washburn, *A Question,* 54–59, 82, 87, 96.

It supervised two kinds: Edward N. Doan, "Organization and Operation of the Office of Censorship," *Journalism Quarterly* 21, September 1944, 200.

71   *Chastised "volunteer firemen":* Byron Price, "Memoir" (unpublished), 424–25, Byron Price Papers, Archives Division, State Historical Society of Wisconsin, Madison.

Necessary "that prohibitions against": Franklin D. Roosevelt, *Complete Presidential Press Conferences of Franklin D. Roosevelt,* vol. 18 (New York: Da Capo Press, 1972), 369–70.

Those words had been written: Price, 315.

72   *Only one journalist:* Sweeney, *Secrets,* 114–15.

Wartime public opinion: Daniel Katz et al., eds., *Public Opinion and Propaganda* (New York: Dryden Press, 1954), 43.

72 *A Supreme Court ruling:* Near v. Minnesota, 283 U.S. 697 (1931).

73 *Price's background:* Sweeney, *Secrets,* 37–38.
"No such thing": Price, 286.

74 *AP as his "religion":* Current Biography, 1942, s.v. "Price, Byron."
He loved reading: Sweeney, *Secrets,* 37.
He "always considered": Current Biography.
He enjoyed nothing more: Sweeney, *Secrets,* 37.
He set up: Doan, 205–10.

75 *Lists of sensitive topics:* Office of Censorship, *Code of Wartime Practices for the American Press* (Washington, D.C.: Government Printing Office, 15 January 1942).
Office of Censorship published: Theodore F. Koop, *Weapon of Silence* (Chicago: University of Chicago Press, 1946), 169–70.
One ad hoc memo: Sweeney, *Secrets,* 200.
News of atomic research: Patrick S. Washburn, "The Office of Censorship's Attempt to Control Press Coverage of the Atomic Bomb during World War II," *Journalism Monographs* 120, 1990, passim.
Bomb's successful production: Sweeney, *Secrets,* 152–53, 204–5.

76 *"If you blow off":* Price, 479.
Groves released one: Sweeney, *Secrets,* 205.
News reports focusing: Robert Jay Lifton and Greg Mitchell, *Hiroshima in America: Fifty Years of Denial* (New York: G. P. Putnam's Sons, 1995), 44–55.
George Weller defied: Amy Goodman and David Goodman, "The Hiroshima Cover-Up," *Mother Jones,* 5 August 2005, www.motherjones.com/commentary/columns/2005/08 /hiroshima.html.

77 *"Japanese are still":* William L. Laurence, "U.S. Bomb Site Belies Tokyo Tales," *New York Times,* 12 September 1945, 1, 4.
"Voice of the Dove": Price, 223.
Missionaries were respected: Sweeney, *Secrets,* 54–56.

78 *It issued a news release:* Ibid., 61–62.

78 *Price had the legal authority:* Price, 341–44.

79 *His daughter Anna:* Goodwin, 519–21.
       Biggest challenge: Sweeney, *Secrets,* 165–74.

80 *"Customary rule":* "Editors Fear Public Distrust from Too Strict
       a Censorship," *Editor and Publisher,* 10 October 1942, 3.

81 *Code restricted radio:* Office of Censorship, *Code of Wartime
       Practices for American Broadcasters* (Washington, D.C.: Gov-
       ernment Printing Office, 15 January 1942).
       Elson kept broadcasting: Stanley P. Richardson to R. E. Spencer,
       29 August 1942, box 351, "Weather Reports/Sports"
       folder, Office of Censorship, Record Group 216, National
       Archives, College Park, Md.
       "Umpires have called": J. Harold Ryan to Maynard Marquardt,
       16 July 1943, Ibid.

82 *Five children:* Lisa Murphy, "One Small Moment," *American
       History* 30, June 1995, 66–70.
       Restrictions remained: Sweeney, *Secrets,* 194.

83 *Advisers such as Stimson:* Horten, 41.
       "Soften up": Holly Cowan Shulman, *The Voice of America: Pro-
       paganda and Democracy* (Madison: University of Wisconsin
       Press, 1990), 14–18, 25–26.

84 *Office followed "the 'strategy of truth'":* Clayton D. Laurie, *The
       Propaganda Warriors: America's Crusade against Nazi Germany*
       (Lawrence: University of Kansas Press, 1996), 64–65.
       "Seems to boil down": Winkler, 29–31.

85 *Commentator "with the funny voice":* Ibid., 31–34.

86 *Davis as "clear-headed, sensible":* "Man of Sense," *Time,* 22 June
       1942, 21.
       Rhodes scholar: Winkler, 36.
       OWI to "formulate and carry out": Ibid., 48–49.

87 *"Admiral King's idea":* Ibid., 49–50.
       Ninety percent: Horten, 118.

88 *For example, Benny supported:* Ibid., 122, 131–32.

88   *"Save the grease":* Kathleen E. R. Smith, *God Bless America: Tin Pan Alley Goes to War* (Lexington: University Press of Kentucky, 2003), 118–19.

Were "escapist and delusive": Winkler, 58.

89   *Office of Censorship could deny:* Clayton D. Koppes and Gregory D. Black, *Hollywood Goes to War: How Politics, Profits, and Propaganda Shaped World War II Movies* (New York: Free Press, 1987), 125–26.

Hollywood remained defensive: Taylor, *Munitions,* 230.

Tarzan defeating "Nadzies": Winkler, 59.

Edward G. Robinson: Robert Fyne, *The Hollywood Propaganda of World War II* (Lanham, Md.: Scarecrow Press, 1994), 149.

Of the sixty-one: George H. Roeder Jr., *The Censored War: American Visual Experience during World War II* (New Haven, Conn.: Yale University Press, 1993), 21.

Hollywood's greatest: Taylor, *Munitions,* 231.

90   *Davis had difficulties:* Winkler, 39–40.

"We are in a sense": Roger Burlingame, *Don't Let Them Scare You: The Life and Times of Elmer Davis* (Philadelphia: J. B. Lippincott, 1961), 197.

"We are leaving": Ibid., 64–65.

91   *"Making bricks":* Ibid., 65–72.

92   *"From this we can":* Herbert Brucker, *Freedom of Information* (New York: Macmillan, 1949), 183.

CHAPTER FOUR

93   *"It matters":* "The American Purpose," *Life,* 5 July 1943, 39.

94   *Roughly 300 million:* Charles J. Rolo, *Radio Goes to War: The "Fourth Front"* (New York: G. P. Putnam's Sons, 1942), 12.

83 percent: Voss, 120.

95   *"Singing and tossing":* Joseph E. Persico, *Edward R. Murrow: An American Original* (New York: McGraw-Hill, 1988), 136–38.

96   *"Listener's sensation":* Ibid., 136.

Only 16 percent: Sweeney, *From the Front,* 181.

96   *"More than five hundred"*: Persico, 230.

97   *Hollywood movies helped:* Vicki Goldberg, *Margaret Bourke-White: A Biography* (New York: Harper and Row, 1986), 173.
By 1940: Roeder, 4.
Content analysis found: Fielding, 288.

98   *Transmission of halftones:* Goldberg, 173.
Readership to 17.3 million: Goldberg, 229.
Three years later: Roeder, 4.
"Total war is fought": Peter Maslowski, *Armed with Cameras: The American Military Photographers of World War II* (New York: Free Press,1993), 7.
Military censors checked: Barney Oldfield, *Never a Shot in Anger* (New York: Duell, Sloan, and Pearce, 1956), 139.
1,646 accredited: John Hohenberg, *Foreign Correspondence: The Great Reporters and Their Times* (New York: Columbia University Press, 1964), 383.
127 women: Penny Colman, *Where the Action Was: Women War Correspondents in World War II* (New York: Crown, 2002), viii.

99   *As the "mud-rain":* Ernie Pyle, *Here Is Your War* (New York: Henry Holt, 1943), 247.
"I haven't written": Ibid., 304.

100   *Men fought better:* Lee G. Miller, *The Story of Ernie Pyle* (New York: Viking, 1950), 227.
Pyle "helped": James Tobin, *Ernie Pyle's War: America's Eyewitness to World War II* (New York: Free Press, 1997), 2.
Achieving nearly universal: Ibid., 5–56.

101   *"Chaplain said":* Ernie Pyle, *Brave Men* (New York: Henry Holt, 1944), 50.

102   *One soldier "squatted down":* Ibid., 156.
Entire front page: Tobin, 137, 218.
"At this spot": Lee G. Miller, *An Ernie Pyle Album: Indiana to Ie Shima* (New York: William Sloan Associates, 1946), 156.
All told: Moeller, 183.

103 *She defied regulations:* Nancy Caldwell Sorel, *The Women Who Wrote the War* (New York: Arcade, 1999), 229–30.

Gellhorn described: Carl Rollyson, *Nothing Ever Happens to the Brave: The Story of Martha Gellhorn* (New York: St. Martin's Press, 1990), 203–4.

104 *News of a single atrocity:* Knightley, *Crimea to Vietnam,* 294.

"We edited ourselves": John Steinbeck, *Once There Was a War* (New York: Penguin, 1986), xvii.

105 *"Yellow bastard":* Sweeney, *Secrets,*156.

Five days later: Knightley, *Crimea to Vietnam,* 320.

Eisenhower said, "You men": Quentin Reynolds, *By Quentin Reynolds* (New York: Pyramid, 1964), 293.

Until Pearson learned: Sweeney, *Secrets,* 157–60.

106 *"Quasi-staff officers":* Knightley, *Crimea to Vietnam,* 315.

"Public opinion must be": Virgil Pinkley, "Eisenhower on Censorship," *Editor and Publisher,* 21 April 1945, 50.

"Tell the full truth": Dwight D. Eisenhower, *Crusade in Europe* (Garden City, N.Y.: Doubleday, 1948), 182.

"By the time you are": Margaret Bourke-White, *They Called It "Purple Heart Valley": A Chronicle of the War in Italy* (New York: Simon and Schuster, 1944), 14.

107 *Arbitrary rank:* Andrew Mendelson and C. Zoe Smith, "Part of the Team: *Life* Photographers and Their Symbiotic Relationship with the Military during World War II," *American Journalism* 12:3 (Summer 1995), 279.

"Senior Officers should not": Ibid., 280–81.

108 *Allowed "soft-gloving":* Pyle, *Here Is Your War,* 54.

Middleton wrote: Knightley, *Crimea to Vietnam,* 308.

"Hell of a beating": "Stillwell, After a 'Beating' in Burma, Would Hit Back," *New York Times,* 26 May 1942, 1.

Like Eisenhower, he: Voss, 29–30.

If journalists dared: Jeffery A. Smith, 158.

Press also underplayed: Voss, 26.

Even the names: Tobin, 233.

109 *Roberts listed the loss:* "Army News Policy," *Army and Navy Register,* 8 April 1944, 9.

Carrying ten tons: Michael A. Feeney, "Mustard as a Chemical Weapon," *Journal of Counterterrorism and Security International* 7:1 (Fall 2000), Lexis/Nexis.

Churchill insisted: Eric Niderost, "Deadly Luftwaffe Strike in the Adriatic," *World War II* 15:6 (February 2001), Academic Search Premier.

110 *Truman's endorsement:* Jeffery A. Smith, 164.

He had heard: A. J. Liebling, "The Wayward Press: The A.P. Surrender," *New Yorker,* 19 May 1945, 57.

"Absurdity of trying": Jeffery A. Smith, 164–65.

111 *"I do not think":* Liebling, 57.

"I pointed out": Walter Cronkite, *A Reporter's Life* (New York: Alfred A. Knopf, 1996), 100–101.

112 *"Voice-cast" copy:* Tobin, 137.

During the invasion: Oldfield, 60, 88–89.

Stanley Johnston witnessed: Sweeney, *Secrets,* 79.

113 *Johnston kept a copy:* Joseph Gies, *The Colonel of Chicago* (New York: E. P. Dutton, 1979), 208.

"Strength of the Japanese": "Navy Had Word of Jap Plan to Strike at Sea," *Chicago Tribune,* 7 June 1942, 1.

Roosevelt initially wanted: Richard Norton Smith, *The Colonel: The Life and Legend of Robert R. McCormick* (Boston: Houghton Mifflin, 1997), 433.

The president had his: "Biddle Attacks the Tribune," *Chicago Tribune,* 8 August 1943, 1.

114 *Code had remained readable:* Sweeney, *Secrets,* 82.

Military censorship of images: Mendelson and Smith, 284–85.

Entitled her to "take pictures": Bourke-White, 21.

Enjoyed raising eyebrows: Goldberg, passim.

115 *Film and caption material:* Bourke-White, 107.

Accredited photographers: Mendelson and Smith, 279.

Decided on a pool system: Moeller, 182.

116 *Reporters filed pool reports:* Burlingame, 246.

116 *"Chamber of Horrors":* Roeder, 1.
Stephen Early told reporters: Winfield, 192–93, 172.
Only photographs released: Moeller, 204–205, 234–35.

117 *Military authorities shocked:* Roeder, 10.
"Nourished the prevalent": Maslowski, 79.
Benefit of "an enlightened people": Roeder, 10–11.

118 *"I'm not arguing for":* Maslowski, 81.
Army Signal Corps restrictions: Voss, 19.
Three of the first photos: Moeller, 206.
"What shall we say?": "Three Americans," *Life,* 20 September 1943, 34.

119 *Dredge company worker's:* "Letters to the Editors," *Life,* 11 October 1943, 4.

120 *"Wounds that you can see":* Lawrence Grobel, *The Hustons* (New York: Avon Books, 1989), 273.

CHAPTER FIVE

121 *"Are you correspondents telling":* Marguerite Higgins, *War in Korea: The Report of a Woman Combat Correspondent* (Garden City, N.Y.: Doubleday, 1951), 84.

122 *"Most consistently raked":* Moeller, 288.
Described as the "most covered": Clarence R. Wyatt, *Paper Soldiers: The American Press and the Vietnam War* (New York: W. W. Norton, 1993), 129.

124 *Created presidential security:* David H. Morrissey, "Disclosure and Secrecy: Security Classification Executive Orders," *Journalism and Mass Communication Monographs* 161 (1997), 10–12.
"The safety and welfare": Jeffery A. Smith, 171–72, 175.
Journalists who angered: Ibid., 187–88.

125 *Their stories vetted:* William Prochnau, *Once Upon a Distant War* (New York: Vintage Books, 1995), 360.
Their bosses threatened: Morley Safer, *Flashbacks: On Returning to Vietnam* (New York: St. Martin's, 1991), 137–38.

125 *Nixon circulated lists:* Jeffery A. Smith, 187.

Report made three key points: "NSC-68: A Report to the National Security Council," *Naval War College Review* 27 (May–June 1975), 51–108.

126 *Government had the right:* Malcolm W. Browne, *Muddy Boots and Red Socks: A Reporter's Life* (New York: Times Books, 1993), 96.

"When the president does it": Jeffery A. Smith, 188.

"Korea ripped away": Higgins, 16.

127 *More than 75 percent:* Moeller, 254.

No war in Asia: Michael Emery, *On the Front Lines* (Washington, D.C.: American University Press, 1995), 89.

128 *"My God":* Higgins, 62.

"Just give me": Ibid., 84, 62, 115, 152.

Lifelong hatred: Virginia Elwood-Akers, *Women War Correspondents in the Vietnam War, 1961–1975* (Metuchen, N.J.: Scarecrow Press, 1988), 20.

129 *First flight into Seoul:* Sweeney, *From the Front,* 230.

Walker banished her: Emery, 102.

"Ban on women": Elwood-Akers, 21.

"Only newsman": Knightley, *Crimea to Vietnam,* 339.

Nearly 300 received: Melvin B. Voorhees, *Korean Tales* (New York: Simon and Schuster, 1952), 81.

Seventeen died: Hohenberg, 390.

130 *Sparks carried a gun:* Higgins, 131.

Only one cable connected: Ibid., 98.

Nondisclosure of "any such information": Moeller, 279.

131 *Slipups occurred:* Higgins, 96.

AP's Tom Lambert: Jeffery A. Smith, 170.

"Essentially responsible": Moeller, 298–99, 279.

"Hundreds" of security: Voorhees, 104.

132 *Refugees died by the score:* Charles J. Hanley et al., *The Bridge at No Gun Ri* (New York: Henry Holt, 2001), 164–65.

132 *Soldiers slaughtered civilians:* Charles Grutzner, "Stranded Enemy Soldiers Merge with Refugee Crowds in Korea," *New York Times,* 30 September 1950, 3.

Army found sufficient: Nancy Ethiel, ed., *The Military, the Media, and the Administration: An Irregular Triangle* (Chicago: McCormick Tribune Foundation, 2002), 163.

"Go back!": Persico, 289–92.

"Clear of error": Moeller, 279.

133 *Stories censored by:* Jeffery A. Smith, 171.

"Pinpoint" aerial: Moeller, 276.

"Many of us who sent": Jeffery A. Smith, 171.

First investigation occurred: Drew Pearson, "MacArthur Puzzles Pentagon," *Washington Post,* 30 December 1950, 9B.

134 *They ended the inquiry:* D. M. Ladd to "The Director," 24 April and 4 May 1951, Federal Bureau of Investigation (FBI) "Drew Pearson" file 65–59762, section 5.

Pearson said his column: Drew Pearson, "Korea Differences Recounted," *Washington Post,* 8 January 1951, 11B.

135 *Western briefing officer:* Knightley, *Crimea to Vietnam,* 353–54.

Television had worked its way: Moeller, 303.

136 *Murrow focused:* Persico, 322.

Place he picked: James Reston, *Deadline: A Memoir* (New York: Random House, 1991), 291.

137 *"War was fought":* Safer, 21.

"In view of the impact": Moeller, 349.

138 *South Vietnam expelled:* Emery, 134–38.

They added a new twist: Wyatt, 159.

Had to be accredited: Ibid., 143.

139 *Forty-five journalists:* Knightley, *Crimea to Vietnam,* 405.

Accreditation card allowed: James Landers, *The Weekly War: Newsmagazines and Vietnam* (Columbia: University of Missouri Press, 2004), 85.

140 *"All of these battles":* David Halberstam, *The Powers That Be* (Urbana: University of Illinois Press, 1975), 352.

140 *"Rounding Le Loi":* Michael Herr, *Dispatches* (New York: Avon, 1978), 37.

Sheehan got a lesson: Prochnau, 53.

141 *"You're right, Admiral":* Harrison E. Salisbury, *Without Fear or Favor: The* New York Times *and Its Times* (New York: Times Books, 1980), 42.

"Why can't you get": Browne, 163.

142 *"Shelling its own troops":* Prochnau, 356–57.

Ran Halberstam's account: "Two Versions of the Crisis in Vietnam," *New York Times,* 23 August 1963, 1.

Within three days: Neil Sheehan, *A Bright Shining Lie: John Paul Vann and America in Vietnam* (New York: Random House, 1988), 350.

"By and large accurate": Prochnau, 360.

Kennedy asked: Halberstam, 445–50.

Analysis of Halberstam's: Daniel C. Hallin, *The "Uncensored War": The Media and Vietnam* (Berkeley: University of California Press, 1986), 40–43.

Known as Cable 1006: William M. Hammond, *United States Army in Vietnam: Public Affairs—The Military and the Media, 1962–1968* (Washington, D.C.: Government Printing Office, 1988), 15.

143 *"What worried me":* Browne, 95.

"Mr. President": Harold W. Chase and Allen H. Lerman, eds., *Kennedy and the Press: The News Conferences* (New York: Thomas Y. Crowell, 1965), 154.

"Maximum candor": Hammond, 82.

144 *One of the more controversial:* Safer, 138–52.

"Have to do something": Browne, 12.

145 *"The power and impact":* Cass D. Howell, "War, Television, and Public Opinion," *Military Review* 67: 2 (February 1987), 72.

A content analysis: Hammond, 238.

Commonly, what passed: Wyatt, 148.

145 *"No empirical evidence":* Wallace B. Eberhard, "A Familiar Refrain but Slightly Out of Tune," *Military Review* 67: 2 (February 1987), 82.

146 *Louis Harris poll:* Wyatt, 148.
   Body counts mattered: Hammond, 262.
   Journalists' interest in sensation: Peter Braestrup, *Big Story* (Boulder, Colo.: Westview Press, 1977), 711–16.
   Months before Tet: Landers, 8, 187.

147 *To Vietnam "a mistake":* Ibid., 182.
   "If I've lost Cronkite": Cronkite, 258.

148 *Government failed to meet:* New York Times v. United States, 403 U.S. 713 (1971).
   Similarly, no journalist: Browne, 99.
   Brokers "forgot at least two": Hammond, 387–88.

CHAPTER SIX

151 *"I had more guns":* "*Newsweek*'s Troops in the Persian Gulf," *Newsweek,* 11 March 1991, 4.
   "If there was one 'lesson'": Philip M. Taylor, *War and the Media: Propaganda and Persuasion in the Gulf War* (Manchester, England: Manchester University Press, 1998), 2.

152 *Discovered the media's worst:* Molly Moore, *A Woman at War: Storming Kuwait with the U.S. Marines* (New York: Charles Scribner's Sons, 1993), 60.
   As a soldier in Vietnam: H. Norman Schwarzkopf, *It Doesn't Take a Hero* (New York: Bantam Books, 1992), 120–21.

153 *Journalists to "help in leading":* Phillip Knightley, *The First Casualty: The War Correspondent as Hero and Myth Maker from the Crimea to Iraq* (Baltimore, Md.: Johns Hopkins University Press, 2004), 478–79.
   Journalists found their reports: Paul Eddy et al., *War in the Falklands: The Full Story* (New York: Harper and Row, 1982), 217.

154 *Called "favorable objectivity":* Arthur A. Humphries, "Two Routes to the Wrong Destination: Public Affairs in the South Atlantic War," *Naval War College Review* 36:3 (May–June 1983), 71.

Even the press offices: John R. MacArthur, *Second Front: Censorship and Propaganda in the Gulf War* (New York: Hill and Wang, 1992), 141.

The navy blockaded: Schwarzkopf, 257.

155 *"I did not want":* Cronkite, 266.

"We would have blown": Schwarzkopf, 258.

Cuban "professional soldiers": Cronkite, 266.

"What really happened": MacArthur, 107.

156 *So-called Sidle Commission:* Ibid., 142.

"Reporters and editors alike": Peter Braestrup, *Battle Lines* (New York: Priority Press, 1985), 162.

157 *Upon arrival, the journalists:* James B. Brown, "Media Access to the Battlefield," *Military Review* 72:7 (July 1992), 13–14.

"Case in point": Robert E. Denton Jr., ed., *The Media and the Persian Gulf War* (Westport, Conn.: Praeger, 1993), 10.

158 *"None of them armed":* Lee Hockstader, "In Panama, Civilian Deaths Remain an Issue," *Washington Post,* 6 October 1990, A23.

159 *Comedy skit reportedly erased:* Jason DeParle, "Keeping the News in Step: Are the Pentagon's Gulf War Rules Here to Stay?" *New York Times,* 6 May 1991, A9.

"Privilege of remaining": Michael Kelly, *Martyrs' Day: Chronicle of a Small War* (New York: Random House, 1993), 33.

160 *Used 7,299 times, "more than":* Bradley S. Greenberg and Walter Gantz, eds., *Desert Storm and the Mass Media* (Cresskill, N.J.: Hampton Press, 1993), 77.

Bush referred to Vietnam: Taylor, *Munitions,* 287.

"Repeat, at all times.": Jason DeParle, "Long Series of Military Decisions Led to Gulf War Censorship," *New York Times,* 5 May 1991 1, 20.

161 *The original pool consisted:* Hedrick Smith, ed., *The Media and the Gulf War* (Washington, D.C.: Seven Locks Press, 1992), 36.

Swelled to nearly 800: Department of Defense, *Conduct of the Persian Gulf War: Final Report to Congress* (Washington, D.C.: Government Printing Office, April 1992), 652.

"Just speed bumps": Moore, 38, 45–46.

162 *"Change the oil":* Molly Moore and Howard Kurtz, "Sweating Out the Gulf Story," *Washington Post,* 18 September 1990, B1.

In Dhahran "to facilitate media": Department of Defense, 652.

"Breakfast at Tiffany's": Moore and Kurtz.

"We wanted to eat sand": Moore, 55.

163 *Cited "widespread abuses":* Associated Press, "Amnesty Report Says Iraqis Tortured and Killed Hundreds," *New York Times,* 20 December 1990, A21.

Variation of the story: MacArthur, 54–55.

It received a boost: "Excerpts from the Bush News Conference on the Budget and the Mideast," *New York Times,* 10 October 1990, A18.

"I volunteered": MacArthur, 56–59.

164 *Saying "although its team":* Ibid., 67, 70.

165 *Media outlets the "ground rules":* Mark Grossman, *Encyclopedia of the Persian Gulf War* (Santa Barbara, Calif: ABC-Clio, 1995), 180–83.

130 initial pool: Ibid., 179.

166 *"Material will be examined":* Ibid., 182.

"Something is definitely": Taylor, *War and Media,* 31, 91.

167 *"Get me on":* U.S. News & World Report, *The Unreported History of the Persian Gulf War* (New York: Times Books, 1992), 233.

"Skies over Baghdad": Peter Arnett, *Live from the Battlefield: From Vietnam to Baghdad, 35 Years in the World's War Zones* (New York: Simon and Schuster, 1994), 366–67.

By describing the fires: Jeffery A. Smith, 214.

168 *The CNN trio went off:* Arnett, 367–72.

168 *Arnett received permission:* Ibid., 385.

169 *"It became necessary":* Ibid., 255–57.
"I was in Baghdad": Hedrick Smith, ed., 331.
Being *"a conduit for Iraqi disinformation":* Arnett, 389.
Labeled *"al-Ban":* Hedrick Smith, ed., 324.
He gave some away: Arnett, 389.

170 *"It was not my job":* Ibid., 412–13.
Senator Alan Simpson: Howard Kurtz, "Sen. Simpson Calls Arnett 'Sympathizer'; CNN Reporter Blasted for Iraq Coverage," *Washington Post,* 8 February 1991, 1B.
Simpson later offered: Al Simpson, "The Word 'Sympathizer' Was Not a Good One," *New York Times,* 20 March 1991, 28A.
Thirty-four members: Arnett, 408.
"Aiding and abetting" Hussein: Patrick E. Tyler, "Schwarzkopf Says Truce Enabled Iraqis to Escape," *New York Times,* 27 March 1991, 9A.

171 *69 percent of Americans:* Greenberg and Gantz, eds., 233, 214.
During the weeks: Ibid., 249–54.
Less than 1 percent: Hedrick Smith, ed., 119.

172 *TV relied heavily:* W. Lance Bennett and David L. Paletz, eds., *Taken by Storm: The Media, Public Opinion, and U.S. Foreign Policy in the Gulf War* (Chicago: University of Chicago Press, 1994), 5.
"A guy was hit": DeParle, "Keeping the News."
Buried alive: MacArthur, 201.
Only 7 percent: Ibid., 161.

173 *Reporters asked to see:* DeParle, "Keeping the News."
Were "100 percent" effective: Knightley, *Crimea to Iraq,* 496.
Patriots' reputation suffered: Eric Schmitt, "U.S. Details Flaw in Patriot Missile," *New York Times,* 6 June 1991, 9A.
Debris from the exploding: Patrick E. Tyler, "Did Patriot Missiles Work? Not So Well, Scientists Say," *New York Times,* 17 April 1991, 11A.
Officers told House: Eric Schmitt, "Missile's War Record Revised," *New York Times,* 8 April 1992, 11A.

174 *Only one journalist:* Denton, ed., 15.

Pool members came to realize: Knightley, *Crimea to Iraq,* 490.

"You could get an angel": Taylor, *War and Media,* 52.

Defense Department's official report: Department of Defense, 655.

"Whenever I began interviewing": MacArthur, 170–71.

175 *"I never saw any organized":* Grossman, 64–65.

While 21 percent traveled: Department of Defense, 653.

Cranking out story after story: Moore, 309.

"You'll prevent us from": Robert Fisk, "Out of the Pool," *Mother Jones* 16:3 (May–June 1991), 58.

176 *Censors changed:* MacArthur, 192.

Veteran war reporter: Hedrick Smith, ed., 138–39.

To the military's credit: Ibid., 173.

Cheney suspended briefings: Moore, 200.

Fitzwater and Schwarzkopf: Hedrick Smith, ed., 388.

177 *McKeown of CBS:* Emery, 271.

"Worked over by a gang": Kelly, 184–85.

Until five years later: Sheldon Rampton and John Stauber, *Weapons of Mass Deception: The Uses of Propaganda in Bush's War in Iraq* (New York: Jeremy P. Tarcher/Penguin, 2003), 4–5.

Bob Simon of CBS: Bob Simon, *Forty Days* (New York: G. P. Putnam's Sons, 1992), 34.

Were told, falsely, the fighting: Jason DeParle, "17 News Executives Criticize U.S. for 'Censorship' of Gulf War Coverage," *New York Times,* 3 July 1991, A4.

178 *Coalition troops detained:* Knightley, *Crimea to Iraq,* 491.

"We have orders": Taylor, *War and Media,* 61.

"I thought, but didn't say": Schwarzkopf, 468.

Plaintiffs argued they sought: Hedrick Smith, ed., 391–402.

179 *"Who can say that during":* Ibid., 414.

CHAPTER SEVEN

181 *"When did we":* Peter Baker, "Inside View," *American Journalism Review* 25:4 (May 2003), 39.

181 *"I am not one":* Katherine M. Skiba, *Sister in the Band of Brothers: Embedded with the 101st Airborne in Iraq* (Lawrence: University of Kansas Press, 2005), 47.

182 *Six hundred accredited:* Bill Katovsky and Timothy Carlson, eds., *Embedded: The Media at War in Iraq* (Guilford, Conn.: Lyons Press, 2003), xiv.

"This is going to be": Rick Atkinson, *In the Company of Soldiers: A Chronicle of Combat* (New York: Henry Holt, 2004), 103.

183 *Nine in ten rated:* Brigitte L. Nacos, *Mass-Mediated Terrorism* (Lanham, Md.: Rowman and Littlefield, 2003), 51.

Support remained high: "TV Combat Fatigue on the Rise," Pew Research Center for the People and the Press, http://people-press.org/reports/pdf/178.pdf.

For example, a Pew: "War Coverage Praised, but Public Hungry for Other News," Pew Research Center for the People and the Press, http://peoplepress.org/reports/display.php3?ReportID=180.

Seventeen percent of Web: David Miller, ed., *Tell Me Lies: Propaganda and Media Distortion in the Attack on Iraq* (London: Pluto Press, 2004), 277.

Most popular Web site: Ibid., 277–78.

Iraq Body Count: Sarah Clark, "Counting Civilian Casualties," *American Journalism Review* 27:4 (August–September 2005), 12.

184 *"We are not just taking":* "ASD PA Clarke Meeting with Bureau Chiefs," *Department of Defense News Transcript,* 30 October 2002, www.defenselink.mil/transcripts/2003/t01152003_t0114bc.html.

Served "only to increase": William David Sloan and Emily Erickson Hoff, eds., *Contemporary Media Issues* (Northport, Ala.: Vision Press, 1998), 115.

185 *"He pulled the cover":* Ethiel, ed., 148.

186 *Journalists grumbled, however:* "ASD PA Clarke Meeting."

186 *Had less access to:* Neil Hickey, "Access Denied: Pentagon's War Reporting Rules Are Toughest Ever," *Columbia Journalism Review* 40:5 (January–February 2002), 26.

"We had greater": Ethiel, ed., 140–49.

187 *An Italian, a Spaniard:* Sweeney, *From the Front,* 311.

When Baker attempted: Baker, 39.

"Minimally restrictive" access: Katovsky and Carlson, eds., appendix.

188 *"We're supposed to be":* Joel Campagna, "Media Concerns about Covering the War," *Op-Ed Articles by CPJ Staff,* Committee to Protect Journalists, 19 March 2003, www .cpj.org/op_ed/Campagna19mar03.html.

"Quite shrewd": Rick Atkinson interview, 28 February 2005.

"Our ultimate strategic": Katovsky and Carlson, eds., appendix.

"Bearer must be escorted": Atkinson, *In the Company,* 43.

189 *"Media products will not":* Katovsky and Carlson, eds., appendix.

Cost of such gear: Philip Seib, *Beyond the Front Lines: How the News Media Cover a World Shaped by War* (New York: Palgrave Macmillan, 2004), 48.

190 *Pentagon encouraged journalists:* Katovsky and Carlson, eds., appendix.

Bloom combined mobile: Seib, *Beyond,* 49.

Images from his vehicle: "NBC's David Bloom Dies in Iraq," Cyberjournalist.Net, 7 April 2003, www.cyberjournalist.net /news/000081.php.

CNN unilateral reporter: Barb Palser, "Online Advances," *American Journalism Review* 25:4 (May 2003), 44.

191 *Freelancer Christopher Allbritton:* Seib, *Beyond,* 93.

"Whole city looked": Miller, ed., 282.

As "L. T. Smash": Seib, *Beyond,* 93.

192 *Web name CBFTW:* Daniel Schulman, "State of the Art: Their War," *Columbia Journalism Review* 44:3 (September–October 2005), 13.

192 *AP's caution paid off:* Anick Jesdanun, "Iraqis, U.S. Forces Restrict Sat Phones," *Editor and Publisher,* 3 April 2003, www .editorandpublisher.com/eandp/news/article_display .jsp?vnu_content_id=1857536.

"Whether you're a hawk": Peter Johnson, "Boot Camp Prepares Journalists for Iraq," *USA Today,* 11 December 2002, 3D.

193 *Participants mainly sat:* Katovsky and Carlson, eds., 111–13.
Reporter Katherine Skiba learned: Skiba, 2.
"The less time soldiers": Johnson, "Boot Camp."
Participants included: Gregg Zoroya, "Course Prepares Journalists in Art of War," *USA Today,* 15 March 2002, 4A.

194 *"If you don't tell":* Jay Price, "Soldiers Get Tips on Dealing with Media," *News and Observer,* 10 January 2005, www .newsobserver.com//nation_world/iraq/story/2008013 p-8388436c.html.
It included "Step 4": Atkinson, *In the Company,* 42.
920 embedding slots: Katovsky and Carlson, eds., 208.
Nearly as many as covered: Atkinson, *In the Company,* 41.

195 *Additional phalanx:* Michael Massing, *Now They Tell Us: American Press and Iraq* (New York: New York Review of Books, 2004), 4–6.
"Go wherever you want": Katovsky and Carlson, eds., 115, 121.
Access to Petraeus's briefings: Atkinson, *In the Company,* 184.
Atkinson reported immediately: Rick Atkinson, "U.S. Soldier Held for Another's Death in Attack; 15 Hurt," *Washington Post,* 23 March 2003, A25.

196 *Perilously close to battle:* Atkinson interview.
Wallace's pessimistic: Atkinson, *In the Company,* 176.
"It cost Wallace": Atkinson interview.
Background in history: Ibid.

197 *"In 20 years of writing":* "Embedded in Iraq: Was It Worth It?" *Washington Post,* 4 May 2003, B3.

198 *Remarkable candor "a riveting":* Ibid.
"No major corporation": Karl Zinsmeister, *Boots on the Ground:*

A Month with the 82nd Airborne in the Battle for Iraq (New York: St. Martin's Press, 2003), 44.

199   *"Slept in fighting holes":* David Zucchino, "The War, Up Close and Very Personal," *Los Angeles Times,* 3 May 2003, A1.

"Just the beginning": Rajiv Chandrasekaran and William Branigin, "Suicide Bombing Kills 4 Soldiers," *Washington Post,* 30 March 2003, A1.

200   *"We dropped a few":* Dexter Filkins, "Either Take a Shot or Take a Chance," *New York Times,* 29 March 2003, 1.

Johnson told his platoon: William Branigin, "A Gruesome Scene on Highway 9; 10 Dead After Vehicle Shelled at Checkpoint," *Washington Post,* 1 April 2003, A1.

Branigin's eyewitness account: Miller, ed., 102.

"Beauty" of embedding: Katovsky and Carlson, eds., 207–8.

201   *Prowar American sources:* Miller, ed., 157.

202   *"Once the war":* Ibid., 165–66.

MSNBC shifting: Ibid., 168–69.

According to Robert Fisk: Lee Artz and Yahya R. Kamalipour, eds., *Bring 'Em On: Media and Politics in the Iraq War* (Lanham, Md.: Rowman and Littlefield, 2005), 201.

CNN toned town: Massing, 11–12.

"Intimidated by the administration": Artz and Kamalipour, 169.

80 percent of Fox's: Ibid., 170.

203   *Fox's quick coverage:* Seib, *Beyond,* 62.

"Fighting to the death": Susan Schmidt and Vernon Loeb, "'She Was Fighting to the Death,'" *Washington Post,* 3 April 2003, A1.

In fact, Lynch: Dana Priest, William Booth, and Susan Schmidt, "A Broken Body, a Broken Story, Pieced Together," *Washington Post,* 17 June 2003, A1.

204   *Rumsfeld reacted:* Rachel Smolkin, "Media Mood Swings," *American Journalism Review* 25:5 (June 2003), 17.

"How can you intelligently": Seib, *Beyond,* 63.

"Yes, at the moment": Smolkin, 23.

205 *"Slices of war":* Seib, *Beyond,* 60.

    Analysis of the embedded: "Embedded Reporters: What Are Americans Getting?" Project for Excellence in Journalism, www.journalism.org/resources/research/reports/war/embed/pejembedreport.pdf.

    Most famous image: Danny Schechter, *Embedded: Weapons of Mass Deception* (Amherst, N.Y.: Prometheus, 2003), 202.

    Of the handful of Iraqis: Miller, ed., 106.

    Arab observers as well as: Schechter, 202.

206 *"But whose history?":* Miller, ed., 107.

    "Riding around in a tank": "Embedded Reporters."

    Four major newspapers' coverage: "Embedded Journalism: How War Is Viewed Differently from the Frontlines versus the Sidelines: Discussion," University of Oklahoma, www.ou.edu/deptcomm/dodjcc/groups/03D1/Discussion.htm.

    However, another study: Dale L. Edwards, "Embed or In Bed? Building the Agendas of Newspaper Coverage of Operation Desert Storm and Operation Iraqi Freedom," unpublished dissertation, University of North Carolina at Chapel Hill, 2005, 195.

207 *Total of thirty-five:* Seib, *Beyond,* 52.

    "You know, guys": Katovsky and Carlson, eds., 78, 182–84.

208 *Though "not deliberate":* Joel Campagna and Rhonda Roumani, "Permission to Fire," 27 May 2003, www.cpj.org/Briefings/2003/palestine_hotel/palestine_hotel.html.

    Ten times more likely: Katovsky and Carlson, eds., xi.

    By August 2005: "Iraq War Journalist Death Toll Rises to 80," International News Safety Institute, 5 August 2005, www.newssafety.com/stories/insi/iraq05.htm.

    Fluent in Arabic: Anthony Shadid, "Pilgrimage of Sorrow: Shiite Faithful Bury Dead," *Washington Post,* 19 April 2003, A1.

    "What's the sin": Anthony Shadid, "A Boy Who Was 'Like a Flower,'" *Washington Post,* 30 March 2003, A1.

209 *"He said it contained"*: Sherry Ricchiardi, "Close to the Action," *American Journalism Review* 25:4 (May 2003), 33.

CHAPTER EIGHT

211 *"Bomb it"*: Philip Seib, "Ethical Issues in the News Coverage of the Iraq War," paper presented to Association for Education in Journalism and Mass Communication convention, 6 August 2004.

"Why are we here?": Katovsky and Carlson, eds., 39.

Ranked a folding cot: Richard Harding Davis, *Notes,* 259–61.

212 *Army's embedding invitation*: Atkinson, *In the Company,* 12, 21–22.

214 *"When stressing speed"*: Seib, *Beyond the Front Lines,* 11.

215 *"We allowed a bonanza"*: Kenneth Payne, "The Media as an Instrument of War," *Parameters: U.S. Army War College Quarterly* 35:1 (Spring 2005), 82.

216 *"The media were in"*: Katovsky and Carlson, eds., 75.

Hersh revealed: Seymour Hersh, "The Debate Within: The Objective Is Clear—Topple Saddam. But How?" *New Yorker,* 4 March 2002, www.newyorker.com/fact/content/articles/020311fa_FACT.

217 *Pentagon shut down:* Eric Schmitt and James Dao, "A 'Damaged' Information Office Is Declared Closed by Rumsfeld," *New York Times,* 27 February 2002, 1.

"Clear, functional distinction": Christopher J. Castelli, "Capitol Hill Cautions DoD on Separating Info Ops and Public Affairs." *Inside the Navy* 18:21, 30 May 2005.

218 *"Fundamental instrument"*: Payne.

Bush administration had spent: Andrea Mitchell, "GOP Under Fire for Producing News 'Reports'" MSNBC, 14 March 2005, http://msnbc.msn.com/id/7183882/.

Apologized to its readers: "The *Times* and Iraq," *New York Times,* 26 May 2004, 10.

Stood virtually alone: Massing, 41–44.

219 *"Abortion today"*: Alvin Toffler and Heidi Toffler, *War and Anti-War: Survival at the Dawn of the 21st Century* (Boston: Little, Brown, 1993), 209.

"We have gotten a very empty": Michelle Ferrari, comp., *Reporting America at War: An Oral History* (New York: Hyperion, 2003), 213.

Only eighty minutes of coverage: Jim Lobe, "Iraq Blotted Out Rest of the World in 2003 TV News," Global Policy Forum, 6 January 2004, www.globalpolicy.org/empire /media/2004/0106blotted.htm.

220 *"If Afghanistan stays"*: Cynthia Tucker, "If Afghanistan Stays Forgotten, It Won't Forget," *Atlanta Journal-Constitution,* 27 April 2003, 10E.

"Chickens are just going": Arnett, 424, 441.

"Is anything getting rebuilt?": Arthur Chrenkoff, "The Terrorists and the Media," WSJ.com Opinion Journal, 16 August 2005, www.opinionjournal.com/extra/?id=110007113.

221 *"Truthful, comprehensive"*: Commission on Freedom of the Press, *A Free and Responsible Press* (Chicago: University of Chicago Press, 1947), 21–29.

"It is the businesspeople": Ferrari, 216.

222 *Grew up in Iran:* Ibid., 208.

Her reporting career: "Anchors and Reporters: Christiane Amanpour," CNN, www.cnn.com/CNN/anchors _reporters/amanpour.christiane.html.

Neutral voice favors: Sweeney, *From the Front,* 280.

"Spokeswoman for al-Qaeda": Peter Johnson, "Amanpour: CNN Practiced Self-Censorship," *USA Today,* 14 September 2003, 4D.

223 *"Dear Traitor" e-mails:* Atkinson interview.

Michael Wolff got 3,000: Miller, ed., 105.

"If you didn't have": Ferrari, 217.

Pew Research Center poll: "War Coverage Praised, but Public Hungry for Other News," Pew Research Center for the

People and the Press, http://peoplepress.org/reports/display.php3?ReportID=180.

224 *"What's the difference"*: Miller, ed., 251.

225 *"It is not the journalist's job"*: Cronkite, 255.
Atkinson also suggested: Atkinson interview.

226 *"To learn as much"*: Jonathan Finer, "Journalist Jill Carroll Freed by Her Captors in Baghdad," *Washington Post,* 31 March 2006, A14.
"Somebody with her sensibilities": "Jill Carroll's Bravery," *Boston Globe,* http://www.boston.com/news/globe/editorial_opinion/editorials/articles/2006/01/20/jill_carrolls_bravery/, 20 January 2006.

227 *"All of us together"*: Pyle, *Brave Men,* 466.
"Men cannot do the work": Walter Lippmann, *Public Opinion* (New York: Harcourt, Brace, 1922), 364.

BIBLIOGRAPHY

American Civil Liberties Union. *Liberty on the Home Front in the Fourth Year of the War.* New York: ACLU, 1945.

"The American Purpose." *Life,* 5 July 1943, 39.

"Anchors and Reporters: Christiane Amanpour." CNN, www .cnn.com/CNN/anchors_reporters/amanpour.christiane .html.

Andrews, J. Cutler. *The North Reports the Civil War.* Pittsburgh: University of Pittsburgh Press, 1955.

————. *The South Reports the Civil War.* Pittsburgh: University of Pittsburgh Press, 1985.

"Army Correspondents." *New York Times,* 25 August 1862, 4.

"Army News Policy." *Army and Navy Register,* 8 April 1944, 9.

Arnett, Peter. *Live from the Battlefield: From Vietnam to Baghdad, 35 Years in the World's War Zones.* New York: Simon and Schuster, 1994.

Artz, Lee, and Yahya R. Kamalipour, eds. *Bring 'Em On: Media and Politics in the Iraq War.* Lanham, Md.: Rowman and Littlefield, 2005.

"ASD PA Clarke Meeting with Bureau Chiefs." *Department of Defense News Transcript,* 30 October 2002. www.defenselink .mil/transcripts/2003/t01152003_t0114bc.html.

Associated Press. "Amnesty Report Says Iraqis Tortured and Killed Hundreds." *New York Times,* 20 December 1990, A21.

Atkinson, Rick. *In the Company of Soldiers: A Chronicle of Combat.* New York: Henry Holt, 2004.

————. "U.S. Soldier Held for Another's Death in Attack; 15 Hurt." *Washington Post,* 23 March 2003, A25.

————. Interview, 28 February 2005.

Baker, Peter. "Inside View." *American Journalism Review* 25:4 (May 2003), 36–39.

Bennett, W. Lance, and David L. Paletz, eds. *Taken by Storm: The Media, Public Opinion, and U.S. Foreign Policy in the Gulf War.* Chicago: University of Chicago Press, 1994.

Biddle, Francis. *In Brief Authority.* New York: Doubleday, 1962.

"Biddle Attacks the *Tribune.*" *Chicago Tribune,* 8 August 1943, 1–2.

Blanchard, Margaret A., ed. *History of the Mass Media in the United States.* Chicago: Fitzroy Dearborn, 1998.

Bourke-White, Margaret. *They Called It "Purple Heart Valley": A Chronicle of the War in Italy.* New York: Simon and Schuster, 1944.

"Brady's Photographs." *New York Times,* 20 October 1862, 5.

Braestrup, Peter. *Battle Lines.* New York: Priority Press, 1985.

––––––. *Big Story.* Boulder, Colo.: Westview Press, 1977.

Branigin, William. "A Gruesome Scene on Highway 9; 10 Dead After Vehicle Shelled at Checkpoint." *Washington Post,* 1 April 2003, A1.

Brown, James B. "Media Access to the Battlefield." *Military Review* 72:7 (July 1992), 10–20.

Browne, Malcolm W. *Muddy Boots and Red Socks: A Reporter's Life.* New York: Times Books, 1993.

Brucker, Herbert. *Freedom of Information.* New York: Macmillan, 1949.

Burlingame, Roger. *Don't Let Them Scare You: The Life and Times of Elmer Davis.* Philadelphia: J. B. Lippincott, 1961.

Campagna, Joel. "Media Concerns about Covering the War." *Op-Ed Articles by CPJ Staff.* Committee to Protect Journalists, 19 March 2003. www.cpj.org/op_ed/Campagna19mar03 .html.

Campagna, Joel, and Rhonda Roumani. "Permission to Fire." Committee to Protect Journalists, 27 May 2003. www.cpj.org/Briefings/2003/palestine_hotel/palestine_hot el.html.

Carlebach, Michael L. *American Photojournalism Comes of Age.* Washington, D.C.: Smithsonian Institution Press, 1997.

Castelli, Christopher J. "Capitol Hill Cautions DoD on Separating Info Ops and Public Affairs." *Inside the Navy* 18:21, 30 May 2005.

Chafee, Zechariah, Jr. *Free Speech in the United States.* New York: Atheneum, 1969.

Chandrasekaran, Rajiv, and William Branigin. "Suicide Bombing Kills 4 Soldiers." *Washington Post,* 30 March 2003, A1.

Chase, Harold W., and Allen H. Lerman, eds. *Kennedy and the Press: The News Conferences.* New York: Thomas Y. Crowell, 1965.

Chrenkoff, Arthur. "The Terrorists and the Media." WSJ.com Opinion Journal, 16 August 2005. www.opinionjournal .com/extra/?id=110007113.

Clark, Sarah. "Counting Civilian Casualties." *American Journalism Review* 27:4 (August–September 2005), 12–13.

Cobb, Irvin S. *Paths of Glory: Impressions of War Written at and near the Front.* New York: George H. Doran, 1915.

Colman, Penny. *Where the Action Was: Women War Correspondents in World War II.* New York: Crown, 2002.

Commission on Freedom of the Press. *A Free and Responsible Press.* Chicago: University of Chicago Press, 1947.

Committee on Public Information. Record Group 63. National Archives, College Park, Md.

Committee on Public Information. "The Kaiserite in America." No date. Special Collections, Harold B. Lee Library, Brigham Young University, Provo, Utah.

Creel, George. *The Creel Report: Complete Report of the Chairman of the Committee on Public Information.* New York: Da Capo Press, 1972.

————. *How We Advertised America.* New York: Harper and Brothers, 1920.

————. "The Plight of the Last Censor," *Collier's,* 24 May 1941, 13, 34–35.

————. *Rebel at Large: Recollections of Fifty Crowded Years.* New York: G. P. Putnam's Sons, 1947.

Creelman, James. *On the Great Highway.* Boston: Lothrop, 1901.

Cronkite, Walter. *A Reporter's Life.* New York: Alfred A. Knopf, 1996.

Crozier, Emmet. *American Reporters on the Western Front, 1914–1918.* New York: Oxford University Press, 1959.

Current Biography. 1942 ed. S.v. "Price, Byron."

Daniels, Josephus. *The Wilson Era: Years of War and After, 1917–1923.* Chapel Hill: University of North Carolina Press, 1946.

Davis, Charles Belmont, ed. *Adventures and Letters of Richard Harding Davis.* New York: Charles Scribner's Sons, 1917.

Davis, Richard Harding. *The Cuban and Porto Rican Campaigns.* New York: Charles Scribner's Sons, 1898.

————. *Notes of a War Correspondent.* New York: Charles Scribner's Sons, 1911.

Denton, Robert E., Jr., ed. *The Media and the Persian Gulf War.* Westport, Conn.: Praeger, 1993.

DeParle, Jason. "Keeping the News in Step: Are the Pentagon's Gulf War Rules Here to Stay?" *New York Times,* 6 May 1991, A9.

————. "Long Series of Military Decisions Led to Gulf War Censorship." *New York Times,* 5 May 1991, 1, 20.

————. "17 News Executives Criticize U.S. for 'Censorship' of Gulf War Coverage." *New York Times,* 3 July 1991, A4.

Department of Defense. *Conduct of the Persian Gulf War: Final Report to Congress.* Washington, D.C.: Government Printing Office, April 1992.

Dicken-Garcia, Hazel. *Journalistic Standards in Nineteenth-Century America.* Madison: University of Wisconsin Press, 1989.

Doan, Edward N. "Organization and Operation of the Office of Censorship." *Journalism Quarterly* 21, September 1944, 200–216.

Eberhard, Wallace B. "A Familiar Refrain but Slightly Out of Tune." *Military Review* 67:2 (February 1987), 71, 80–84.

Eddy, Paul, et al. *War in the Falklands: The Full Story.* New York: Harper and Row, 1982.

"Editors Fear Public Distrust from Too Strict a Censorship." *Editor and Publisher,* 10 October 1942, 3.

Edwards, Dale L. "Embed or In Bed? Building the Agendas of Newspaper Coverage of Operation Desert Storm and Operation Iraqi Freedom." Unpublished dissertation, University of North Carolina at Chapel Hill, 2005.

Eisenhower, Dwight D. *Crusade in Europe.* Garden City, N.Y.: Doubleday, 1948.

Elwood-Akers, Virginia. *Women War Correspondents in the Vietnam War, 1961–1975.* Metuchen, N.J.: Scarecrow Press, 1988.

"Embedded in Iraq: Was It Worth It?" *Washington Post,* 4 May 2003, B3.

"Embedded Journalism: How War Is Viewed Differently from the Frontlines versus the Sidelines: Discussion." University of Oklahoma. www.ou.edu/deptcomm/dodjcc/groups/03D1/Discussion.htm.

"Embedded Reporters: What Are Americans Getting?" Project for Excellence in Journalism. www.journalism.org/resources/research/reports/war/embed/pejembedreport.pdf.

Emery, Michael. *On the Front Lines.* Washington, D.C.: American University Press, 1995.

Ethiel, Nancy, ed. *The Military, the Media, and the Administration: An Irregular Triangle.* Chicago: McCormick Tribune Foundation, 2002.

"Excerpts from the Bush News Conference on the Budget and the Mideast." *New York Times,* 10 October 1990, A18.

Federal Bureau of Investigation. "Drew Pearson" file 65–59762.

Feeney, Michael A. "Mustard as a Chemical Weapon." *Journal of Counterterrorism and Security International* 7:1 (Fall 2000), Lexis/Nexis.

Ferrari, Michelle, comp. *Reporting America at War: An Oral History.* New York: Hyperion, 2003.

Fielding, Raymond. *The American Newsreel, 1911–1967.* Norman: University of Oklahoma Press, 1972.

Filkins, Dexter. "Either Take a Shot or Take a Chance." *New York Times,* 29 March 2003, 1.

Finer, Johathan. "Journalist Jill Carroll Freed by Her Captors in Baghdad." *Washington Post,* 31 March 2006, A14.

Fisk, Robert. "Out of the Pool." *Mother Jones* 16:3 (May–June 1991), 56–59.

Frassanito, William A. *Antietam: The Photographic Legacy of America's Bloodiest Day.* New York: Charles Scribner's Sons, 1976.

————. *Gettysburg: A Journey in Time.* New York: Charles Scribner's Sons, 1975.

Fyne, Robert. *The Hollywood Propaganda of World War II.* Lanham, Md.: Scarecrow Press, 1994.

Gardner, Alexander. *Gardner's Photographic Sketch Book of the Civil War.* New York: Dover, 1959.

"German Atrocities Are Proved, Finds Bryce Committee." *New York Times,* 13 May 1915, 6.

Gies, Joseph. *The Colonel of Chicago.* New York: E. P. Dutton, 1979.

Goldberg, Vicki. *Margaret Bourke-White: A Biography.* New York: Harper and Row, 1986.

Goodman, Amy, and David Goodman. "The Hiroshima Cover-Up." *Mother Jones,* 5 August 2005. www.motherjones.com /commentary/columns/2005/08/hiroshima.html.

Goodwin, Doris Kearns. *No Ordinary Time: Franklin and Eleanor Roosevelt: The Home Front in World War II.* New York: Simon and Schuster, 1994.

Gottschalk, Jack A. "'Consistent with Security' . . . A History of American Military Press Censorship." *Communications and the Law* 5, Summer 1983, 35–52.

Greenberg, Bradley S., and Walter Gantz, eds. *Desert Storm and the Mass Media.* Cresskill, N.J.: Hampton Press, 1993.

Grobel, Lawrence. *The Hustons.* New York: Avon Books, 1989.

Grossman, Mark. *Encyclopedia of the Persian Gulf War.* Santa Barbara, Calif.: ABC-Clio, 1995.

Grutzner, Charles. "Stranded Enemy Soldiers Merge with Refugee Crowds in Korea." *New York Times,* 30 September 1950, 3.

Halberstam, David. *The Powers That Be.* Urbana: University of Illinois Press, 1975.

Hallin, Daniel C. *The "Uncensored War": The Media and Vietnam.* Berkeley: University of California Press, 1986.

Hamilton, Alexander, James Madison, and John Jay. *The Federalist: A Commentary on the Constitution of the United States.* New York: Tudor Publishing, 1937.

Hammond, William M. *United States Army in Vietnam: Public Affairs—The Military and the Media, 1962–1968.* Washington, D.C.: Government Printing Office, 1988.

Hanley, Charles J., et al. *The Bridge at No Gun Ri.* New York: Henry Holt, 2001.

Harris, Brayton. *Blue and Gray in Black and White: Newspapers in the Civil War.* Washington: Brassey's, 1999.

Haverstock, Nathan A. *Fifty Years at the Front: The Life of War Correspondent Frederick Palmer.* Washington: Brassey's, 1996.

Herr, Michael. *Dispatches.* New York: Avon, 1978.

Hersh, Seymour: "The Debate Within: The Objective Is Clear—Topple Saddam. But How?" *New Yorker,* 4 March 2002. www.newyorker.com/fact/content/articles/020311fa _FACT.

Hickey, Neil. "Access Denied: Pentagon's War Reporting Rules Are Toughest Ever." *Columbia Journalism Review* 40:5 (January–February 2002), 26–31.

Higgins, Marguerite. *War in Korea: The Report of a Woman Combat Correspondent.* Garden City, N.Y.: Doubleday, 1951.

Hockstader, Lee. "In Panama, Civilian Deaths Remain an Issue." *Washington Post,* 6 October 1990, A23.

Hohenberg, John. *Foreign Correspondence: The Great Reporters and Their Times.* New York: Columbia University Press, 1964.

Horten, Gerd. *Radio Goes to War: The Cultural Politics of Propaganda during World War II.* Berkeley: University of California Press, 2002.

Howell, Cass D. "War, Television, and Public Opinion." *Military Review* 67:2 (February 1987), 71–79.

Humphrey, Carol Sue. *The Revolutionary Era: Primary Documents on Events from 1776 to 1800.* Westport, Conn.: Greenwood, 2003.

————. "The Vagaries of Original Intent: What Did the Founding Fathers Really Believe about the Freedom of the Press." Paper presented at the Annual Conference, American Journalism Historians Association, October 2000.

Humphries, Arthur A. "Two Routes to the Wrong Destination: Public Affairs in the South Atlantic War." *Naval War College Review* 36:3 (May–June 1983), 56–71.

"Iraq War Journalist Death Toll Rises to 80." International News Safety Institute, 5 August 2005. www.newssafety.com /stories/insi/iraq05.htm.

Jesdanun, Anick. "Iraqis, U.S. Forces Restrict Sat Phones." *Editor and Publisher,* 3 April 2003. www.editorandpublisher.com /eandp/news/article_display.jsp?vnu_content_id=1857536.

"Jill Carroll's Bravery." *Boston Globe.* http://www.boston .com/news/globe/editorial_opinion/editorials/articles /2006/01/20/jill_carrolls_bravery/. 20 January 2006.

Johnson, Peter. "Amanpour: CNN Practiced Self-Censorship." *USA Today,* 14 September 2003, 4D.

————. "Boot Camp Prepares Journalists for Iraq." *USA Today,* 11 December 2002, 3D.

Jowett, Garth S., and Victoria O'Donnell. *Propaganda and Persuasion.* Thousand Oaks, Calif.: Sage Publications, 1999.

Katovsky, Bill, and Timothy Carlson, eds. *Embedded: The Media at War in Iraq.* Guilford, Conn.: Lyons Press, 2003.

Katz, Daniel, et al., eds., *Public Opinion and Propaganda.* New York: Dryden Press, 1954.

Kelly, Michael. *Martyrs' Day: Chronicle of a Small War:* New York: Random House, 1993.

Kendall, George Wilkins. *Dispatches from the Mexican War.* Ed. and intro. by Lawrence Delbert Cress. Norman: University of Oklahoma Press, 1999.

Kluger, Richard. *The Paper: The Life and Death of the* New York Herald Tribune. New York: Alfred A. Knopf, 1986.

Knightley, Phillip. *The First Casualty: From the Crimea to Vietnam— The War Correspondent as Hero, Propagandist, and Myth Maker.* New York: Harcourt Brace Jovanovich, 1975.

————. *The First Casualty: The War Correspondent as Hero and Myth Maker from the Crimea to Iraq.* Baltimore, Md.: Johns Hopkins University Press, 2004.

Koop, Theodore F. *Weapon of Silence.* Chicago: University of Chicago Press, 1946.

Koppes, Clayton D., and Gregory D. Black. *Hollywood Goes to War: How Politics, Profits, and Propaganda Shaped World War II Movies.* New York: Free Press, 1987.

Kurtz, Howard. "Sen. Simpson Calls Arnett 'Sympathizer'; CNN Reporter Blasted for Iraq Coverage." *Washington Post,* 8 February 1991, B1.

Lande, Nathaniel. *Dispatches from the Front: News Accounts of American Wars, 1776–1991.* New York: Henry Holt, 1995.

Landers, James. *The Weekly War: Newsmagazines and Vietnam.* Columbia: University of Missouri Press, 2004.

Lasswell, Harold D. *Propaganda Technique in the World War.* New York: Peter Smith, 1938.

Laurence, William L. "U.S. Bomb Site Belies Tokyo Tales." *New York Times,* 12 September 1945, 1, 4.

Laurie, Clayton D. *The Propaganda Warriors: America's Crusade against Nazi Germany.* Lawrence: University of Kansas Press, 1996.

"Letters to the Editors: Three Americans." *Life,* 11 October 1943, 4.

Liebling, A. J. "The Wayward Press: The A.P. Surrender." *New Yorker,* 19 May 1945, 57–62.

Lifton, Robert Jay, and Greg Mitchell. *Hiroshima in America: Fifty Years of Denial.* New York: G. P. Putnam's Sons, 1995.

Lippmann, Walter. *Public Opinion.* New York: Harcourt, Brace, 1922.

Lobe, Jim. "Iraq Blotted Out Rest of the World in 2003 TV News." Global Policy Forum, 6 January 2004. www.globalpolicy.org/empire/media/2004/0106blotted.htm.

London, Jack. "Japanese Officers Consider Everything a Military Secret." *San Francisco Examiner,* 26 June 1904, 1.

Lubow, Arthur. *The Reporter Who Would Be King: A Biography of Richard Harding Davis.* New York: Charles Scribner's Sons, 1992.

MacArthur, John R. *Second Front: Censorship and Propaganda in the Gulf War.* New York: Hill and Wang, 1992.

"Man of Sense." *Time,* 22 June 1942, 21.

Maslowski, Peter. *Armed with Cameras: The American Military Photographers of World War II.* New York: Free Press, 1993.

Massing, Michael. *Now They Tell Us: American Press and Iraq.* New York: New York Review of Books, 2004.

Mendelson, Andrew, and Zoe C. Smith. "Part of the Team: *Life* Photographers and Their Symbiotic Relationship with the Military during World War II." *American Journalism* 12:3 (Summer 1995), 276–89.

Miller, David, ed. *Tell Me Lies: Propaganda and Media Distortion in the Attack on Iraq.* London: Pluto Press, 2004.

Miller, Lee G. *An Ernie Pyle Album: Indiana to Ie Shima.* New York: William Sloan Associates, 1946.

————. *The Story of Ernie Pyle.* New York: Viking, 1950.

Milton, Joyce. *The Yellow Kids: Foreign Correspondence in the Heyday of Yellow Journalism.* New York: Harper and Row, 1989.

Milwaukee Social Democratic Publishing Co. v. Burleson, 255 U.S. 407 (1921).

Mindich, David T. Z. *Just the Facts: How "Objectivity" Came to Define American Journalism.* New York: New York University Press, 1998.

Mitchell, Andrea. "GOP Under Fire for Producing News 'Reports.'" MSNBC.com, 14 March 2005. http://msnbc.msn.com/id/7183882/.

Mock, James R. *Censorship 1917.* New York: Da Capo Press, 1972.

Moeller, Susan D. *Shooting War: Photography and the American Experience in Combat.* New York: Basic Books, 1989.

Moore, Molly. *A Woman at War: Storming Kuwait with the U.S. Marines.* New York: Charles Scribner's Sons, 1993.

Moore, Molly, and Howard Kurtz. "Sweating Out the Gulf Story." *Washington Post,* 18 September 1990, B1.

Morrissey, David H. "Disclosure and Secrecy: Security Classification Executive Orders." *Journalism and Mass Communication Monographs* 161 (1997), 10–12.

Murphy, Lisa. "One Small Moment." *American History* 30, June 1995, 66–70.

Nacos, Brigitte L. *Mass-Mediated Terrorism.* Lanham, Md.: Rowman and Littlefield, 2003.

Nasaw, David. *The Chief: The Life of William Randolph Hearst.* Boston: Houghton Mifflin, 2000.

"Navy Had Word of Jap Plan to Strike at Sea." *Chicago Tribune,* 7 June 1942, 1.

"NBC's David Bloom Dies in Iraq." Cyberjournalist.Net, 7 April 2003. www.cyberjournalist.net/news/000081.php.

Near v. Minnesota, 283 U.S. 697 (1931).

New York Times v. United States, 403 U.S. 713 (1971).

"*Newsweek*'s Troops in the Persian Gulf." *Newsweek,* 11 March 1991, 4.

Niderost, Eric. "Deadly Luftwaffe Strike in the Adriatic." *World War II* 15:6 (February 2001), Academic Search Premier.

"NSC-68: A Report to the National Security Council." *Naval War College Review* 27, May–June 1975, 51–108.

Office of Censorship. *Code of Wartime Practices for American Broadcasters.* Washington, D.C.: Government Printing Office, 15 January 1942.

————. *Code of Wartime Practices for the American Press.* Washington, D.C.: Government Printing Office, 15 January 1942.

————. Record Group 216. National Archives, College Park, Md.

O'Higgins, Harvey. "The Daily German Lie." N.d. Committee on Public Information. Record Group 63, CPI-1CI, entry 15, box 1, "Propaganda Reports" folder, National Archives, College Park, Md.

Oldfield, Barney. *Never a Shot in Anger.* New York: Duell, Sloan, and Pearce, 1956.

Palmer, Frederick. *The Folly of Nations.* New York: Dodd, Mead, 1921.

————. *My Second Year of the War.* New York: Dodd, Mead, 1917.

————. *With Kuroki in Manchuria.* New York: Charles Scribner's Sons, 1906.

Palser, Barb. "Online Advances." *American Journalism Review* 25:4 (May 2003), 40–45.

Payne, Kenneth. "The Media as an Instrument of War." *Parameters: U.S. Army War College Quarterly* 35:1 (Spring 2005), 81–93.

Pearson, Drew. *Drew Pearson Diaries.* New York: Holt, Rinehart, and Winston, 1974.

————. "Korea Differences Recounted." *Washington Post,* 8 January 1951, 11B.

————. "MacArthur Puzzles Pentagon." *Washington Post,* 30 December 1950, 9B.

Persico, Joseph E. *Edward R. Murrow: An American Original.* New York: McGraw-Hill, 1988.

Peterson, H. C. *Propaganda for War: The Campaign against American Neutrality, 1914–1917.* Norman: University of Oklahoma Press, 1939.

Pinkley, Virgil. "Eisenhower on Censorship." *Editor and Publisher,* 21 April 1945, 50.

"The Press Agents' War." *New York Times,* 9 September 1914, 8.

Price, Byron. "Memoir" (unpublished). Byron Price Papers, Archives Division, State Historical Society of Wisconsin, Madison.

Price, Jay. "Soldiers Get Tips on Dealing with Media." *News and Observer,* 10 January 2005. www.newsobserver.com//nation_world/iraq/story/2008013p-8388436c.html.

Priest, Dana, William Booth, and Susan Schmidt. "A Broken Body, a Broken Story, Pieced Together." *Washington Post,* 17 June 2003, A1.

Prochnau, William. *Once Upon a Distant War.* New York: Vintage Books, 1995.

Pyle, Ernie. *Brave Men.* New York: Henry Holt, 1944.

————. *Here Is Your War.* New York: Henry Holt, 1943.

Rampton, Sheldon, and John Stauber. *Weapons of Mass Deception: The Uses of Propaganda in Bush's War on Iraq*. New York: Jeremy P. Tarcher/Penguin, 2003.

Read, James Morgan. *Atrocity Propaganda 1914–1919*. New Haven, Conn.: Yale University Press, 1941.

Regulations for Press Correspondents, n.p., 1904. Box 20, folder 1, Jack and Charmian London Papers. Special Collections, Utah State University, Logan.

Reston, James. *Deadline: A Memoir*. New York: Random House, 1991.

Reynolds, Quentin. *By Quentin Reynolds*. New York: Pyramid, 1964.

Ricchiardi, Sherry. "Close to the Action." *American Journalism Review* 25:4 (May 2003), 28–35.

Risley, Ford. "Peter Alexander: Confederate Chronicler and Conscience." *American Journalism* 15:1 (Winter 1998), 35–50.

Roeder, George H., Jr. *The Censored War: American Visual Experience during World War II*. New Haven, Conn.: Yale University Press, 1993.

Rogers, Lindsay. "Freedom of the Press in the United States." *Contemporary Review* 114, August 1918, 177–83.

Rollyson, Carl. *Nothing Ever Happens to the Brave: The Story of Martha Gellhorn*. New York: St. Martin's Press, 1990.

Rolo, Charles J. *Radio Goes to War: The "Fourth Front."* New York: G. P. Putnam's Sons, 1942.

Roosevelt, Franklin D. *Complete Presidential Press Conferences of Franklin D. Roosevelt*. New York: Da Capo Press, 1972.

Ross, Stewart Halsey. *Propaganda for War: How the United States Was Conditioned to Fight the Great War of 1914–1918*. Jefferson, N.C.: McFarland, 1996.

Safer, Morley. *Flashbacks: On Returning to Vietnam*. New York: St. Martin's, 1991.

Salisbury, Harrison E. *Without Fear or Favor: The* New York Times *and Its Times*. New York: Times Books, 1980.

Sandweiss, Martha A., et al., *Eyewitness to War: Prints and Daguerreotypes of the Mexican War, 1846–1848.* Fort Worth, Texas: Amon Carter Museum, 1989.

Schechter, Danny. *Embedded: Weapons of Mass Deception.* Amherst, N.Y.: Prometheus, 2003.

Schenck v. United States, 249 U.S. 47 (1919).

Schmidt, Susan, and Vernon Loeb. "'She Was Fighting to the Death'; Details Emerging of W. Va. Soldier's Capture and Rescue." *Washington Post,* 3 April 2003, A1.

Schmitt, Eric. "Missile's War Record Revised." *New York Times,* 8 April 1992, A11.

———. "U.S. Details Flaw in Patriot Missile." *New York Times,* 6 June 1991, A9.

Schmitt, Eric, and James Dao. "A 'Damaged' Information Office Is Declared Closed by Rumsfeld." *New York Times,* 27 February 2002, 1.

Schulman, Daniel. "State of the Art: Their War." *Columbia Journalism Review* 44:3 (September–October 2005), 13.

Schwarzkopf, H. Norman. *It Doesn't Take a Hero.* New York: Bantam Books, 1992.

Seib, Philip. *Beyond the Front Lines: How the News Media Cover a World Shaped by War.* New York: Palgrave Macmillan, 2004.

———. "Ethical Issues in the News Coverage of the Iraq War." Unpublished paper presented to the Annual Convention of the Association for Education in Journalism and Mass Communication, 6 August 2004, Toronto.

Seldes, George. *Witness to a Century: Encounters with the Noted, the Notorious, and the Three SOBs.* New York: Ballantine Books, 1987.

Shadid, Anthony. "A Boy Who Was 'Like a Flower.'" *Washington Post,* 30 March 2003, A1.

———. "Pilgrimage of Sorrow: Shiite Faithful Bury Dead." *Washington Post,* 19 April 2003, A1.

Shafter, William R. "The Capture of Santiago de Cuba." *The Century Illustrated Monthly Magazine,* February 1899, 612–30.

Sheehan, Neil. *A Bright Shining Lie: John Paul Vann and America in Vietnam*. New York: Random House, 1988.

Shulman, Holly Cowan. *The Voice of America: Propaganda and Democracy*. Madison: University of Wisconsin Press, 1990.

Simon, Bob. *Forty Days*. New York: G. P. Putnam's Sons, 1992.

Simpson, Al. "The Word 'Sympathizer' Was Not a Good One." *New York Times,* 20 March 1991, 28A.

Skiba, Katherine M. *Sister in the Band of Brothers: Embedded with the 101st Airborne in Iraq*. Lawrence: University of Kansas Press, 2005.

Sloan, William David, and Emily Erickson Hoff, eds. *Contemporary Media Issues.* Northport, Ala.: Vision Press, 1998.

Smith, Hedrick, ed. *The Media and the Gulf War.* Washington, D.C.: Seven Locks Press, 1992.

Smith, Jeffery A. *War and Press Freedom: The Problem of Prerogative Power.* New York: Oxford University Press, 1999.

Smith, Kathleen E. R. *God Bless America: Tin Pan Alley Goes to War.* Lexington: University Press of Kentucky, 2003.

Smith, Richard Norton. *The Colonel: The Life and Legend of Robert R. McCormick.* Boston: Houghton Mifflin, 1997.

Smolkin, Rachel. "Media Mood Swings." *American Journalism Review* 25:5 (June 2003), 17–23.

Sorel, Nancy Caldwell. *The Women Who Wrote the War.* New York: Arcade, 1999.

Stein, M. L. *Under Fire: The Story of American War Correspondents.* New York: Julian Messner, 1968.

Steinbeck, John. *Once There Was a War.* New York: Penguin, 1986.

Stephens, Mitchell. *A History of News: From the Drum to the Satellite.* New York: Penguin, 1988.

Stevens, John D. *Shaping the First Amendment: The Development of Free Expression.* Beverly Hills, Calif.: Sage Publications, 1982.

"Stillwell, After a 'Beating' in Burma, Would Hit Back." *New York Times,* 26 May 1942, 1.

Sweeney, Michael S. *From the Front: The Story of War Featuring Correspondents' Chronicles.* Washington, D.C.: National Geographic Press, 2002.

—————. *Secrets of Victory: The Office of Censorship and the American Press and Radio in World War II.* Chapel Hill: University of North Carolina Press, 2001.

Taylor, Philip M. *Munitions of the Mind: A History of Propaganda from the Ancient World to the Present Era.* Manchester, England: Manchester University Press, 1995.

—————. *War and the Media: Propaganda and Persuasion in the Gulf War.* Manchester, England: Manchester University Press, 1998.

"Three Americans." *Life,* 20 September 1943, 34.

"The *Times* and Iraq." *New York Times,* 26 May 2004, 10.

Tobin, James. *Ernie Pyle's War: America's Eyewitness to World War II.* New York: Free Press, 1997.

Toffler, Alvin, and Heidi Toffler. *War and Anti-War: Survival at the Dawn of the 21st Century.* Boston: Little, Brown, 1993.

Tucker, Cynthia. "If Afghanistan Stays Forgotten, It Won't Forget." *Atlanta Journal-Constitution,* 27 April 2003, 10E.

"TV Combat Fatigue on the Rise." Pew Research Center for the People and the Press, http://people-press.org/reports /pdf/178.pdf.

"Two Versions of the Crisis in Vietnam." *New York Times,* 23 August 1963, 1.

Tyler, Patrick E. "Did Patriot Missiles Work? Not So Well, Scientists Say." *New York Times,* 17 April 1991, A11.

—————. "Schwarzkopf Says Truce Enabled Iraqis to Escape." *New York Times,* 27 March 1991, A9.

United States. *Laws, etc. (United States Statutes at Large).* Washington, D.C.: Government Printing Office, 1937– .

"U.S., British Censors in Harmony." *Editor and Publisher,* 15 April 1944, 10.

U.S. News & World Report. *The Unreported History of the Persian Gulf War.* New York: Times Books, 1992.

Vaughn, Stephen. *Holding Fast the Inner Lines.* Chapel Hill: University of North Carolina Press, 1980.

"Virtual News Censorship Set by War Department." *New York Times,* 14 June 1940, 12.

Voorhees, Melvin B. *Korean Tales.* New York: Simon and Schuster, 1952.

Voss, Frederick S. *Reporting the War: The Journalistic Coverage of World War II.* Washington, D.C.: Smithsonian Institution Press, 1994.

"War Coverage Praised, but Public Hungry for Other News." Pew Research Center for the People and the Press, http://peoplepress.org/reports/display.php3?ReportID=180.

Washburn, Patrick S. "The Office of Censorship's Attempt to Control Press Coverage of the Atomic Bomb during World War II." *Journalism Monographs* 120, 1990.

————. *A Question of Sedition: The Federal Government's Investigation of the Black Press during World War II.* New York: Oxford University Press, 1986.

Winfield, Betty Houchin. *FDR and the News Media.* New York: Columbia University Press, 1994.

Winkler, Allan M. *The Politics of Propaganda: The Office of War Information 1942–1945.* New Haven, Conn.: Yale University Press, 1978.

Wyatt, Clarence R. *Paper Soldiers: The American Press and the Vietnam War.* New York: W. W. Norton, 1993.

Zinsmeister, Karl. *Boots on the Ground: A Month with the 82nd Airborne in the Battle for Iraq.* New York: St. Martin's Press, 2003.

Zoroya, Gregg. "Course Prepares Journalists in Art of War." *USA Today,* 15 March 2002, 4A.

Zucchino, David. "The War, Up Close and Very Personal." *Los Angeles Times,* 3 May 2003, A1.

INDEX

Wellington House, 38, 42, 64
Westmoreland, William C., 137
WGN, 81
White House (*see also individual
    presidents' names*), 67, 79, 80,
    124–25, 154, 159, 178, 188,
    224
Whitman, Walt, 28, 74
Why We Fight, 89–90
Wildermuth, Ron, 160
Wilderness, Battle of, 22
Wilkeson, Sam, 21
Williams, Pete, 160, 164, 166,
    173
Williams, Wythe, 57
Wilson, Woodrow, 38, 45–46, 47,
    49, 54, 74, 79
Winchell, Walter, 95
Windom, William, xx
Wing, Henry, 21
Winkler, Allan M., 84
Wolff, Michael, 211, 223
Wood, David, 181
World Trade Center (*see also*
    September 11 terrorist at-
    tacks), 220
World War I (*see also* censorship;
    Committee on Public Infor-
    mation), xi, xvii, 63, 64, 65,
    68, 70, 73, 74, 85, 86, 93, 97,

107, 120; American prepara-
    tion, 43–45; atrocity allega-
    tions, 41–43; British propa-
    ganda, 38–41, 97; combat
    zone coverage, 52–61; effect
    on press-military relations,
    35–37
World War II (*see also* censor-
    ship; Office of Censorship;
    Office of Facts and Figures;
    Office of War Information),
    xi, xvii, 6, 44, 55, 123, 128,
    133, 136, 137, 145, 167, 174,
    185, 197, 213; American
    preparation, 63–68; combat
    zone coverage, 93–94,
    96–120; comparison with
    World War I, 68, 69–70, 107,
    120; relations with Allies,
    109–110
World Wide Web, 182, 183, 217,
    223; broadens war coverage,
    190–92, 209, 213
Worth, William J., 17–18
Wyatt, Clarence, 122
Wyler, William, 89

Zinsmeister, Karl, 198
Zorthian, Barry, 143, 148
Zucchino, David, 198–99

Michael S. Sweeney is a professor of print journalism and the head of the Department of Journalism and Communication at Utah State University in Logan. He is the author of *From the Front: The Story of War Featuring Correspondents' Chronicles* and *Secrets of Victory: The Office of Censorship and the American Press and Radio in World War II*.

Roy Gutman is the foreign editor of *Newsday* and the winner of both a Pulitzer Prize for International Reporting and a Polk Award for Best Foreign Reporting. He is the author of *A Witness to Genocide: The 1993 Pulitzer Prize-Winning Dispatches on the "Ethnic Cleansing" of Bosnia*.